C000228887

Stalin's Loyal Ex
People's Commissar Nikolai Ezhov

Stalin's Loyal Executioner

People's Commissar Nikolai Ezhov, 1895–1940

Marc Jansen and Nikita Petrov

HOOVER INSTITUTION PRESS
Stanford University
Stanford, California

20087294
MORAY COUNCIL
LIBRARIES &
INFORMATION SERVICES
363·28

The Hoover Institution on War, Revolution and Peace, founded at Stanford University in 1919 by Herbert Hoover, who went on to become the thirty-first president of the United States, is an interdisciplinary research center for advanced study on domestic and international affairs. The views expressed in its publications are entirely those of the authors and do not necessarily reflect the view of the staff, officers, or Board of Overseers of the Hoover Institution.

www.hoover.org

Hoover Institution Press Publication No. 502

Copyright © 2002 by the Board of Trustees of the
  Leland Stanford Junior University

All rights reserved. No part of this publication may be reproduced, stored in a retrieval system, or transmitted in any form or by any means, electronic, mechanical, photocopying, recording, or otherwise, without written permission of the publisher.

First printing 2002

Manufactured in the United States of America

07 06 05 04 03 02   9 8 7 6 5 4 3 2 1

The paper used in this publication meets the minimum requirements of American National Standard for Information Sciences—Permanence of Paper for Printed Library Materials, ANSI Z39.48-1984. ⊗

Library of Congress Cataloging-in-Publication Data

Jansen, Marc.
    Stalin's loyal executioner : People's Commissar Nikolai Ezhov,
  1895–1940 / Marc Jansen and Nikita Petrov.
      p. cm.
    Includes bibliographical references.
    ISBN 0-8179-2902-9
    1. Ezhov, Nikolaæ Ivanovich, 1895–1940. 2. Soviet Union.
  Narodnyæ komissariat vnutrennikh del—Officials and employees—
  Biography. 3. Kommunisticheskaëi partiëi Sovetskogo Soëïza—
  Purges. 4. Political purges—Soviet Union—History. I. Petrov,
  N. V. (Nikita Vasil'evich). II. Title.
  DK268.E93 J36 2002
  363.28'3'092—dc21
    [B]   2001039836

Contents

Illustrations

Preface

I don't know of any more ideal functionary than Ezhov. After charging him with a task, you don't have to check up on him: he will accomplish the mission. He has only one, indeed essential, shortcoming—he does not know where to stop.

—I. M. Moskvin, 1936–37

If during this operation an extra thousand people will be shot, that is not such a big deal.

—N. I. Ezhov, July 1937

Better too far than not far enough.

—N. I. Ezhov, October 1937

Recent literature on the Stalinist period of Soviet history has dwelt heavily on the significance and scope of the terror, and historians are still much divided on both facts and interpretation, but there is little difference of opinion on the central role of what is now generally called the Great Terror of 1937–38. In the course of some fifteen months, approximately 1.5 million people were arrested; almost half of them were executed. The main executor of this gigantic operation was Stalin's state security chief of those years, Nikolai Ezhov.

Until quite recently, very little was known about this man, and what was known was to a large extent the product of invention. It was hard to realize that Ezhov had been one of the secret police chiefs praised most by Soviet propaganda. The extremely short lived Ezhov cultus of the years 1937–38 was indeed unprecedented. During this period Stalin was very favorably disposed toward Ezhov; according to Khrushchev, he had a pet name for

The Netherlands Organization for Scientific Research (NWO) has contributed to the realization of this book with a grant to the authors.

him: *ezhevichka,* "little bramble."[1] Stalin put his boundless trust in Ezhov. He was personally allowed to impose death sentences in the so-called "national operations," whereas the responsibility to impose death sentences in the operation with respect to order No. 00447 was passed on to an even lower level, that is, the regional NKVD chiefs. Since the Red Terror years 1918–21, neither before nor later in Soviet history have there been similar examples. During the 1920s and 1930s all death sentences were confirmed at the highest level, that is, by the Politburo. Even Ezhov's predecessors Menzhinskii and Iagoda, who had an OGPU Board issuing death sentences, officially needed prior permission by the Politburo. So from early 1937 until November 1938 Ezhov was not only the troubadour but the symbol of the new Soviet terror. His name is strongly linked to the Great Terror.

His short period of greatness, amounting to only one and a half years, was followed by a sudden complete, and well enforced, oblivion. Stalin forbade mention even of his name—not, perhaps, simply because it may have called up unpleasant memories, but because it annoyed him. For example, in 1949 in a conversation with Vulko Chervenkov and other Bulgarian leaders, when explaining how to organize the work of their national Department of the Interior, Stalin referred to the Soviet experience and in that connection also mentioned the name of Iagoda; but he kept silent about Ezhov.[2] According to the aircraft designer A. Iakovlev, some months after his fall Stalin recalled his former favorite with the words: "Ezhov was a scoundrel. He ruined our best cadres. He had morally degenerated."[3] Stalin seemed to put the burden of guilt for the terror of 1937–38 on the executors.

The historian analyzing the life and activity of Ezhov is confronted by a great deal of vagueness and inconsistencies. This is partly a result of the shortcomings of his official biography, published in the 1930s, which, as usual with a "model" biography of a Kremlin leader, omitted much and falsified when convenient, all in order to present an exemplary revolutionary career. Biographical facts were adjusted to the accepted cliché; all that was considered dubious or superfluous was cut out, or altered. After Ezhov's fall in the late 1930s, the situation was turned upside down: he was accused of having been a spy, a drunkard, a "pederast," the murderer of his wife. Nothing good remained. Stalin's famous *Short Course in the History of the All-Union Communist Party (Bolsheviks)*, which began appearing in installments in *Pravda* in September 1938, mentions Ezhov just twice—once in connection with his role during the civil war and again in the verification of Party documents campaign of the mid-1930s.[4] The second edition omits him altogether.[5] From the late 1930s on, Party censorship banned his works.[6] Since then, he has mainly been described in very negative terms. During the de-Stalinization campaign of the 1950s, the term *ezhovshchina* was even invented as a synonym for the bloody purges of 1936–38, as if it had all been Ezhov's work.

In the 1990s, the doors of the former Soviet archives were set ajar. New information on Ezhov's life and work began to appear. The authors of the present biography have used the following hitherto unpublished information to fill the gaps: materials from Ezhov's personal file (*lichnoe delo*) as nomenklatura functionary of the Party Central Committee apparatus at the Tsentr khraneniia sovremennoi dokumentatsii (TsKhSD,* the former archive of the General Department of the CPSU Central Committee); Ezhov's papers (*fond* 57) in the Arkhiv Prezidenta Rossiiskoi Federatsii (APRF, the former Politburo archive), later transferred (as *fond* 671) to the Rossiiskii tsentr khraneniia i izucheniia dokumentov noveishei istorii, or RTsKhIDNI[†] (the former Central Party Archive, where as yet they have not been completely declassified and are only sparsely accessible to researchers; most of these materials have been studied by the authors when they were still in the Presidential Archive, as a consequence of which in the notes they refer to this archive); other documents from the APRF and the RTsKhIDNI; Ezhov's interrogation and other documents from the Tsentral'nyi arkhiv Federal'noi sluzhby bezopasnosti (TsA FSB, the former

---

*Since 1999 renamed Rossiiskii gosudarstvennyi arkhiv noveishei istorii, or RGANI.
†Since 1999 renamed Rossiiskii gosudarstvennyi arkhiv sotsial'no-politicheskoi istorii, or RGASPI.

KGB archive), as well as from the archive of the Moscow Province
FSB Directorate; papers of the People's Commissariat of Water
Transportation of 1938–39 at the Rossiiskii gosudarstvennyi ark-
hiv ekonomiki (RGAE); and documents from the Gosudarstven-
nyi arkhiv Rossiiskoi Federatsii (GARF), all of them in Moscow.
In addition, a number of photographs have been obtained from
the Rossiiskii gosudarstvennyi arkhiv kinofotodokumentov
(RGAKFD) in Krasnogorsk.

A word on the archival investigation cases (*arkhivno-sledst-
vennye dela*) in the FSB Archive studied by us: they are a unique
source of immense importance. It is true that they contain the
most fantastic confessions of people tortured during interrogation; NKVD officers, for instance, confessed to having taken part
in nonexistent conspiracies, having prepared attempts on the life
of Stalin and other leaders, and so on. However, if handled in a
critical way, such evidence can reveal totally truthful information
about the way of life and mutual relations of the various NKVD
clans, the character of the NKVD conferences at which campaigns
of repression were discussed, private conversations of NKVD
leaders, their reactions to remarks by Stalin and Molotov—the list
goes on. Moreover, the truthfulness of such information can be
examined for compatibility with other sources, such as Stalin's
and Ezhov's visitors' registers. Another important source is that
of the stenographic reports of the operational NKVD conferences
of December 1936 and January 1938. Having been the first to
study them, we are able to publish Ezhov's original words with
respect to the repressions.

It should be pointed out that there may be serious discrepancies with Ezhov's accepted official biography, which created for
Ezhov a totally fictitious revolutionary past. That work states, for
example, that "comrade Ezhov prepared the soldiers in Belorussia
for the [October 1917] uprising," whereas Ezhov's role until the
mid-1930s was in fact of rather secondary importance. But we
shall also critically examine Ezhov's image in the anti-Stalinist his-
toriography as "bloodthirsty dwarf," "moral and physical
pygmy," or "bloody degenerate."[7]

*   *   *

This book is a coproduction researched and written in two places, Moscow and Amsterdam. Both authors have participated in all stages of the work and are fully responsible for the whole text. Nikita Petrov has traced most of the archival sources, Marc Jansen the published sources; the writing has primarily been done by Jansen, but always in close cooperation with Petrov. We are much obliged to Shirley Taylor for the constructive and respectful way in which she has edited our frequently inadequate English, and we want to thank the Netherlands Organization for Scientific Research (NWO) for their financial support in this respect. We also thank the Russian institutions mentioned above, together with their employees, for having made available archival materials for this study, especially APRF and RGAKFD and its director, Liudmila Petrovna Zapriagaeva, as well as the institutions where we have been able to research published sources, especially the Institute of Russian and East European Studies of Amsterdam University and the International Institute of Social History, also in Amsterdam. Moreover, we have made use of documents, photographs, and information from the archives of Moscow Memorial's Research and Information Center and want to express our special gratitude to Arsenii Roginskii and Nikita Okhotin. Others we should like to thank for their help in tracing materials, commenting on the manuscript or parts of it, and in other ways are Nanci Adler, Rolf Binner, Alex Lande, and Erik van Ree, as well as O. Kapchinskii. The authors very much appreciate the practical help in realizing this book offered by Robert Conquest and Stephen Cohen.

Marc Jansen
Nikita Petrov

1

Early Career

According to his official biography, Nikolai Ivanovich Ezhov had the right proletarian origin. He was born on 1 May (19 April, OS) 1895 in the Russian capital St. Petersburg, the son of a poor metalworker, a founder. But during interrogation, after his arrest in April 1939, he stated that he had been born in Mariiampole, a provincial town in southwest Lithuania, not far from the Polish border (later Kapsukas) and at that time part of the Russian empire. He had moved to Petersburg only in 1906, when he was eleven years old. After the revolution he started to assert that he was born there.

Ezhov also confessed that his father had not been an industrial worker at all. On the contrary, having been called up for military service, Ivan Ezhov, a Russian from Volkhonshino village in the Krapivna district to the southwest of Tula, joined a musical detachment in Mariiampole, where he married the conductor's maid. After demobilization he became a forest warden and then a pointsman in the railway service. In 1902–3, according to his son's words, he kept a tearoom, in fact serving as a brothel. From 1905 to 1914, after the tearoom closed, the elder Ezhov worked as a house painter. Even worse from the proletarian point of view, he was a small contractor who employed two wage laborers. Ivan Ezhov died in 1919, after some years of a debilitating illness.[1]

Nor did the other half of Nikolai Ezhov's origins suit later requirements. His official biography fails to note that his mother, Anna Antonovna Ezhova (born c. 1864)—the conductor's maid— was Lithuanian. Ezhov himself acknowledged in a questionnaire in 1924 that since childhood he could make himself understood in Polish and Lithuanian as well as Russian; three years later such origins were no longer appropriate and he stated that he knew only Russian.[2]

Ezhov had a sister, Evdokiia, some two years his senior, and also a brother, Ivan, who was born in 1897 in Veivery, Mariiam-pole district.[3] The two brothers did not get along well. Later, Nikolai told his nephew Viktor, Evdokiia's son, that Ivan, though two years younger, beat him up systematically, and once did so with a guitar in a street fight, an act that Nikolai never forgot. In 1939, during investigation, Nikolai related that before being called up for the army in 1916, Ivan had belonged to a criminal gang.[4] In the autumn of 1938, in a letter intended for Stalin, he wrote that his brother had been a "half-criminal element" and that since childhood he had not maintained any ties with him.[5]

Nikolai Ezhov attended primary school (probably a parish school) for no more than a year; according to the data of his later criminal case, he had an "unfinished primary education." In 1906, at eleven years of age, he was sent to Petersburg as apprentice to a tailor. From 1909 on, he was an apprentice and then a metalworker at several Petersburg factories. He spent more than a year in Lithuania and Poland in search of work, holding jobs in Kovno (later Kaunas), as an apprentice metalworker at the Til'-mans works, and in other towns as hired help to craftsmen.[6]

In 1914–15 he was employed in a Petrograd frame workshop, the Nedermeier and the Putilov works. At that time he took part in some strikes and demonstrations. In spite of his lack of schooling, he was rather well read and among workers had the nickname "Nicky the booklover" (*Kol'ka knizhnik*).[7] In a questionnaire of the early 1920s he stated that he was "literate (self-taught)."[8] In connection with a strike at the Treugol'nik factory he was arrested and exiled from Petrograd. In 1915 (he was then twenty years old), he was called up for army duty, first in the 76th infantry depot regiment and then in the 172d infantry Libavskii regiment, but he was soon wounded on the German front near Alitus (just to the west of Vilnius) and sent on leave for six months. He returned to the Putilov works. Later in the same year he was called up again, assigned first as a soldier in the 3d infantry regiment in Novo-Petergof, and then as a soldier-worker in a noncombatant detachment in the Dvinsk military district. In 1916 he became a foreman in the Fifth Artillery Workshop of the Northern Front in Vitebsk.[9]

Later, a fellow soldier of those days described how Ezhov once, in some way having got hold of the right ribbon, had posed as a holder of the St. George Cross.[10] During the 1930s, such an episode was not, of course, correct form, and this part of Ezhov's biography accordingly was painted in the style of revolutionary romanticism, emphasizing rebelliousness and punishment.[11] In the late 1930s, Aleksandr Fadeev was commissioned to write Ezhov's biography. He fulfilled the task, and the manuscript of a small book went to the publishing house. Although Ezhov was arrested before the biography could be printed,[12] part of Fadeev's manuscript was preserved among Ezhov's papers, under the title "Nikolai Ivanovich Ezhov: Child of Indigence and Struggle" (1937–38). "He was a small, dark-haired young man, with an open and stubborn face, with a sudden boyish smile and adroit precise movements of his small hands," Fadeev wrote. He goes on to say:

> He was a small Petersburg workman, very restrained and modest, with a clear, calm, and firm look from under his dark, beautiful eyebrows. He loved reading and poetry and now and then scribbled a few lines himself. He was a thoughtful and cordial friend, a good chap, in leisure time loving to play the guitar, to sing and dance, fearless in front of the authorities. Among his comrades he enjoyed a great deal of love and influence.[13]

Rather a similar description was that of A. Drizul, who knew Ezhov as a fellow workman at the artillery workshop No. 5. In

N. I. Ezhov (right), Vitebsk, 1916. (Memorial collection)

an interview with Isaak Mints of the Institute of Party History, Drizul described "Kolia" as "a smart, lively chap," "loved by all, sharp in conversations with other workmen." According to Drizul, Ezhov had been active in the Red Guard even before joining the Party, but he was "not much of a platform speaker." Drizul added: "He was a painstaking orator, a characteristic he kept to this day. He did not like to make speeches."[14] This is how the Institute of Party History edited Drizul's recollections: "Many workers . . . knew Nikolai Ivanovich as a cheerful, sociable person, in conversations knowing how to put before them political questions of the most vital importance and finding convincing, correct answers to them. . . . His characteristic was—'fewer words, more deeds.' "[15]

In his work of 1937, *The Great Socialist Revolution in the USSR*, Mints further glamorized Ezhov's past: "The Bolshevik fortress in Vitebsk was the Fifth Artillery Workshop of the Northern Front. It employed N. I. Ezhov, who had been dismissed from the Putilov works together with a few hundred fellow workers for their struggle against the imperialist war. Ezhov was sent to the army, to a depot battalion." After a strike, Mints went on, Ezhov was "thrown into a military convict prison, a penal battalion."[16] In actual fact, there is no evidence that he took part in any soldiers' strike or rebellion.

Some present-day authors do continue to suggest that Ezhov's class instincts were formed in a highly politicized environment, at a time of increasing tension between workers and employers. R. W. Thurston, for example, suggests: "Perhaps this background made Ezhov less tolerant of managers and bureaucrats, on whom the Terror of the late 1930s fell particularly harshly."[17] O. V. Khlevniuk, however, rightly points to the fact that Ezhov's later activity was not in the first place directed against the so-called economic specialists and that in several cases he even defended them.[18] (For example, in 1933 he is said to have defended coal enterprise managers, who in some regions were sacked too frequently, strongly interfering with coal extraction.)[19]

Ezhov's association with the Communist Party is equally unclear. His own testimony suggested that on 5 May 1917, following the February revolution, he joined the RSDRP(b), Lenin's Bolshevik (or Communist) Party; in a questionnaire of the early 1920s he reported that he had been a Party member since then.[20] Evidence from the Institute of Party History indicates that on 3 August 1917 he joined the Vitebsk organization of the RSDRP (Internationalists); the United Internationalists, to whom the Vitebsk organization belonged, were an intermediate group between Bolshevism and Menshevism.[21] At any rate, Ezhov did become the leader of the Party cell of artillery workshop No. 5, and from October 1917 to January 1918, he was assistant commissar and then commissar of Vitebsk station of the Riga-Orel railway line, organizing unit cells.[22] With respect to the February and October revolutions of 1917, in the questionnaire of the early 1920s he responded that he "very actively participated in both of them," and in another questionnaire he stated that during the October revolution he took part in "disarming Cossacks and Polish legionaries."[23] Mints exaggerated: "Lively and impetuous, he plunged into organization work from the very beginning of the revolution of 1917 on. Ezhov created a Red Guard, himself picked participants, himself instructed them, and obtained weapons."[24] In any case, his active participation in the revolution of 1917 in Petrograd is a legend.[25]

In early 1918 Nikolai Ezhov joined his family in Vyshnii Volochek, Tver' province, where he got a job at the Bolotin glassworks. He became a member of the factory committee, and from June 1918 to April 1919 he was a member of the district committee and head of the Party club. He also worked in a battalion of special destination in Zubtsov in the same province, until May 1919, when he was called up for the Red Army. He served in Saratov in a depot electrical engineering battalion, where he presided over the Party group and was presidium member of the military district. Twenty years later, during interrogation, Vladimir Konstantinov, who had evacuated the battalion from Petrograd to Saratov, recollected how in 1919, after quartering, Ezhov, "an urchin with torn boots," was appointed political instructor (*polit-*

ruk). They became friends, serving together until 1921.[26] In August 1919, after evacuating to Kazan', Ezhov was appointed military commissar of the school of the Second Base of Radio Telegraph Units—which meant that he was charged with political work such as agitation. His biographer Fadeev again sparks up the image: he was actively engaged in battle, like the assault on Ivashchenko village, in which he was wounded by three shell-splinters, one of which pierced his jaw. "The severe injury disabled Ezhov for a long time. Throughout his life there remained a scar to the right of his chin"; and he describes a portrait of Ezhov of the time: "a still very young, black-haired chap with black eyebrows; a dreamy expression of his eyes with a strong curve in his lips—an inspired, strong-willed face."[27]

In February 1920 Ezhov was reprimanded by the military tribunal of the Depot Army, of which his base was part, for insufficient vigilance that had resulted in the admission to the school of a number of deserters. This misstep had no consequences for his

Radio technicians leaving for the front, Kazan', June 1920, with Ezhov in the middle of the front row. (Memorial collection)

career, however, and in May he was promoted to military commissar of the Radio Units Base in Kazan'.[28] Although his discipline and diligence in executing orders had already been noticed, still another stain was subsequently found on his reputation. After his fall, the Chekist S. F. Redens testified that Ezhov had on at least one occasion privately boasted about having come out against Lenin and having been an adherent of the anti-intellectual Machajski movement.[29] In 1936 in a registration form Ezhov stated that he had belonged to the "Workers' Opposition" within the Communist Party but had broken with it before the Tenth Party Congress of March 1921. Four years later, before the court, he admitted only to having sympathized with the Opposition, adding that he had never been a member and that after Lenin's criticism of March 1921 he had recognized its deceit and had lined up behind Lenin.[30]

That was a good move, for in April 1921 Ezhov became a member of the bureau and head of the agitation and propaganda department of one of Kazan's district Party committees, and in July he assumed the same functions in the Tatar provincial Party committee. At about the same time, he was demobilized from the army[31] and was then elected to the Presidium of the Central Executive Committee of the Tatar Republic. In August, suffering from work stress, he was granted a leave and the right to enter one of Moscow's sanatoriums for medical treatment; at the recommendation of the Central Committee, he was in the Kremlin hospital from 18 January to 13 February 1922, for treatment of colitis, anemia, and lung catarrh.[32] By then, clearly, he was already fairly prominent, and in Moscow he probably associated with influential people from the Central Committee apparatus, like Lazar' Kaganovich and Mendel' Khataevich, people who had become acquainted with him in Belorussia.[33] It resulted in a responsible assignment: on 15 February 1922 the Central Committee Secretariat appointed him Secretary of the Party Committee of the Mari Autonomous Province.[34] Because this was an important assignment, it is conceivable that in this connection he had his first conversation with Stalin.

Ezhov's assignment in the small provincial capital, Krasno-kokshaisk (now Ioshkar-Ola), got off to a bad start in March: the Bureau of the Provincial Party Committee only accepted him after an initial refusal, and I. P. Petrov, the chairman of the Provincial Executive Committee, from the very beginning was openly hostile, mainly because of Ezhov's dismissal of concern for the native language or culture as "national chauvinism." Ezhov's biographers agree that "the worst sides of his character revealed themselves," and they note his "lust for power, arrogance, rudeness." He showed a purely administrative attitude, refusing to take into account the national peculiarities of the province. Even an instructor from the central apparatus did not succeed in calming people's feelings.[35] In October 1922 Ezhov requested a leave of absence, again citing stress: "From the February revolution on I have not taken a holiday. In February of this year I was sent to the Mari province straight from the hospital. I have been worn out completely. At present I suffer from almost seven illnesses." The Bureau of the Provincial Committee complied with the request and granted him a leave of one month, plus an allowance of 300 million rubles (not a huge amount at the time) for medical treatment "in view of a number of serious illnesses." His place was filled temporarily by a colleague.[36] He had served in Krasnokokshaisk for only seven months.

Instead of going straight to a health resort, however, Ezhov returned to Kazan', writing in a letter that he liked "Tatariia better than Marlandiia."[37] From there he went to Moscow, where in late October he attended a session of the Central Executive Committee of Soviets. (On that occasion a photograph seems to have been taken of Lenin, surrounded by a group of delegates, one of them Ezhov.)[38] The Central Committee authorities had agreed not to send him back to Krasnokokshaisk but rather, after a rest period of a month, to transfer him to another province or another branch. The expensiveness of Moscow during the NEP seemed shocking, and on 6 November he wrote that he "had already started to be pretty much out of commission" and was going to the North Caucasian health resort of Kislovodsk for medical treatment, though he "did not have a red cent."[39] On 28 November he was already in a Kislovodsk sanatorium, apparently having applied for an extension of his leave period; in a telegram of that date he asked the Central Committee authorities to let him know in case his request had been positively judged.[40]

The request seems to have been granted, for on 1 March 1923, at a meeting of the Orgburo and the Secretariat of the Central Committee in Moscow (with Stalin present), Ezhov was appointed Secretary of the Party committee of Semipalatinsk province in the northeast of what was then called the Kirgiz (later Kazakh) Republic.[41] Although Ezhov himself was not at the meeting, as in 1922, Stalin may have interviewed him in connection with the important appointment. Ezhov was granted nine days' leave to go to Krasnokokshaisk in order to hand things over, but instead he went again to Kazan', perhaps hoping to find work there.[42] On 9 March, in a letter to his former colleague from the Mari provincial Party committee, P. N. Ivanov, he noted that he had heard that "you have sacked Petrov" but that to his displeasure an Orgburo commission had decided to send Petrov back to the Mari province.[43] Nine days later he wrote that he was going to Semipalatinsk.[44]

All in all, Ezhov had stretched out his month-long leave to half a year. One gets the impression that in this period he was a rather bad functionary, sickly and not very hardworking. Not surprisingly, he was given bad references with respect to his work in the Mari province: "In a leading function, the absence of sufficient theoretical training and versatile practical skill make it impossible for comr. E. to orient himself straight away in an especially complicated situation. This is confirmed by the blunders made by him during his first time in the Mari province." A "certain obstinacy, sometimes bordering on irascibility," was established as a trait of his character. Because of insufficient theoretical training and "polished accumulated experience in leading work," for the time being a promotion was not recommended. He only qualified for a provincial Party function as second or third in charge: organization or agitation head, or district secretary.[45]

These recommendations were clearly not followed, however, for on 27 March Ezhov was confirmed as having arrived in Semipalatinsk and begun work as Party Secretary.[46] According to his biographers, in his new function he again behaved "high-handedly" in front of the secretaries of the district committees.[47] Fadeev says that in some districts anti-NEP sentiments prevailed. Advocates of equalizing "poor man's communism" proclaimed the independent "Bukhtarma Republic"* in northeast Kazakhstan, and Ezhov quickly discovered that "among the provincial 'leaders' there were quite a few secret and overt enemies sympathizing with the insurrection and supporting it." He went to the rebellious peasant districts without any military protection. The expedition was full of hardships, Fadeev wrote. The rebels were after his life. But in the end the insurrection was suppressed peacefully.[48] A photograph of the time shows Ezhov in front of a group of soldiers returning after the insurrection had been suppressed.

A year or so later, in May 1924, Ezhov was delegated to the Thirteenth Party Congress in Moscow.[49] The following month he was transferred to Orenburg to head the organization department of the Provincial Party Committee of the Kirgiz Republic, which looks rather like a demotion, except that in November of the same year the Orgburo appointed him Secretary of the Kirgiz Provincial Committee.[50] Here, too, he had a frustrating experience with the locals. As a former Gulag prisoner recalled later on, Ezhov was so unable to deal with the strong local Trotskiist opposition that he went into hiding in a saloon car.[51] In April 1925, the Kirgiz Republic was renamed the Kazakh Republic and the capital was transferred to Kzyl-Orda. That summer, Ezhov became Secretary of the Regional Party Committee of the Kazakh Republic and head of the organization department. According to Fadeev, he proved himself a passionate opponent of concessions to foreign capitalists, such as the British businessman Leslie Urquhart. During the same time he taught himself Marxism-Leninism. Fadeev notes: "With the exceptional capacity for work characteristic of him, for nights he sat over his books in order to master the theory of

*Fadeev incorrectly calls it the Baturminskaia respublika.

Marx-Lenin-Stalin."[52] (In 1924, in a questionnaire, Ezhov had answered to knowing the basic Marxist literature; at one point, during two months, two evenings a week, he had participated in a Marxist self-education circle.)[53]

Ezhov's career was on its way. In December 1925 he was delegated to the Fourteenth Party Congress in Moscow, finishing on 31 December, and on 18 January 1926 the Central Committee Secretariat informed the Kazakh Regional Committee that Ezhov was to attend a one-year course in Marxism-Leninism at the Communist Academy, where professional Party functionaries were being trained. Ezhov had returned to Kzyl-Orda after the Congress, and on 25 January, he left for Moscow, with new prospects for advancement.[54] Among his fellow students were his later close colleague E. G. Evdokimov and the future chief of the Red Army Political Directorate, L. Z. Mekhlis.[55] If Ezhov did indeed complete the course in early 1927, then there is a gap in our information about his activities during the first half of that year. According to his Russian biographers, in February 1927 he was appointed instructor of the Organization and Distribution Department (Orgraspredotdel) of the Central Committee.[56] It is also possible that during the first half of 1927 he prolonged his studies or, as in the months after his service in the Mari province, sickly and inactive, was awaiting a new appointment.

In early July 1927, when he underwent a koumiss cure in a sanatorium in Shafranovo near Ufa in the Urals, Orgraspredotdel was looking for him in connection with his appointment as its assistant head.[57] Only in mid-July he reacted, explaining the delay with an operation he had been undergoing in Ufa. Although the cure was to finish only on 1 August, he left for Moscow the following day.[58] The Orgburo confirmed the appointment on 15 July.[59] It implied an unusually fast promotion. According to Lev Razgon, it was Ivan Mikhailovich Moskvin, Razgon's father-in-law and Orgraspredotdel head since February 1926,[60] who "found, fetched, brought up, and fostered" Ezhov: he summoned the "quiet, modest, and dependable secretary of a distant Party committee" to Moscow and made him instructor in the Orgraspredotdel, subsequently assistant, and then his deputy.[61] Ezhov had, of course, gone to Moscow to study at least a year before his Orgraspredotdel appointment. It is beyond a doubt, however, that by then he had become acquainted with Stalin, for it was Stalin's practice to know his apparatchiks, especially at this level.

Ezhov was made deputy head of Orgraspredotdel in November 1927.[62] In this important function he became initiated in the niceties of the Party's personnel policy. His department was engaged in the selection and assignment of nomenklatura personnel over the whole country and all branches; moreover, it checked the activities of the local Party organizations. In this capacity, he attended the Fifteenth Party Congress (December 1927) and the Sixteenth Party Conference (April 1929).[63] By now he was so highly respected that in 1928 the Secretary of the Tatar Provincial Party Committee, M. M. Khataevich, asked to be replaced by him: "You have in the Central Committee a tough guy, Nikolai Ezhov. He will establish order among the Tatars." Although the Central Committee seems to have complied with Khataevich's request, for one reason or another the new appointment did not materialize.[64]

Nikolai Ezhov's name appeared in the central press for the first time in August 1929 as one of three authors—along with Lev Mekhlis and Petr Pospelov—of an article entitled "The Right Deviation in the Practical Work and the Party Swamp," published in the theoretical Party journal *Bol'shevik*. The authors pointed out that, in addition to the public ones, there were also secret Rightists in the Party—"Party swamp" meaning "Rightist practice in the everyday practical work." The fight was against not only known Rightists but also the Party swamp.[65]

In December 1929 Ezhov moved from Ograspredotdel to a new post as Deputy People's Commissar of Agriculture responsible for personnel selection, under Iakov Iakovlev.[66] For the first time he came to deal with real mass repressions. When in February 1930 the state security service OGPU began arresting and deporting hundreds of thousands of peasants who had been labeled "kulaks," the People's Commissariat of Agriculture did not stand on the sidelines. In June–July 1930 the People's Commissariat delegated him to the Sixteenth Party Congress.[67]

In several articles of this period Ezhov corroborated his radicalism. In March 1930 he published "The City to the Aid of the Village," an article dealing with the mobilization by the November 1929 Central Committee Plenum of 25,000 workers in order to collectivize agriculture—a demonstration, he pointed out, of the aid of the working class to the kolkhoz movement.[68] Another article that appeared in the autumn of the same year, "Kondrat'evism in the Struggle for Cadres," advocated the training of proletarian specialists, in spite of the strong opposition from "bourgeois" specialists, who preferred the education of "universal" specialists instead of specialized specialists, or technicians; according to Ezhov, this was precisely what the proletarian state needed.[69] An article in *Pravda* in March 1932, "Some Questions with Respect to the Training and Placing of Cadres," continued Ezhov's radical views on education. He was pleased to establish that the old-fashioned universities were a thing of the past. Because of the need to train economic and technical cadres, they had made way for specialized institutions of higher education that were indissolubly related to production and within three to four years trained engineers in a definite speciality: "Our institutions of higher education have been transformed into a sort of factory, and carry out the orders of the economy to train the necessary specialists."[70]

Ezhov returned to the Party apparatus in November 1930 as head of the Distribution Department or Raspredotdel, one of the two departments resulting from the division of Orgraspredotdel.[71] This was a key position with control over the selection and assignment of Party personnel. On 21 November—one week after his appointment—he was received by Stalin in the Kremlin.[72] He was clearly admitted to Stalin's inner circle. Four days later, at the suggestion of his direct chief in the Central Committee apparatus, L. Kaganovich, the Politburo allowed him to attend its meetings and to receive all materials sent to Central Committee members.[73] In other words, Ezhov, though not a Central Committee member, was, like Politburo members, informed about state and Party matters.

On 9 November 1931 he was again received by Stalin, accompanied by Kaganovich, V. Molotov, and K. Voroshilov; among the others present were OGPU deputy chairman Genrikh Iagoda, E. P. Berzin, and S. A. Bergavinov.[74] As a result, two days later Stalin signed a Politburo decision on the mining of gold in the far north. The Dal'stroi state trust was to be organized under the direction of Berzin, supervised by Iagoda, in order to speed up the exploitation of gold mining on the upper reaches of Kolyma River. Bergavinov, as First Party Secretary of the Far East, was to explore the possibilities of using icebreakers; Ezhov, together with a few others, was to "work out privileges to be enjoyed by both deported prisoners and volunteers for good work in Kolyma (reduction of their terms of punishment, rehabilitation, security for the families of volunteers, increase of salary, etc.)."[75] This was the origin of the infamous forced labor system in Kolyma.

After the meeting there was a characteristic incident. When Ezhov left the Kremlin, together with Iagoda and Bergavinov, Iagoda offered the other two a lift in his car. On the way Ezhov, who was dressed in an ordinary summer coat, got very cold. Iagoda protested indignantly that Ezhov's coat was too light: while money was spent for his treatment, with his sick lungs he dressed like that! Ezhov answered that he had no winter coat. Then Bergavinov thought that in that case he should receive fur for a coat. Within two weeks he was sent some strips of squirrel fur, without any account. Apparently, the Central Control Commission heard about this, after which Ezhov sent a note to Matvei Shkiriatov of the Commission explaining that the fur lay unused in his apartment and that he was prepared to yield it any moment.[76]

The episode should be considered against the background of Ezhov's health problems. Earlier, in June of 1931, the head of the Kremlin Medical Directorate had reported to Kaganovich and Postyshev that Ezhov suffered from tuberculosis of the lungs, myasthenia, neurasthenia owing to work stress, anemia, and malnutrition. He needed an immediate sick leave of two months, to be spent in a sanatorium in the south, like Abastuman (Georgia) or Kislovodsk.[77] In November of the next year the same functionary informed the Central Committee that Ezhov had moreover contracted angina and suffered from sciatica. He needed an urgent checkup in the Kremlin hospital and a diet in order to be able to return to work soon.[78]

In Kazan', no later than in June 1921, Ezhov had married Antonina Titova, a lower Party functionary, who was a few years younger than he. She accompanied him to Krasnokokshaisk and Semipalatinsk, but in the summer of 1923 she left for Moscow to study at the Timiriazev agricultural academy. In late 1925 the two reunited in Moscow. With them lived Ezhov's mother, who was then in her early sixties, and two children of his sister, Evdokiia, the teenagers Liudmila and Anatolii Babulin, who studied in Moscow (Evdokiia herself with her four other children lived as a peasant in a village near Vyshnii Volochek in Tver' province). After finishing the agricultural academy in 1928, Antonina was also employed by the People's Commissariat of Agriculture, as subdepartment head. With her husband's help, she published a book, *The Collectivization of Agriculture and the Peasant Woman*. But around 1930 they divorced because Ezhov, who had never been much of a true husband, had seriously fallen in love with another woman.[79]

Her name was Evgeniia Solomonovna (or Zalmanovna), born Feigenberg in 1904 to a large Jewish family in Gomel', where her father was a small tradesman. There, while young, she had married Lazar' Khaiutin. After divorcing him, she had married the journalist and diplomat Aleksandr Gladun. They had lived in London since September 1926 but were expelled from Great Britain in connection with the raid in May 1927 by British authorities on the Soviet trade delegation and the resulting break in diplomatic relations between Moscow and London. Gladun returned to Moscow, Evgeniia became a typist for a time at the Soviet Trade Mission in Berlin, where in the summer of 1927 she met the writer Isaak Babel' and apparently had an affair with him. (According to Babel's widow, Babel' had known Evgeniia since the time when she worked in an Odessa publishing house.)

Before too long Evgeniia was back at her husband's side in

Moscow, and in November 1927 Ezhov must have appeared in their apartment for the first time; they seem to have met in a Black Sea sanatorium. In 1939, during interrogation, Gladun testified: "She said that Ezhov was a rising star and that it was profitable for her to be with him and not with me." Around 1930 Ezhov married Evgeniia, who took his name. They lived in central Moscow. Evgeniia worked as a typist for the newspaper *Krest'ianskaia gazeta*, edited by Semen Uritskii, with whom she seems to have had an affair as well. Uritskii took her away from the typewriter to make her a journalist. She had a sort of salon where she received writers, artists, and diplomats. Apart from Babel', regular guests were other writers like Lev Kassil' and Samuil Marshak and the musician Leonid Utesov.[80]

Ezhov not only had heterosexual relations. On 24 April 1939, after his arrest, he wrote a statement for the NKVD investigation department about his "vice of long standing—pederasty." Of course, the word "pederasty" meant homosexuality, but except for that the confession seems to have been well founded, and the statement needs to be quoted at length:

> It started already when at a very young age I was a tailor's apprentice. Approximately from fifteen to sixteen I had some cases of perverted sexual acts with apprentices of the same tailor's workshop who were of the same age. This vice was resumed in the old tsarist army under front conditions. Apart from an accidental liaison with a soldier of our company, I had a liaison with a certain Filatov, a friend of mine from Leningrad who served in the same regiment. The liaison was mutually active [*vzaimnoaktivnaia*], i.e. now the one, now the other side was the "woman." Later Filatov was killed at the front.
>
> In 1919 I was appointed commissar of the Second Base of Radio Telegraph Units. My secretary was a certain Antoshin. . . . In 1919 I had a mutually active pederastic liaison with him. In 1924 I worked in Semipalatinsk. My friend of long standing Dement'ev went there together with me. In 1924 I had also some cases of pederasty with him in which I alone was active. In 1925 in Orenburg I established a pederastic liaison with a certain Bo-

iarskii, then chairman of the Kazakh provincial trade union council. At present, as far as I know, he is director of the Moscow Arts Theater.* The liaison was mutually active. He and I had then just arrived in Orenburg, we lived in the same hotel. The liaison was brief, until shortly after his wife arrived.

In 1925 the capital of Kazakhstan was transferred from Orenburg to Kzyl-Orda, and I went to work there also. Soon F. I. Goloshchekin (now Chief Arbitrator) arrived there as secretary of the provincial committee [*kraikom*]. He arrived as bachelor, without wife, and I also lived as bachelor. Until my departure to Moscow (approximately within two months) I practically moved to his apartment and frequently passed the night there. Soon I also established a pederastic liaison with him, which continued periodically until my departure. Just like the previous ones, the liaison with him was mutually active.[81]

In the late 1920s–early 1930s, Ezhov had already developed drinking habits. Later, during interrogation, Zinaida Glikina, Evgeniia's old friend from Gomel' times on and an habituée of their apartment, testified that Ezhov "drank systematically and often got awfully drunk." He also "incredibly indulged in debauchery, and lost the appearance not only of a communist, but of a man as well."[82] One of the close friends with whom he used to spend nights hitting the bottle was his colleague from the People's Commissariat of Agriculture, Fedor Mikhailovich Konar (Polashchuk); they probably became acquainted in 1927. After arrest, Ezhov stated that "Konar and I always drank in the company of prostitutes he had brought to his apartment."[83] Having become Deputy People's Commissar of Agriculture, in January 1933 Konar was arrested on a charge of espionage for Poland; two

---

*Ia. I. Boiarskii (Shimshelevich), born 1890, Party member, Central Committee chairman of the Trade Union of Artistic Functionaries *Rabis*, first deputy of the Soviet government Committee for Art Questions. In July 1937 the Politburo appointed him director of the Moscow Arts Theater, a function he held for more than a year; in July 1939 he was arrested, then sentenced to death: *Vlast' i khudozhestvennaia intelligentsiia: Dokumenty TsK RKP(b)-VKP(b), VChK-OGPU-NKVD o kul'turnoi politike. 1917–1953 gg.* (Moscow, 1999), pp. 201, 250, 269, 699, 774; Memorial archive, execution lists, No. 25D–928.

months later he was condemned to death for "sabotage activity in agriculture," and shot.[84]

Another drinking pal was Lev Efimovich Mar'iasin, Ezhov's co-deputy head of Orgraspredotdel from November 1927 on. In 1930 he was appointed to the governing board of the USSR State Bank; the next year he became its deputy president and in 1934 its president; at the same time, he was Deputy People's Commissar of Finances. There is evidence about how Mar'iasin and Ezhov loved to kill time. Having gotten drunk, the two organized a competition to see who, with their pants off and squatted, was faster and better at blowing away a handful of cigarette ash from a penny by farting.[85]

Via Mar'iasin, Ezhov came to know his chief, Georgii Leonidovich Piatakov, since 1928 deputy president and since the following year president of the board of the USSR State Bank, until in 1932 he became Deputy People's Commissar of Heavy Industry. During his trial in 1940, Ezhov gave details of their relationship: "Usually Piatakov, when he became slightly tight, loved to mock partners. In one case, being drunk, he pricked me with a pin twice. I flared up, slapped his face, and cut his lip. After this we swore and did not talk anymore." Mar'iasin tried to reconcile the two, but Ezhov refused and eventually broke with Mar'iasin.[86] All these and other acquaintances were subsequently condemned as "Trotskiists," etc., and when in 1939 Ezhov was arrested himself, he was accused of having had the wrong contacts.

In these early years Ezhov did not yet have the reputation of being a cruel and merciless henchman. He was not considered to be all that bad. In the province he gave the impression of "a nervous but well-meaning and attentive person, free of arrogance and bureaucratic manners." When Iurii Dombrovskii met Ezhov's Kazakhstan Party colleagues, not one of them had anything negative to say about him: "He was a responsive, humane, gentle, tactful man. . . . Any unpleasant personal matter he without fail tried to solve quietly and to slow down." "He responded to any request, even of little importance, and always helped as best he could," a colleague of Ezhov from Kazakhstan told Anna Larina (Bukharina). When Nadezhda Mandel'shtam met him at a holiday resort for Party bosses in 1930, she found him "a modest and rather agreeable person." A Russian who knew him in the same period wrote that he "made the impression of a good lad, a good comrade."[87]

During the late 1920s Lev Razgon, who was married to Ivan Moskvin's stepdaughter, met Ezhov a couple of times in the family circle: "Ezhov did not at all resemble a vampire. He was a small slender man, always dressed in a crumpled cheap suit and a blue satin shirt. He sat at the table quietly, not talking much, somewhat shy, drank little, did not interrupt, only listened attentively, slightly bending his head." Moskvin's wife was anxious about his not eating enough; she was very concerned about his health (he had suffered from tuberculosis). He had a good voice and in company used to sing folk songs sometimes. Moskvin esteemed him as an irreproachable executor. When his former protégé was already NKVD chief, he told Razgon:

> I don't know of any more ideal functionary than Ezhov. Rather, he is not a functionary, but an executor. After charging him with a task, you don't have to check up on him: he will accomplish the mission. Ezhov has only one, indeed essential, shortcoming—he does not know where to stop. . . . Sometimes you have to take care to stop him in time.[88]

Ezhov's later colleagues in the Party leadership testified that he had "great organizational talents and an iron grasp," was "very energetic, a strong hand."[89] And he was "boundlessly devoted to Stalin."[90] According to Roy Medvedev, Stalin's influence on Ezhov became "total, unlimited, almost hypnotic."[91] The Party leader made him a key figure in the struggle against the "enemies of the people"—against, that is, those who opposed his personal rule.

2

Directing the Purges and Supervising the NKVD

In April 1933 the Central Committee entrusted a commission, including Raspredotdel chief Ezhov, with a large-scale purge, similar to earlier purges organized in 1921 and 1929.[1] All Party members were subjected to a review to establish whether they could remain in the Party; for the time being, no new members were admitted. The purge resulted in many expulsions.[2] It lasted until May 1935 and was followed by two successive purge campaigns under Ezhov's direction, lasting until September 1936.[3]

When in January–February 1934 the Seventeenth Party Congress convened, Ezhov was elected to its Secretariat and (as chairman) to the Mandate (credentials) Commission.[4] During the Congress he was elected to the Central Committee and (as deputy head) to the newly instituted Party Control Commission.[5] Reportedly, the commission head, Kaganovich, personally chose him as his deputy.[6] At the Central Committee Plenum following the Congress he was made a member of the Organization Bureau (Orgburo).[7] In March he was charged with presiding over the Central Committee Industrial Department, and in December he succeeded Andrei Zhdanov as chairman of the Commission for Foreign

Travel.[8] He was rising extraordinarily fast, as if Stalin trusted him more than anyone else.

From this early moment on, Ezhov was involved in state security matters. On 20 February 1934 he attended his first Politburo meeting;[9] on Stalin's initiative, it was decided to institute an all-Union People's Commissariat of Internal Affairs (NKVD), with a reorganized state security organization OGPU incorporated within it.[10] A month later, in this connection, the Politburo charged a commission, presided over by Kuibyshev and including Ezhov, with reforming the judiciary.[11] A few days later, together with Stalin, Ezhov was included in another Politburo commission, presided over by Kaganovich and charged with working out draft regulations for the NKVD and a "Special Board."[12] As a result, on 10 July the OGPU was abolished, its police functions being incorporated in the newly instituted NKVD under Genrikh Iagoda, with Ia. S. Agranov and G. E. Prokof'ev as deputies; the Chief Directorate of State Security (GUGB) and the camps system (GULag) were part of it. Unlike the OGPU, the NKVD was not authorized to pass death sentences or administrative sentences above five years; with respect to "people recognized as socially dangerous," an NKVD Special Board (Osoboe soveshchanie, OSO) was authorized to pass sentences up to five years (from April 1937 on, eight years) exile or camp. Treason cases were referred to the courts.[13] In May 1935, the NKVD ordered its regional bodies to organize triumvirates or troikas, enjoying the same powers as the OSO.[14] These were the so-called "militia troikas" (headed by the regional militia chief); the main targets were people who had transgressed the passport regime, and tramps.

As before, Ezhov suffered from bad health. By now he ranked high enough to earn the privilege of traveling abroad. In July 1934, the Politburo sent him to Italy for medical treatment, with a disbursement of 1,200 rubles in foreign currency (later supplemented with an additional 1,000 gold rubles); he had to be forbidden to return until the end of his rest.[15] Instead of Italy he went to Vienna, where he was treated in a sanatorium for several weeks. (After arrest he gratuitously stated that while there he had had intimate intercourse with a nurse; when a doctor found out about it, he had himself recruited as an "agent of the German intelligence service.")[16] In early October he returned to Moscow, informing Stalin (who was on leave in Sochi) that he was at work again. He wrote that he felt all right but was on a diet and in half a year's time had to have his appendix removed in order to improve the working of the alimentary canal. Apparently, when abroad he had not lost sight of state security interests: he told Stalin that he had had a look at the work of Soviet institutions there and wanted to report on it.[17]

Stalin indeed took personal care of Ezhov, whom he had selected as his main assistant in realizing plans for a political purge. This became clear after the murder of the Leningrad Party chief, Sergei Kirov, on 1 December 1934. According to one version of events, on the morning of that day, after the news of the murder had reached Moscow, Ezhov was summoned to Stalin's office and spent a good part of the day there.[18] The day's register of visitors to Stalin's office does not mention Ezhov at all.[19] Yet when on the same day late at night Stalin left for Leningrad on a special train, Ezhov was among those accompanying him, and after arriving in Leningrad the next morning, he attended Stalin's interrogation of the murderer, Nikolaev.[20] Two days after the murder, the Politburo approved an emergency decree enabling the conviction and execution in an abbreviated procedure of persons accused of terrorism. During the purges of the following years, this Law of 1 December 1934 was used extensively.[21]

Stalin charged Ezhov with supervising the investigation, together with Komsomol leader A. V. Kosarev and Iagoda's deputy in charge of state security Agranov.[22] Notwithstanding the lack of any facts, Stalin gave orders to fabricate the story that Zinov'ev, Kamenev, and the other former Party oppositionists were responsible for the murder. The NKVD leadership, however, treated this version of events with distrust and tried to disregard Stalin's orders. Then Ezhov came to play his role. Stalin in fact appointed him his representative in the NKVD. This was not appreciated by Iagoda, and later, under arrest, he testified that after the Kirov murder Ezhov "systematically and persistently began to creep into NKVD matters"; passing over Iagoda, he went straight to the operative departments and meddled in everything.[23] Indeed, at an NKVD conference in December 1936, Ezhov confirmed to having been very closely connected with NKVD work during the past two years.[24]

Delving into the details of the investigation, Ezhov gave it the direction Stalin wanted: in a detailed report, he unmasked the culpable enemies and spies. The NKVD, accustomed to acting on its own, resented the interferences; as Ezhov explained later, the NKVD looked in another direction and would not allow him access to the case until Stalin intervened. The Party leader threatened Iagoda, "Take care, or we'll punch you in the mug." He ordered the NKVD chief to arrest those against whom Ezhov had collected evidence, which Iagoda did, but only reluctantly.[25]

By February, Ezhov reported to Stalin that he had rounded up about one thousand former Leningrad oppositionists, three hundred of whom had been arrested, the rest exiled; in addition, several thousand so-called "former people" had been deported from the city.[26] In December 1934 Kirov's murderer, Nikolaev, was tried; next month followed the trial of the "Moscow Center" of Zinov'ev, Kamenev et al., who received five-to-ten-year sentences for "ideological involvement" in the murder.[27] Henceforth, Iagoda sent Ezhov all examination records of the main oppositionists and plotters.

Ezhov's authority was not limited to overseeing the investigation of these cases; increasingly he gained control of the whole NKVD. In a memorandum, he directed Stalin's attention to NKVD "deficiencies," criticizing its policy of drift with respect to the work of informers and agents. The way agents were recruited was "bordering on counterrevolution": "Under such conditions of recruiting, foreign intelligence services can easily implant their people under the guise of Cheka agents." The NKVD, he complained, was much less competent in investigating than in searching. On the whole, its people were insufficiently qualified, and the purge that he had carried out personally of the Leningrad NKVD, in his opinion, "should yet be extended." (In Leningrad Ezhov had checked 2,747 NKVD employees and 3,050 militia employees, resulting in the firing or transferring to other work of 298 and 590 of them, respectively). Ezhov asked Stalin for permission to address a conference of NKVD executives with sharp criticism of these deficiencies.[28] Stalin approved, and in February 1935 Ezhov addressed such a conference.[29] On 31 March, the Politburo decided to give him for examination the regulations pertaining to the NKVD and the GUGB.[30] USSR Procurator Ivan Akulov also sent him his complaints about NKVD methods.[31] In short, from December 1934 on he was the supreme supervisor of the NKVD.

On 1 February the Central Committee appointed Ezhov its secretary. He was given an office in the Central Committee building on Staraia ploshchad', on the fifth floor, where also were offices of the Orgburo and the Secretariat.[32] (As Raspredotdel head, he already must have had an office there.) Apart from Stalin and Ezhov, the Secretariat now consisted of Kaganovich, Zhdanov, and (from 28 February on) Andreev. As Secretary, Ezhov got three assistants: S. A. Ryzhova, V. E. Tsesarskii, and I. I. Shapiro, the last two already having served under him in the Industrial Department; they stayed with him during the following years.[33] Moreover, on 27 February the Politburo appointed him chairman of the Party Control Commission, succeeding Kaganovich, who became People's Commissar of Communications.[34] Now he was the supreme Party judge as well, investigating and punishing cases of ideological deviance, corruption, and violation of Party rules.

On 10 March he took over the key function of head of the Department of Leading Party Organizations (ORPO). This department had been established straight after the Seventeenth Party Congress in the place of Raspredotdel and was engaged in the selection and distribution of personnel in the Party, but not in industry, which was the Industrial Department's responsibility. The first ORPO head had been D. A. Bulatov, but since his transfer in December 1934 to another Party function, the post had been vacant. Already since then, Ezhov had signed the ORPO documents, and now he was officially appointed its head.[35] He had to hand over the Industrial Department to Andrei Andreev, who also became head of the Orgburo, but with Ezhov as second man.[36] On 31 March the Politburo replaced Kaganovich in several of its commissions by Iakovlev, Andreev, and Ezhov. Ezhov was charged with purging the Komsomol and checking the NKVD staff.[37]

According to O. V. Khlevniuk, as a consequence of this redistribution of leading functions, Kaganovich lost his position as Stalin's second man. Formally he was succeeded by Andreev, but Andreev's influence was strongly limited by his having to share responsibility in the Orgburo with Ezhov, and furthermore Kaganovich remained Central Committee secretary and Orgburo member. The roles of Andreev and Ezhov were more or less balanced. Although not (like Andreev) a Politburo member, Ezhov controlled the Party personnel policy and the conduct of the main political campaigns. Moreover, he took an active part in Politburo work and was charged by Stalin with the task of controlling the NKVD and organizing the political purges.[38] A relative unknown, in Central Committee circles Ezhov's rapid promotion was explained by his great firmness and "good nose" (*ogromnyi niukh*), as well as by the strong support of Kaganovich and Stalin.[39]

According to a number of authors, on 13 May 1935 the Politburo secretly instituted a special State Security Commission, headed by Stalin, with Ezhov as his deputy. The members were Zhdanov, Malenkov, Matvei Shkiriatov (secretary of the Party Collegium of the Party Control Commission), and USSR Deputy Procurator Andrei Vyshinskii; an executive staff was added under Ivan Serov from the NKVD. Supposedly, the commission's task was to prepare the coming liquidation of the "enemies of the people," and with this aim it began collecting information on former oppositionists and others. The commission was, the story goes, in effect a state security staff within the Party apparatus, parallel to the NKVD. Moreover, in addition to a public verification of Party documents, there was to be a secret check of the political conduct of all Party members. In this vision, the commission played a key role in the organization of the Great Terror. According to

A. Avtorkhanov, a former Party functionary who emigrated during World War II, it planned the mass terror that surfaced in 1937.[40]

A. Kolpakidi even quotes the relevant Politburo decision, in quotation marks but without any reference.[41] This, however, must be a falsification. As the authors of the present work have verified in the archives, neither the Politburo minutes (*protokol*) of 13 May 1935, or any other date, nor the special files (*osobye papki*) contain any reference to such a commission. Moreover, it is improbable that Serov was made head of an executive staff, since in 1935 he entered the Military Frunze Academy in Moscow and did not finish the study before February 1939.[42] This does not alter the fact that in January 1935, on the instruction of the Central Committee apparatus, the regional Party organizations started drawing up lists of Party members who had earlier been expelled for belonging to the "Trotskiist and Trotskiist-Zinov'evist bloc." According to Khlevniuk, the later arrests were carried out on the basis of these lists.[43]

What did happen at the 13 May Politburo meeting was that after a report by Ezhov, the Politburo approved his draft Central Committee letter to all Party organizations "on disorders in the registration, issuing, and keeping of Party cards, and on measures for regulating these."[44] The letter charged that Party organizations were guilty of "the most flagrant arbitrariness in the handling of Party cards" and of "a totally intolerable chaos in the registration of communists." In numerous cases, enemies had succeeded in seizing Party documents. He had found "uttermost neglect of and disorganization in the registration of communists" and an absence of investigation with respect to new members. All this attested to "organizational lack of discipline of the Party organizations" and to "intolerable complacency [*blagodushie*] and idleness [*rotozeistvo*] among Party members."

Ezhov recommended that in order to facilitate the exposure and liquidation of Party enemies, the "organizational lack of discipline" should be overcome as soon as possible, all expressions of "idleness" and "complacency" among communists should be completely eradicated, and order should be instituted within the Party. Until this was accomplished, the admission of new members was out of the question. The letter formulated a number of organizational measures the Party organizations had to take in order to institute order within two to three months, all boiling down to more control and more discipline. The second secretary of each Party committee and the regional ORPO head were charged with carrying out the verification operation.[45]

Later, Ezhov explained that the letter had been inspired by Stalin. He reported that during 1934 the Central Committee had taken a number of decisions on disorders in the issuing and keeping of Party documents with respect to separate Party organizations. Under Ezhov's direction, the ORPO controlled the execution of these decisions. Then in the Orgburo, facts of "scandalous disorders" in the issuing of Party documents were revealed. Stalin attended the Orgburo meeting and put the question "on a completely different track." He announced that "as long as such arbitrariness in the issuing of Party documents and chaos in the admission of Party members and candidates were reigning," an exchange of Party cards, as intended by the Central Committee, and especially the admission of new Party members, were out of the question. The result of this formulation of the question, according to Ezhov, was the Central Committee letter of 13 May 1935.[46]

Indeed, on 27 March Stalin in the Orgburo had declared himself opposed to admitting new members as long as the membership administration was in such a mess: "Good guys sometimes are expelled from the Party, while scoundrels remain, because they dodge very adroitly." Stalin had thought it necessary to send the Party organizations a special Central Committee letter on this issue: "We gained power and took it into our own hands, but we don't know how to handle it. Get this clear, we turn it over, like a monkey smelling at a pair of spectacles, we lick it, and that's all. . . . We are bad heirs: instead of accumulating new moral capital, we run through it."[47]

In this way Ezhov came to direct the verification of Party documents campaign, aiming at "exposing the alien people who have wormed their way into the Party."[48] It continued the purge started in April 1933. During the next one and a half years he was engaged in organizing Party purges.[49]

In early 1935 Zinov'ev and the others had been punished relatively mildly, but the matter had not been settled. In consultation with Stalin, Ezhov was writing a book on the Zinov'evists entitled "From Factionism to Open Counterrevolution." On 17 May 1935 he sent Stalin the first chapter, "The Stages of the Anti-Party Struggle of the Zinov'evist-Kamenevist and Trotskiist Groups." The intended four following chapters were not yet ready. He asked Stalin's instructions because the journal *Bol'shevik* wanted to publish the chapter before the rest of the book was completed.[50] Stalin indeed gave his comment, as did Shkiriatov and Iaroslavskii, but neither the chapter nor the book was ever published.[51]

The book's title pointed to the fact that, according to the author, there was a straight line from the inner-Party factionism of Zinov'ev, Kamenev, and their supporters since the mid-1920s to their involvement in the Kirov murder: in a logical development, the Zinov'evists had passed from inner-Party opposition to counterrevolution. As early as 1925 a "bloc of Trotskiists and Zinov'evists" had been formed, "uniting all anti-Party groupings in the struggle against the Party." In the absence of any support within the Party, the Zinov'evists had repeatedly retracted their positions in public, promising to abstain from factionism, but that had been no more than a false maneuver in order to escape annihilation, and by late 1927 an "explicitly terrorist" mood was reigning among them toward Stalin. They "tried to decapitate the revolution, by destroying comrade Stalin."

Ezhov further charged that in the late 1920s the Zinov'evists had set up leading clandestine Moscow and Leningrad centers, hoping to make use of the appearance of the Rightists in order to return to power. Zinov'ev and Kamenev took steps "for a deal" with the object of a possible "joint action of the Rightists and the Zinov'evists." Bukharin and Kamenev (who indeed had had a conversation in April 1928) "on behalf of their groups negotiated about a concrete plan for an action against the Party." In 1929 the plans were thwarted by the annihilation of the Rightist opposition, but in 1932 the activity of the Zinov'evist organization revived. There were negotiations with the "Leftists" (Lominadze et al.) and with the Rightist Riutin group, and contacts were searched with the Trotskiist underground. Zinov'ev, Kamenev, and their supporters set their hopes on a military attack by the imperialists on the Soviet Union so that a favorable situation could be created for the overthrow of the Party leadership. When this turned out to be hopeless, they seriously considered "terror against the most prominent Party and government leaders" as a method. A "clandestine terrorist group" was formed within the "Leningrad Center" "with the object of organizing the murder of comrades Kirov and Stalin." The group succeeded only in the first object. At the same time there was a close relationship with the Trotskiists, who were also informed of the terrorist activity of the Zinov'evist organization. What is more, the Trotskiists "also took the course of organizing terrorist groups."

Stalin slightly edited the text, making no substantial corrections. One may safely conclude that he agreed.[52]

Ezhov's papers contain another, more extensive (probably later) version of the same work. In it Ezhov expanded on details with respect to the so-called "Kremlin affair." During the early months of 1935 a large group of Kremlin staff had been arrested, among them Kamenev's brother. They were accused of having prepared an attempt on Stalin's life. (At the June 1935 Central Committee Plenum Ezhov used the evidence in attacking the Secretary of the Central Executive Committee, Avel' Enukidze.) According to Ezhov, it had now been proved that the Zinov'evists and Trotskiists had passed to terror, in the first place, attempts on Kirov and Stalin. Zinov'ev had organized the terror in Leningrad, and Kamenev in Moscow; they kept in touch with the Trotskiists. The Kirov murder, organized by Zinov'ev and Kamenev, was "just a link in the terrorist chain of the plans of the Zinov'evist-Kamenevist and Trotskiist groups."[53]

Ezhov's work initiated the prosecution of the former Party opposition. It was specific in making inner-Party opposition a criminal act, by means of linking it to concrete terrorist activity. This was done on Stalin's initiative. The several Party oppositions were closely linked together, as "blocs." But Ezhov did not yet explicitly point to a joint bloc of Zinov'evists, Trotskiists, and Rightists, nor did he link the Rightists to terror. That may explain why the text was not published: Stalin needed more evidence. In any case, the attribution of terrorist plans to the former opposition leaders inevitably implied a program for their physical liquidation.

It was not only a question of prosecuting former Party oppositionists, however. On 11 February 1935 a Politburo commission consisting of the control commissions functionaries Z. M. Belen'kii and M. F. Shkiriatov and directed by Ezhov was charged with checking the personnel of the USSR Central Executive Committee apparatus (together with that of its Russian Republic counterpart) for evidence of "elements of decay."[54] In June 1935 Kaganovich informed the Central Committee Plenum that as soon as Stalin received the news of the "Kremlin affair," he had convened his entourage, establishing that "there was something rotten here," and raised the question of removing Enukidze from the post of USSR Central Executive Committee (TsIK) Secretary.[55] On 3 March the Politburo indeed transferred him to the Transcaucasian TsIK.[56] Thus, the information on the "Kremlin affair" had probably been received shortly before that date, and Stalin personally had taken the first step leading to Enukidze's dismissal.

Ezhov had the NKVD examination records at his disposal and on their basis wrote a draft Central Committee report concerning "the USSR Central Executive Committee apparatus and comrade Enukidze." On 21 March, after being edited by, probably, Stalin and Molotov, the text was approved by the Politburo. It said that in the beginning of the year counterrevolutionary activity directed against Stalin and the Party leadership had been established among the Kremlin personnel; recently, the NKVD had even discovered several mutually allied counterrevolutionary groups that had set themselves to organizing terrorist attempts on Stalin and other leaders. Many members of these groups had enjoyed the support and protection of Enukidze, who had appointed them and had even cohabited with some of the females. The report admitted that, indeed, Enukidze had not known about the preparations for an attempt on Stalin; but the class enemy had used him as "a man who has lost political vigilance and has shown an attraction toward former people [*byvshie liudi*] that is uncharacteristic for a communist."[57]

A few days later, the leadership agreed to Enukidze's request for the time being not to send him to Tiflis but rather to Kislovodsk for medical treatment. On 8 May Enukidze even requested to be dismissed as Transcaucasian TsIK president for health reasons and to be given work in Moscow or, if this was impossible, in the Northern Caucasus, for example, as local TsIK representative.[58] Although Ezhov asked Stalin's permission to summon Enukidze for interrogation, Stalin agreed to Enukidze's request, and on 13 May, on his proposal, the Politburo dismissed Enukidze and gave him the job of representative of the USSR TsIK for the North Caucasian mineral resorts.[59]

Two weeks later Enukidze returned to Moscow for a Central Committee Plenum. Here, on 6 June, Ezhov made his first Plenum speech. It had been approved by Stalin.[60] He reported that although the investigation into the Kirov murder had not yet fully revealed the role of Zinov'ev, Kamenev, and Trotskii in the preparation of terrorist acts against Soviet leaders, it appeared from the new facts of the "Kremlin affair" that they had been not just the instigators but the "direct organizers" of the Kirov murder as well as of an attempt on Stalin's life that had been prepared within the Kremlin. Ezhov further said that the NKVD had rounded up five terrorist groups within and outside the Kremlin that had been after Stalin's life; they were all linked to Zinov'ev, Kamenev, and Trotskii. Thus, Kamenev's and Zinov'ev's "direct participation in the organizing of terrorist groups" had been proved, as well as Trotskii's responsibility for organizing the terror.

Continuing, Ezhov turned his attack on Enukidze. The terrorist groups had made use of the lack of vigilance of many communists with respect to the enemies, their "loss of class vigilance, criminal idleness, complacency, and decay." The clearest example of such "political myopia" was TsIK Secretary Enukidze, head of the Kremlin apparatus. As a result of his lack of vigilance, the Zinov'evists and Trotskiists had succeeded in penetrating the Kremlin and organizing terrorist groups there. Owing to Enukidze's personnel policy, the TsIK apparatus had become "extremely contaminated with elements alien and hostile to the Soviet regime," who could thus freely weave their "counterrevolutionary nest" inside it. These and other counterrevolutionary elements had been patronized by Enukidze. In this way, a situation had been created within the Kremlin "in which terrorists were able with impunity to prepare an attempt on comrade Stalin's life." Enukidze, Ezhov charged, was "the most typical representative of the corrupt and self-complacent communists, playing the 'liberal' gentlemen at the expense of the Party and the state." They "not only fail to see the class enemy, but in fact affiliate themselves with them, become their involuntary accomplices, opening the gates to the enemy for their counterrevolutionary acts." On this account, Ezhov recommended Enukidze's expulsion from the Central Committee.[61]

At the Plenum, Enukidze was attacked from all sides. When in his defense he argued that the Kremlin personnel were hired only after a thorough check by the NKVD, this was labeled a lie by its chief Iagoda. It did not alter the fact that Iagoda was also pushed into the defense. He felt forced into taking part of the responsibility: "I admit my guilt in that I have not seized Enukidze by the throat and forced him to kick out all this scum." He demanded that Enukidze be arrested and tried.[62]

Enukidze's main fault had been, Ezhov explained in his concluding remarks, that "from day to day you supported all this White Guard rubbish that had settled down in the Kremlin, defended them in every way, rendered them material help, created conditions, in which these inveterate counterrevolutionaries and terrorists felt themselves at home in the Kremlin, felt themselves master of the situation." The speaker advocated a decision, that "will harden even more the Party ranks and allow us to finally root out political myopia, moral and political corruption, rotten liberalism, from which unfortunately—as we have seen in Enukidze's example—some communists still suffer."[63] The Central Committee decided to expel Enukidze from the Party because of "political and social corruption."[64]

Thus, through Ezhov's doing, approved by Stalin, the June 1935 Plenum introduced a new element. From now on, not only former Party oppositionists were outlawed. Communists who—in contrast to Stalin and his supporters—practiced a conciliatory attitude toward the oppositionists were also called to account for their lack of vigilance regarding the enemy. Enukidze's case was exemplary. As appears from Kaganovich's words, the initiative here had again been taken by Stalin, just as in the preparation of the Central Committee letter of 13 May 1935. On 27 July the "Kremlin affair" ended in a trial, in which Kamenev and the other defendants were accused of having instigated the plan for a terrorist act. Two of them were condemned to death; Kamenev got ten years.[65]

The June 1935 Plenum had put the NKVD chief Iagoda on the defensive for having missed the "Kremlin affair," and conflict with his supervisor Ezhov was unavoidable: "When the NKVD is to be blamed, nobody has ever obscured it," Ezhov had said in his concluding Plenum remarks.[66] But the two still had to cooperate in the verification operation. In July they sent a joint instruction to the regional NKVD and Party chiefs on involving the NKVD in the conduct of the operation. The regional NKVD chiefs were ordered to help the Party chiefs by examining questionable Party members, "for the sake of arresting and thoroughly investigating the activities and contacts of the exposed spies, White Guards, speculators, etc."[67]

The Party leadership was not impressed by the conduct of the verification operation at the local level. On two occasions, in June and August, it criticized the "overtly unsatisfactory" course of the operation in quite a number of Party organizations. According to the criticism, the rules formulated in the letter of 13 May were handled "formally-bureaucratically," and almost no defects were exposed. The vigilance was not heightened but weakened. Accordingly, some province and district Party leaders were reprimanded or even expelled.[68]

At some point during the summer Ezhov reported to Stalin on the course of the verification operation, observing that the term originally fixed for its end—early August—was unrealizable and should be extended for another three months, until 1 November. He attributed the delay to the Party organizations, which only after one, sometimes even two months, had understood the seriousness of the matter, after which almost all of them had had to start the operation all over again. In addition, "the contamination of the Party ranks turned out to be greater than we supposed." Foreign intelligence services had instructed their agents to penetrate the Party, it contained complete Trotskiist organizations, and so on. In particular, Ezhov noted, Stalin's anxiety with respect to the verification operation in the Ukraine had been justified, for a new verification round in several Ukrainian provinces had revealed how much the Party organizations had been contaminated with Polish, Romanian, and German agents. Because the Party could not on its own "expose all this scum to the end," this was a job for the NKVD. However, until very recently it had stood aside; only during the past months had Ezhov succeeded in involving it in this work. He asked Stalin's permission to organize an operative conference of NKVD executives in order to instruct them how even better to track down Trotskiists and spies within the Party. In the meantime, he and his team would begin work on a new operation, the exchange of Party cards. In this connection he directed Stalin's attention to the utter disorder in the registration of Party members; it should be organized more professionally.[69]

On 25 September 1935, at a conference of regional ORPO representatives, their chief Ezhov criticized the "criminal idleness and complacency" initially shown by many Party organizations with respect to the verification.[70] He urged the Party organizations to cooperate closely with the NKVD. When during the course of the verification they ran across swindlers, adventurists, scoundrels, spies, and that sort, they should hand them over to the NKVD.[71]

In September 1935 Ezhov had again become overworked. Stalin pressed him to "go on leave straight away, to a Soviet health resort or abroad, as you like it, or as the doctors say."[72] The Politburo granted him a leave of two months and sent him abroad for treatment, in accordance with the conclusions of the doctors; he was to be accompanied by his wife.[73] In early October he apologized to Stalin that he should already have gone on leave, but that he had lingered because he had gotten the flu.[74] Later, in 1939, during interrogation, Ezhov confirmed that in 1935 he had indeed gone again to Vienna to be treated for pneumonia by Dr. Noorden and that he had been accompanied by his wife, who had gone shopping. (As was expected of him by then, he confessed to having used the visit for contacting the German intelligence service.)[75]

Ezhov was back in Moscow by 15 December, for on that day he visited Stalin in his Kremlin office.[76] Ten days later he reported to the Central Committee Plenum on the results of the verification campaign: on the basis of the verification of documents of every member and candidate, the Party should be "cleaned of swindlers, rascals, and elements who had attached themselves to it," and there should be an end to the disorder in the issuing and keeping of Party documents: the registration of communists should be put in a model way. The organizational licentiousness in the Party organizations should be overcome, and the "complacency and idleness among communists" be finally extirpated. Ezhov stressed how much Stalin was concerned about the organization of the verification campaign: "He interrogated me at least five times. Who will verify, and how. Who will be responsible for the verification in the provincial committee, who in the city and district committee. How will the organizations report to the Central Committee and how will the course of the verification work be controlled."

In Ezhov's opinion the campaign enabled the Party committees to "unmask the enemies who had crept into the Party." The secretaries of the district committees personally verified the Party documents of all members and candidates, talked extensively with many of them, and in this way "often to their surprise discovered overt Party enemies." Ezhov disapprovingly reported how at the beginning of the campaign many Party organizations had requested some deviations from the established order; they had asked permission to verify without necessarily summoning every Party member to the district committee, since this was "unpleasant" to them. But all these proposals had been rejected. There had also been many Party organizations that considered the campaign a mere technicality and wished it to be over as soon as possible.

According to Ezhov, as a result of the campaign the most malicious and active Party enemies had been expelled. Many of them had deliberately penetrated the Party in order to undermine it and had not been unmasked during earlier purges. Data of 1 December showed that 177,000 members and candidates had been expelled (9.1 percent of the Party membership); 8.7 percent of these, or 15,218 people, had been arrested. But, Ezhov added, this figure was incomplete—"in fact it is considerably higher." He blamed the penetration of so many malicious enemies into the Party on subjective guilt and bad work and stressed that Bolshevik vigilance should not be forgotten.[77]

During the Plenum, the Belorussian Party chief, Nikolai Gikalo, indicated how closely Ezhov had supervised the course of the verification campaign: on Ezhov's instructions, the Central Committee apparatus had called almost every day.[78]

The resolution of the Central Committee Plenum, drafted by Ezhov, declared that as a result of the verification campaign the Party organizations had unmasked "alien persons who had made their way into the Party." But there was still insufficient awareness of the need for a "comprehensive increase of Bolshevik alertness and discipline"; the class enemy could still take advantage of the "opportunistic complacency and idleness" of communists. Therefore, although the verification operation had not yet been completed, its results should be consolidated by means of one more purge operation, an "exchange of Party documents of all Party members and candidates," from 1 February to 1 May 1936.[79]

On 25 January, at an ORPO conference devoted to the results of the verification operation, Ezhov warned that the purge had not yet been completed and that among those expelled there were still enemies against whom criminal proceedings had not yet been instituted. He urged the regional Party leaders to "get in touch with the NKVD organs and give us a personal list of people who immediately should be deported from the region by administrative means."[80] (It was one of Ezhov's last actions as ORPO head; on 4 February he was succeeded in this function by his deputy, Georgii Malenkov.) Later, Ezhov claimed that during the verification campaign "many enemies and spies" had been pointed out but that the NKVD had only arrested them after Stalin's intervention.[81]

Since early 1935, Ezhov had also been directing a campaign against foreign influences. In March of that year he summoned Evgenii Varga,* director of the Institute of World Economy and World Politics, which employed many foreign communists who had found refuge in the Soviet Union. Ezhov inquired why so many "enemies of the people" had "nested" themselves at the institute, making clear he did not trust political émigrés or people who had lived abroad. He urgently reminded Varga of Stalin's teaching that "vigilance requires the obligatory discovery of anti-Party and hostile elements and the subsequent purging of them."[82] In September he again requested Varga's help in "disclosing the counterrevolutionary underground" in his institute, which he believed to be "filled with dark personalities who were tied to foreign countries." He therefore demanded "secret references regarding each employee, with detailed indication of his activities and foreign links."[83] Varga proved extremely uncooperative and half

---

*The Hungarian communist Jenö (Russian: Evgenii) Varga (1879–1964) had been People's Commissar of the Hungarian Soviet republic of 1919; after its suppression, he lived in exile in the Soviet Union.

a year later, in March 1936, was reprimanded by an angry Ezhov for ignoring Stalin's "appeals for high-level vigilance." In Ezhov's opinion, Varga underestimated the counterrevolutionary danger lurking in his institute, since among the employees—the foreign émigrés as well as Russians who had lived abroad—there were probably foreign intelligence agents. Varga was instructed to produce at once the mandatory references as well as a special list of those who had been in close contact with Zinov'ev, Kamenev, Radek, Bukharin, and others. When Varga failed to comply, Stalin personally interfered, explaining that Varga insufficiently understood the complexity of the political situation and was "excessively trusting": "And because of that the enemy wins."[84]

In the summer of 1935, on Stalin's proposal, Ezhov was

Dimitrov, Ezhov, and Manuil'skii at the Seventh Comintern Congress, summer 1935. (RGAKFD collection)

elected to the Comintern Executive Committee.[85] This assignment was connected with preparations of a campaign with respect to the political émigrés, especially from Poland. More than a million Poles were living in the USSR, mainly peasants in the Ukrainian and Belorussian border regions but also many political émigrés. Already in 1933 a group of Poles had been arrested for alleged membership in the "espionage and sabotage organization of the Polish Military Organization (POV)," which had been set up in 1915 under General Józef Pilsudski for the independence struggle against Austria-Hungary and Germany, as well as against Russia. It had suspended its activity in 1921 and therefore in 1933 did not in fact exist. Nonetheless, several of those arrested were condemned to death. In September 1935 a new wave of arrests started, with a view to end an alleged "POV network."[86] During the same month, the representative of the Polish Communist Party in the Comintern Executive Committee, B. Bronkowski (Bortnowski), sent Ezhov a memorandum on deficiencies in the NKVD work concerning the exposure of the agent provocateur and espionage role of Polish agents.[87]

Agents of foreign intelligence services, disguised as political émigrés and members of sister parties, allegedly had penetrated the Russian Communist Party. This is what Ezhov had reported to Stalin in the summer of 1935, and at an ORPO conference of late September he reached the same conclusion.[88] In particular, he mentioned the Poles, Romanians, Germans, Finns, and Czechs. Following this report, the December 1935 Central Committee Plenum decided on checking the political émigrés, charging Ezhov with preparing a Politburo resolution in this respect.[89] On 19 January 1936 the Secretary of the Comintern Executive Committee, Dmitrii Manuil'skii, asked to be received by Ezhov within the next few days in order to discuss measures to "stop the infiltrating in the USSR of spies and saboteurs under cover of political émigrés and members of sister parties." Manuil'skii proposed to curtail the inflow of political émigrés and to require registration and verification of all such persons in the USSR. He especially insisted on a verification of the Polish Communist Party as "one of the main suppliers of spies and agent provocateur elements in the USSR."[90] He recommended that the check should be completed before 8 March. Although from nine to ten thousand people had already been checked, many still remained, about whom neither the Comintern personnel department nor the International Red Help had information.[91] Reporting to Stalin on the course of the resolution work, Ezhov pointed to "political émigrés, suspected of espionage, whose cases are being worked out in the NKVD."[92]

On 28 February, after many revisions, Ezhov's draft of "On Measures to Protect the USSR Against the Penetration of Spy, Terrorist, and Sabotage Elements" was accepted as a Central Committee resolution stating that among the numerous political émigrés in the USSR there were "direct agents of spy organizations of capitalist states." In order to track them down, the Comintern and the NKVD were charged with carrying out within three months a complete new registration of all political émigrés who had arrived in the USSR by way of the International Red Help, the Comintern, or the Red Trade Union International.[93] To this end a special Central Committee commission on political émigrés was created, including Ezhov, Manuil'skii, and the head of the GUGB counterintelligence department (*osobyi otdel*), M. I. Gai. After taking stock of the émigrés, the commission was to submit to the Central Committee for confirmation lists with three categories: those who should be exiled from the Soviet Union on suspicion of espionage or hostile anti-Soviet activity, those who could be sent abroad for clandestine work by way of the Comintern or the International Red Help, and those who should remain in the Soviet Union because in their own country they would be in danger.[94]

At its first meeting, on 15 March, the commission decided not to wait until the registration of political émigrés had been completed but from 1 April on to examine the lists of the Comintern sections, starting with the Polish one. The NKVD began collecting compromising materials against Polish political émigrés.[95] There had already been some arrests. In November 1935 the Ukrainian NKVD chief, V. Balitskii, had reported the arrest of 184 Poles, 61

Galicians, and 57 Germans, some of them on suspicion of espionage under the cover of a Party card.[96] Although the Central Committee resolution had only provided for exile abroad, the commission also sanctioned the arrest of political émigrés. Of the 368 cases of Polish political émigrés examined, 53 ended in arrest and 238 in exile. In early July 1936 a total of 811 political émigrés from Germany had been registered, and compromising evidence had been collected against 414 of those.[97] During 1935–36, authorities arrested 126 members of the German Communist Party in the USSR—38 as "Trotskiists" and 50 for "connections with the Gestapo and the German consulate" (in Moscow).[98]

Ezhov was most active in the campaign against the Poles, especially those who worked in the NKVD (during the terms of the Poles Dzerzhinskii and Menzhinskii, from 1917 until 1934, the VChK-OGPU had employed many Poles). On 7 February 1936 he sent Stalin a note on the GUGB counterintelligence department head of Omsk province, Iu. I. Makovskii, who had recently been arrested on charges of being an agent of the Polish intelligence service. In addition to Makovskii's former department, Ezhov also implicated Iagoda: the NKVD chief had failed to report, and in the counterintelligence department there were "friends" of Makovskii.[99]

In January 1936, a commission headed by the member of the Presidium of the Executive Committee, M.A. Trilisser-Moskvin (a former Chekist), was charged with verifying the Comintern Executive Committee staff and purging the Comintern apparatus.[100] The Executive Committee leadership instructed the representatives of all affiliated parties to make a further check of all political émigrés and decide on each individually, in writing; information on all suspected persons had to be passed on.[101] On 23 August Comintern Secretary General Georgii Dimitrov reported that the personnel department of the Executive Committee had made available to the NKVD material on 3,000 persons who were "under suspicion of being saboteurs, spies, agents provocateur, etc."[102]

*   *   *

Party leaders on top of the Lenin Mausoleum viewing the 1 May parade, 1936. From left to right: Andreev, unknown (effaced), Ezhov, Ordzhonikidze, Kaganovich, Molotov, Dimitrov, Stalin, Khrushchev, Kalinin. (RGAKFD collection)

On 3 June 1936, Ezhov was able to report to the Central Committee Plenum that during the verification campaign over 200,000 people had been expelled and that the number of people arrested had also increased beyond the figure given at the December 1935 Plenum. Ezhov seemed to show a more "liberal" face here, questioning that the matter was now closed. First, the appeals of those who wanted to be reinstated into the Party had to be examined because most Party organizations adopted a formally bureaucratic attitude—not out of vigilance but simply through carelessness. After all, most of those expelled were not enemies; they had consciously concealed their past or committed some other minor offenses, and Ezhov thought it inadmissable that many of them were automatically dismissed from their jobs, expelled from universities, deprived of their apartment, and so on, and that similar actions were sometimes taken in regard to their families. He also reported that 3.5 percent of Party members had not received new Party cards, half of them on account of their "passivity." He considered this percentage to be too high, the result of an arbitrary determination. He also insisted on the need of an active policy of bringing in new members.[103]

These objections hardly made Ezhov an overnight liberal, but they do suggest that the distinction that has sometimes been made in the historical literature between "hawks" and "doves" within the Stalinist leadership is artificial. The purges were directed against people who were considered *real* enemies. The intention was not at any price to expel as many members as possible for their mere "passivity." In the opinion of the Party leadership, the regional Party officials often wrongly directed their attention to such "passives," at the same time leaving untouched the real enemies, who were often among themselves. Ezhov thought this was an incorrect attitude "dictated not by reasons of vigilance but by a striving by certain party officials to protect themselves against any eventuality."[104] His denunciation was endorsed by Stalin and the Plenum.[105] In accordance with Ezhov's report, on 24 June the Central Committee issued a letter, "On Errors in the Examination of Appeals from Persons Expelled from the Party During the Verification and Exchange of Party Documents," denouncing the frivolous, and in many instances callously bureaucratic, attitude of the Party organizations in processing the appeals of persons expelled from the Party.[106]

According to Stalin, the verification and exchange of Party documents were completed no earlier than September 1936. The ban on admitting new members into the Party was lifted only on 1 November of the same year.[107] Before the purges ended, the terror in the Party began, culminating first in the show trial of August 1936 against Zinov'ev, Kamenev, et al.

The current operations took so much of his time that Ezhov seems to have been unable to take his usual annual leave. Indeed, in April 1936 the Politburo had discussed the matter.[108] According to one source, he underwent medical treatment in Vienna in 1936, but this was stated after his arrest, when he was gratuitously accused of having stopped in Warsaw for a day on his return trip to

Moscow and had there established espionage ties with the Poles.[109] If we check Stalin's visitors' book for 1936 and add the other information we have of Ezhov's whereabouts, the longest hiatus is of a month, from late March to late April; he may have taken a leave within that period. In any case, as Iagoda confirmed later, when being interrogated, "during the summer of 1936 Ezhov worked all the time, did not take a leave, and, it seems, was not even ill."[110]

He took a leading part in preparing and organizing the Zinov'ev trial. According to Khlevniuk, the situation of early 1935 was repeated: Stalin used Ezhov to push through his version against a certain amount of opposition from the NKVD leadership. Having carried out mass arrests among Trotskii's former adherents, the NKVD leadership wanted to try and execute them. But Stalin demanded the fabrication of a case of a united "Trotskiist-Zinov'evist Center" that on behalf of Trotskii abroad gave instructions to use terror against the Party leaders. When the NKVD leadership seemed skeptical of these plans, Ezhov undertook the preparation of the case.[111]

Ezhov had already, in mid-1935, ordered Iagoda's deputy, Agranov (as the latter reported afterward), to carry out an operation against the Trotskiists in Moscow—according to his information and "in the opinion of the Central Committee" (that is, Stalin), there existed "an undiscovered center of Trotskiists that should be tracked down and liquidated." (Indeed, in his letter to Stalin of the summer of 1935 as well as in his address to the ORPO conference of late September of the same year, Ezhov concluded that the Trotskiists must have been directed by a center within the USSR.) Agranov then instructed the head of the GUGB Secret Political Department, G. A. Molchanov, to carry out the operation, but Molchanov did not believe in the reality of an active Trotskiist underground, and with Iagoda's support the operation was obstructed.[112]

Essential in the preparation of the Zinov'ev trial was a united Trotskiist-Zinov'evist bloc, allegedly having been formed in 1932.[113] As Ezhov reported afterward, the NKVD almost immediately had information about the bloc but did not use it and picked up the thread only in late 1935. Stalin "correctly sensed in all this something was not quite right, and ordered the case to be continued," with Ezhov overseeing the investigation.[114] In February 1936 Stalin gave instructions to hand over to Ezhov all documents regarding Trotskii and to have him participate in the interrogation of arrested Trotskiists.[115] In June, after Iagoda's plan of a trial of the Trotskiists alone had been dismissed, Stalin ordered Ezhov to organize a trial against both the Trotskiists and Zinov'evists.[116] Ezhov then summoned Agranov and passed on Stalin's order to "expose the real Trotskiists center."[117]

Around the same time, more definite information concerning the 1932 "bloc" reached Stalin. In July 1936 Ezhov sent Stalin a draft Central Committee resolution "on the terrorist activities of the Trotskiist-Zinov'evist-Kamenevist Counterrevolutionary Group," a summary of the preliminary investigation results. Stalin carefully edited the text, changing the title to "On the Terrorist Activities of the Trotskiist-Zinov'evist Counterrevolutionary Bloc," and on 29 July sent the letter to the regional and local Party committees.[118] It was the basis of the August 1936 trial. The 1932 "bloc" was blown up to a terrorist conspiracy. "New materials gathered by the NKVD in 1936" had led to the assertion that Kamenev and Zinov'ev had plotted an attempt on Stalin and that already since 1932 a united Trotskiist-Zinov'evist bloc had been directing the terrorist activities. In view of the dangerous situation, the Party should "come to understand that the vigilance of Communists is necessary in every area and in every situation." According to the letter, every Bolshevik now should be able to "recognize and identify the enemies of the Party, no matter how well they may have camouflaged their identity."[119]

Ezhov's important role in organizing the trial is evident from the fact that his papers contain no less than ten related files on matters like providing information about the trial, photos and films, the admittance of the press, and so on.[120] Among them is also a manuscript by Zinov'ev of eleven chapters, entitled "A Deserved Sentence," sent to Ezhov and Molchanov two weeks before

Ezhov, Voroshilov, Kaganovich, and Stalin on their way to a gymnastic parade in Red Square, July 1936. (RGAKFD collection)

the trial, on 4 August.[121] He had the disposal of all materials both of the NKVD and the Central Committee, uniting their work in view of conducting a political and legal investigation regarding the former oppositionists and their sympathizers. He supervised the investigation with respect to the trial and occasionally attended the interrogations in person. As a rule, these took place at night, and at Ezhov's insistence the prisoners were not handled with "kid gloves."[122] The trial of the "United Trotskiist-Zinov'evist Center" against Zinov'ev, Kamenev, and fourteen others took place from 19 to 24 August 1936 and resulted in their death sentences, which were carried out immediately.

The trial was only the beginning. In July and August, some of the accused in the case against Zinov'ev et al. testified that there was yet another Trotskiist "parallel" center with Piatakov et al. Piatakov had been under suspicion after a search of his ex-wife's apartment in July had turned up compromising materials on his Trotskiist past. On 11 August Ezhov reported to Stalin on his conversation with Piatakov. Ezhov had explained to his former drinking companion why he could not be a prosecutor at the Zinov'ev trial, as had been intended. Piatakov had pleaded guilty only to not having seen the counterrevolutionary activities of his ex-wife. When he had volunteered to "personally execute all those sentenced to death at the trial, including his own former wife," Ezhov had declined the offer as "absurd." A month later Piatakov was expelled from the Party and arrested.[123]

Late in 1935 evidence had also been collected against the Rightists, Bukharin et al., but Iagoda had not acted on it.[124] However, during the August 1936 trial, USSR Procurator Vyshinskii officially announced that, in view of the testimonies, an investigation would be started against Radek and Piatakov, as well as the Rightist leaders.[125] The next day one of the latter, Mikhail Tomskii, committed suicide. Immediately, Ezhov, together with Politburo members Kaganovich and Ordzhonikidze, informed Stalin (who was at his holiday resort in Sochi) that Tomskii, knowing he could "no longer hide his connections with the Zinov'evist-Trotskiist gang," had decided to "remove his traces" by committing suicide.[126] A letter that Tomskii had left behind was for-warded to Stalin. Kaganovich and Ordzhonikidze sent Ezhov to Tomskii's widow.

On 9 September Ezhov wrote to Stalin about the visit. Tom-skii's widow had told him that, according to her late husband, during the late 1920s Iagoda had played a leading role among the Rightists; Ezhov was not sure whether this was "a counterrevolu-tionary kick from the grave by Tomskii, or a real fact." He rather thought that Tomskii had "chosen a peculiar means of revenge." "In the light of the latest testimonies of those arrested, the role of the Rightists appears quite different," Ezhov informed Stalin. Previously "we did not dig down far enough," and that was why on his orders some of the Rightists were interrogated anew, with interesting results: "There is every reason to suppose that we will be able to discover a lot of new things and that the Rightists will look different to us, including Rykov, Bukharin, Uglanov, Shmidt, et al."

Ezhov further reported that he had carried out Stalin's order in organizing a revision of the lists of all those arrested in connec-tion with the latest cases, including those having to do with the Kirov murder. For the final examination a commission had been formed, including Ezhov, Vyshinskii, and Iagoda. The main orga-nizers and direct participants in terrorist groups, double agents, and the like should be executed; the others were to get prison terms of five to ten years. Further, Ezhov expressed the opinion that at the August trial the accused had not told the whole truth and that the Trotskiists must still have "some unexposed officers" in the army. With respect to the NKVD, he thought its contacts with the Trotskiists had not been sufficiently investigated, since it had been revealed that, although the NKVD had had at its disposal signals about the terrorist activities of the Trotskiist-Zinov'evist bloc as early as 1933–34, it had paid little attention to them. Ezhov expressed the wish to inform Stalin privately about some deficiencies in the NKVD work that could no longer be tolerated: "Without your intervention things will come to no good."[127]

In a draft of the same letter that has been found among his papers, Ezhov wrote with respect to the NKVD deficiencies:

> I restrained myself from it as long as the main emphasis was on unmasking the Trotskiists and Zinov'evists. But now, it seems to me, one should also get down to some conclusions from this whole affair for the restructuring of the work of the NKVD itself. This is especially necessary since within its leadership moods of complacency, calmness, and bragging are increasingly developing. Instead of drawing conclusions from the Trotskiist affair, criticizing their own deficiencies and correcting them, they now only dream about decorations for the discovery. It is even hard to believe that they don't understand that in the end it is not to their credit that the Cheka discovered the truth, already known by hundreds, five years *after* the organization of a serious plot.[128]

Ezhov was obviously after a change of the NKVD leadership, probably wanting to confirm Stalin's opinion. Within a month Stalin announced that the NKVD was lagging in the exposure of the plot and that Iagoda would be replaced. It is interesting that only after the change, on 29 September, Stalin sent Ezhov's letter on to his closest colleagues, Kaganovich and Molotov.[129] There may have been no earlier opportunity, but it is also possible that Stalin feared Iagoda's finding out about it, including Ezhov's sharp criticism directed at him and the invitation that Stalin should intervene.

In the draft letter Ezhov was more explicit with respect to the Rightists. He wrote that he doubted "whether the Rightists entered into a direct organizational bloc with the Trotskiists and Zinov'evists. The Trotskiists and Zinov'evists were politically so discredited that the Rightists must have feared such a bloc with them." The Rightists had their organization, supported the use of terror, knew about the activities of the Trotskiist-Zinov'evist bloc, but bided their time, wishing to make use of the results of the Trotskiist terror in their own interest. The time had come for taking measures, Ezhov wrote. He considered the "most minimal punishment" for the Rightists to be their expulsion from the Central Committee and exile to remote places. He urged Stalin's "firm instructions" in this respect. As for Piatakov, Radek, and Sokol'nikov, though he had no doubt that they were the leaders of a "counterrevolutionary gang," he considered the organization of a new trial "hardly expedient":

> The arrest and punishment of Radek and Piatakov without a trial undoubtedly will leak out to the foreign press. Nevertheless, it needs to be done. . . . It is understandable that no trials should be organized. It can be done by way of a simplified procedure, on the basis of the law of 1 December [1934] and even without a formal court session.[130]

The draft letter was never sent to Stalin. It seems that Ezhov was not informed about Stalin's plans for new trials and a large-scale purge—if Stalin himself had already made up his mind. "But in any case, it was not Ezhov who suggested to Stalin new scenarios and 'inspiring' ideas," writes Khlevniuk.[131]

It is also interesting to note that on 9 September Ezhov urged Stalin to investigate the Rightists more actively. For only a day later a report from the USSR Procurator, Vyshinskii, was published in the press to the effect that there was insufficient evidence to proceed against Bukharin and Rykov and that therefore the case was now regarded as closed.[132] The conclusion must be that the report was only intended to set Bukharin and Rykov at rest and that the cases with respect to the Rightists in actual fact were not closed at all. The trial of Piatakov et al. had priority now.

3

State Security Chief

While collecting incriminating evidence against Iagoda, Ezhov took advantage of the anti-Iagoda sentiments of some of his subordinates, like the Voronezh NKVD chief Semen Dukel'skii. On 13 July 1936 Dukel'skii informed him about the slowing down by the NKVD leadership of the investigation of Trotskiist cases.[1] On 11 September, Dukel'skii sent Ezhov another note and immediately, probably on the next day, was received by him. On 14 September Ezhov wrote Stalin that, according to Dukel'skii, the NKVD had been informed about the existence of a Trotskiist center in early 1933, but instead of sorting it out, they had consciously slurred over it. Explicitly, Dukel'skii had put the "organizational question" with respect to the GUGB "arrangement of forces," which in his eyes was not good.[2] By sending the information on, Ezhov was aiming at Iagoda, whom Stalin wanted to dispense with by then anyway. Iagoda reacted by dismissing Dukel'-skii.[3]

However, Iagoda was the one to be dismissed. On 25 September Stalin, also on behalf of Zhdanov, sent Kaganovich, Molotov, and the other Politburo members a telegram from his holiday resort in Sochi: "We deem it absolutely necessary and urgent to have comrade Ezhov appointed People's Commissar of Internal Affairs. Iagoda has definitely proved himself incapable of unmasking the Trotskiist-Zinov'evist bloc. The OGPU [*sic*] is four years behind in this matter." Iagoda was to be appointed People's Commissar of Communications. Ezhov was to retain his functions of Central Committee Secretary and of chairman of the Control Commission, on the condition that "he will devote nine-tenths of his time to the NKVD." As Stalin informed his colleagues, "Ezhov agrees with our proposals."[4] The "four years" referred to the formation in 1932 of a Trotskiist-Zinov'evist bloc, which had been discovered no earlier than in June–July 1936, as well as to Dukel'skii's information cited above.[5] The following day, carrying out Stalin's order, the Politburo appointed Ezhov People's Commissar of Internal Affairs.[6] (As a result, Shkiriatov became the acting head of the Control Commission.)[7]

Of course, Iagoda's dismissal was not the result of Dukel'skii's statement; that served only as an extra argument. Iagoda had not expected such a rapid outcome, and for him the decision was a complete surprise. He left for Sochi immediately, assuming it was a misunderstanding that could still be corrected. But his, now former, subordinate K. V. Pauker, heading the guard department, did not even let him enter Stalin's dacha.[8]

Stalin did, however, receive Ezhov.[9] As we have seen, in his telegram Stalin wrote that Ezhov had agreed with his being appointed, which means that they had already discussed it. Possibly as early as the day before his appointment Ezhov had left for Sochi with the information of Tomskii's widow about Iagoda. On 29 September, back in Moscow, he started his new job of state security chief in the Lubianka.[10] The leadership received his appointment favorably. On 30 September Politburo member Kaganovich wrote to his colleague Sergo Ordzhonikidze:

This remarkably wise decision of our father [*roditel'*], which had been pending for some time, has met with a splendid reception in the Party and the country. Iagoda had absolutely turned out to be too weak for such a role; to be organizer of construction is one thing, but to be politically mature and expose enemies *in good time* is something else. And the OGPU is several years behind in this matter, and failed to forestall the vile murder of Kirov. Surely, under Ezhov things will go smoothly. According to my information among the Chekists, with few exceptions, the change in leadership was favorably received also.

Two weeks later Kaganovich confirmed that "under Ezhov things are going well! He set to work firmly, in a Stalinist way."[11]

Ezhov's appointment was no sudden decision; it had ripened for a long time. According to E. G. Evdokimov (when being interrogated in 1939), already during the June 1936 Plenum Ezhov had shown interest in going to work in the NKVD, "even as deputy to Iagoda." Somewhat later, when Evdokimov had urged him to take the NKVD leadership, Ezhov had given the impression that "the question of his appointment as People's Commissar of Internal Affairs is being decided [*reshaetsia*]."[12] Stalin may have wanted to make Ezhov Iagoda's deputy first, in order to force the other out—a maneuver he would use later when replacing Ezhov with Beriia. As things worked out, he decided to appoint Ezhov immediately.

The first person that Ezhov received on returning from Sochi was his protégé G. S. Liushkov, the former deputy head of the NKVD Secret Political Department whom Iagoda had recently appointed NKVD chief of the Azov–Black Sea province. M. I. Litvin, an old acquaintance of Ezhov's from his Kazakhstan times and later his subordinate in Raspredotdel, was made NKVD personnel chief. The Moscow NKVD chief, S. F. Redens, was also promised a promotion. Ezhov put his special trust in Chekists from North Caucasia, like Efim Evdokimov (since early 1937 the Party chief of the Azov–Black Sea province), V. M. Kurskii, I. Ia. Dagin, N. G. Nikolaev-Zhurid, and P. F. Bulakh. On 16 October the head of the NKVD Chief Directorate of Frontier and Internal Troops, Mikhail Frinovskii, was appointed Deputy People's Commissar of Internal Affairs, though for the time being Agranov— whom Ezhov thought too closely connected with Iagoda—was retained as First Deputy; in December 1936 Agranov was even appointed head of the Chief Directorate of State Security (GUGB). From the Control Commission and the Central Committee Secretariat, apart from Litvin, Ezhov took along V. E. Tsesarskii (NKVD Special Plenipotentiary, charged with investigating work offenses by NKVD employees and from November 1936 on head of the GUGB registration department), S. B. Zhukovskii (head of the Administrative-Economic Department), and I. I. Shapiro (deputy head, then head of the NKVD Secretariat). Other acquaintances appointed to high positions were S. G. Gendin, P. A. Korkin, A. R. Stromin, G. N. Lulov, L. V. Kogan, M. S. Alekhin, and Z. I. Passov.[13] Ezhov had been acquainted with Liushkov, Gendin, and Korkin since the Kirov murder investigation and with Frinovskii since supervising the NKVD. He knew Frinovskii, Evdokimov, and Redens to be at odds with Iagoda.

In the eyes of the public, Ezhov's appointment did not point to an intensification of the terror. Bukharin, for example, was even pleased, according to his widow. His relations with Ezhov were reasonable, and until late 1936 he believed that the new NKVD chief would not engage in forgeries.[14] Unlike Iagoda, Ezhov did not come out of the "organs," which was considered an advantage. "The majority of Old Chekists," one of them writes in his memoirs,

> were convinced that with the coming to the NKVD of Ezhov we would at last return to the traditions of Dzerzhinskii, overcome the unhealthy atmosphere and the careerist, degenerating, and forging tendencies introduced in the organs during the last years by Iagoda. For, as a Central Committee Secretary, Ezhov was close to Stalin, in whom we then believed, and we thought that now the firm and reliable hand of the Central Committee would reign in the organs.[15]

Dagin thought that with the coming of Ezhov a "Party atmosphere" would be brought into the NKVD work, an idea in which he was later disappointed.[16]

The campaign against the Party opposition continued. Ezhov drafted the Politburo resolution "On the Attitude to Counterrevolutionary Trotskiist-Zinov'evist Elements," which Stalin signed on 29 September; the "Trotskiist-Zinov'evist scoundrels" should from now on be considered "foreign agents, spies, subversives, and wreckers on behalf of the fascist bourgeoisie in Europe," and one needed to make short work of them all.[17] Stalin did delete one point from the draft: a demand for the summary execution of several thousand Trotskiists and the exile of thousands of others to Iakutiia.[18] Within a few days, Ezhov, together with Vyshinskii, requested the Politburo to sanction the conviction of 585 listed participants in the Trotskiist-Zinov'evist counterrevolutionary terrorist organization; on 4 October the Politburo agreed with the request.[19]

On 7 October Ezhov sent Stalin the testimony of a minor Rightist who had admitted to the existence of a "terrorist organization of the Rightists" with plans to murder Stalin and also to having been informed by Tomskii of a Rightist center with Bukharin, Rykov, Tomskii, et al.[20] For the time being, Bukharin and Rykov were only approached via their surroundings; little by little, evidence accumulated. Though only recently, in August, Ezhov had expressed himself rather moderately concerning the Rightists; after the August 1936 trial, interest in them continued. It has been assumed that Stalin removed Iagoda for being inattentive to the Rightists, whereas in September 1936, not long before his dismissal, Iagoda had in fact sent Stalin the testimonies of some minor Rightists who had recently been arrested, incriminating Bukharin, Rykov, and Tomskii. And he had added, "The testimony of Kulikov concerning terrorist activity of a counterrevolutionary organization of Rightists is especially interesting."[21]

It was to become clear that Stalin's lifting of the accusations against Bukharin and Rykov was only temporary; until more evidence had been accumulated, there was no sense in diverting the attention of the public. For the time being, the next in line were the arrested Trotskiists—Piatakov, Sokol'nikov, and Radek. At this point Ezhov was himself opposed to the preparation of a new public trial and, apparently, contributed to Vyshinskii's decision to drop the proceedings against Bukharin and Rykov, published on 10 September.[22]

Although Ezhov was not the first to draw Stalin's attention to the Rightists—Iagoda had also done so—Ezhov had the advantage of grasping what Stalin wanted at a given moment, and how to act on it. Iagoda's attack against Bukharin and Rykov was not backed by compelling evidence, and he had to retreat. Possibly, Stalin had explained to him how to act properly. Later in September Iagoda began to accumulate evidence from the Rightist small fry, mentioning terrorist Rightist groups, as well as Bukharin and Rykov, and send it to Stalin. The more such evidence of small people accumulated, the harder it would be for the Rightist leaders to refute it, and the more well founded their prosecution would be later. Ezhov did not discover this line, as has generally been assumed; in his new function of People's Commissar, he only continued it.

Soon the offensive against the Rightists went public. On 4 December 1936 at the Central Committee Plenum Ezhov accused them of having been informed of the plans of the Trotskiist-Zinov'evist bloc regarding attempts on Stalin and others and of having approved of them; they had even "immediately directed terrorist groups." But Stalin in his concluding words acknowledged that there were no straightforward indications that Bukharin and Rykov were related to a terrorist group. The Central Committee decided to carry on the examination and postpone the decision until the next Plenum.[23]

While the case against the Rightists was still pending, the second great Moscow show trial, that of the "Parallel Anti-Soviet Trotskiist Center" against Piatakov, Radek, Sokol'nikov, and others, took place. At the December 1936 Plenum Ezhov had reported that another "conspiracy" by these people had been revealed and that the Central Committee had expelled Piatakov and Sokol'nikov from the Party because of their close ties with terrorist Trotskiist and Zinov'evist groups.[24] The trial was conducted between 23 and 30 January 1937, and from the indictment to the death sentence was directly predetermined by Stalin and Ezhov.[25] On 13 January, when Radek was confronted with Bukharin, Ezhov directed the interrogation with Stalin and other Politburo members in attendence.[26] Three days before the trial ended, Ezhov was rewarded with the title of Commissar-General of State Security, a rank equivalent to that of marshal.[27]

At the notorious February–March 1937 Central Committee Plenum, Stalin sketched the background of the unfolding terror. According to him, the "Zinov'evist-Trotskiist bloc" had turned into an "espionage and saboteur-terrorist agency of the German secret police" and was in a kind of alliance with the surrounding bourgeois states—Finland, the Baltic states, Poland, Romania, Turkey, and Japan—supported by France and Great Britain, as always intending to crush the USSR. Following their plan, the Trotskiists had undermined the Soviet state by committing espionage, terrorism, and sabotage so as to make it ripe for military intervention. This was all clear enough, but some of the leading Party comrades, too "careless, complacent, and naïve" to see it, had helped foreign agents to advance to important positions.[28] But now the time had come to round up the saboteurs without mercy.

Ezhov's report to the Plenum on the "Lessons from the Wrecking, Sabotage, and Espionage by the Japanese-German-Trotskiist Agents" accused Bukharin, Rykov, and the other Rightists of having, since the early 1930s, aimed at seizing power by means of force and having formed a de facto bloc with the Trotskiists, Zinov'evists, and anti-Soviet parties. In his words, they had resorted to terror and collaboration with foreign fascists. When Bukharin refused to confess, Ezhov demanded that he and Rykov be expelled from the Party, tried, and condemned to death. Some of the participants thought the death penalty was too severe, and at Stalin's suggestion the Central Committee decided first to refer the matter to the NKVD. Bukharin and Rykov were arrested on the site.[29] Ezhov also shook his finger at several Soviet departments for reportedly protecting pseudo-loyal saboteurs within their ranks. According to him, even within the "armed vanguard of our Party" (Stalin's designation of the state security organs) vigilance had been lacking, and traitors had penetrated there so that he had had to arrest lots of people.[30]

Ezhov had requested the Central Committee Secretariat, in addition to those invited ex officio, to permit nineteen NKVD executives to be present at the Plenum. One of those making a speech was his first deputy, Agranov, who seized the opportunity to praise his chief. The appointment of Ezhov, he declared, had "cleared the air with its strong, bracing Party spirit," and since then "the state security organs have begun to consolidate swiftly, made compact by a powerful Party-Bolshevik cement."[31]

The Central Committee approved Ezhov's stern measures in removing from the GUGB those "decayed bureaucrats, who have lost all Bolshevik sharpness and vigilance in the struggle against the class enemy," as was apparent in the much too lenient prison procedures regarding the political enemies of the Soviet regime: "The political isolation facilities have been quite comfortable, resembling involuntary rest homes rather than prisons." Moreover, the NKVD was four years behind in unmasking the Trotskiist-Zinov'evist bloc. The former chief of the GUGB Secret Political Department, Molchanov, was declared "one of the main culprits in the shameful failure of the state security organs in the struggle against the Zinov'evists and Trotskiists." His arrest, one month before, and his trial were duly approved of. The GUGB apparatus was to be augmented with new Party cadres, and its reorganization (started on 28 November 1936) should be continued, in order to make it a "real fighting organ," able to guarantee the security of the Soviet state and society.[32]

Ezhov carried out a large-scale purge operation within the NKVD. The Saratov NKVD deputy chief, Ignatii Sosnovskii, of Polish origin, had already been arrested the previous November, and his arrest was followed by that of others from Poland, Germany, and elsewhere whom Ezhov suspected of being "foreign agents." In February 1937 his deputy, Agranov, from the regional departments requested lists of former Trotskiists, Zinov'evists, and Rightists employed in the NKVD.[33]

On 19–21 March 1937 Ezhov convened a Party meeting of state security officers at NKVD headquarters for a report on the results of the February–March Plenum. He announced that the conspirators had penetrated even the heart of the NKVD and that Iagoda himself was the main traitor.[34] Stalin, he said, no longer trusted the NKVD leadership: people in key functions, Iagoda's protégés like Molchanov, Gorb, Gai, Volovich, and Pauker, had turned out to be German spies and had been removed. In the mid-1920s even Dzerzhinskii's policy had sometimes been "hesitating": "What is needed is purging, purging, and again purging."[35] As a result, former Dzerzhinskii people were arrested, especially the Poles.

After the meeting, more arrests followed among the NKVD leadership, forming the base of a "Iagoda conspiracy," which on 29 March culminated in the arrest of Iagoda himself, along with the head of his secretariat, P. P. Bulanov. Two days later, Stalin informed the Central Committee members that "anti-state and criminal acts" had been brought to light, committed by Iagoda when he was NKVD chief and after. In view of the "danger of leaving Iagoda at liberty for so much as one day," the Politburo had been "compelled to order Iagoda's immediate arrest"; now, afterward, it asked the Central Committee to sanction his expulsion and arrest.[36]

On 12 April it was the turn of Iagoda's former deputy (since 29 September 1936 Deputy People's Commissar of Communications), G. E. Prokof'ev. Also arrested were the state security department heads K. V. Pauker (guard department, 17 April), A. M. Shanin (transport department, 22 April), G. I. Bokii (special [*spetsial'nyi*] department, 16 May), and M. I. Gai (former head of the counterintelligence [*osobyi*] department and since November 1936 Eastern Siberian NKVD chief, 1 April). In April the head of the counterespionage department, L. G. Mironov, was sent on a mission in order to "destroy the spies and wreckers" in the Siberian and Far Eastern railways. He even took part in interrogating Iagoda, but on 14 June was arrested himself.

On 4 April, right after press reports of Iagoda's arrest, his close ally, the Gor'kii NKVD chief, M. S. Pogrebinskii, shot himself. During the spring of 1937, fear caused more NKVD suicides. So on 17 April the assistant head of the counterespionage department, I. I. Chertok, threw himself out of the window. In May Ezhov continued to purge the NKVD of Iagoda's adherents. On 17 May Agranov was dismissed as Deputy People's Commissar, having already lost his function of First Deputy and GUGB chief to Frinovskii on 15 April; he became NKVD chief of Saratov, after his predecessor, R. A. Piliar, was arrested as an agent of the "Polish Military Organization." Agranov was arrested on 20 July and tried and executed on 1 August 1938.

Ezhov paid close attention to Iagoda's interrogation, seeing to it that his own protégés were not put in an unfavorable light. This was no easy task, since Stalin himself was following the investigation and Ezhov had to send all examination records of important prisoners to the Kremlin without delay. Although Frinovskii was charged with directing the investigation of Iagoda, the Leningrad NKVD chief, L. M. Zakovskii, also took part in it, together with V. M. Kurskii, L. V. Kogan, and N. M. Lerner. In accordance with Ezhov's and Frinovskii's instructions, the names of certain high NKVD officers were kept out of the examination records—for example, Liushkov's.[37] Based on this evidence, "anti-Soviet conversations" were ascertained among Chekists.[38] But this was still not enough; because Stalin wanted Iagoda exposed as a real conspirator, coup plans were attributed to him and his close collaborators, like Pauker, Sosnovskii, Piliar, Prokof'ev, and Shanin.[39]

Iagoda was also accused of attempted murder. During interrogation, he testified that right after his dismissal he had tried to poison his successor. On 28 or 29 September he had ordered his secretary, Bulanov, to spray Ezhov's office with mercury dissolved in an acid; Bulanov had done this, aided by Iagoda's messenger, Savolainen, with Iagoda watching the procedure. Allegedly, the spraying had been continued after Iagoda's departure (on 1 October).[40] At their trial in March 1938 Iagoda and Bulanov confirmed the testimony.[41] Later, during the proceedings instituted against Ezhov, it was concluded that Ezhov had himself launched the affair; he was said to have had the cloth in his apartment sprinkled with mercury and then when the attempt was "discovered" to have had an NKVD employee arrested and forced to confess that it was done by order of Iagoda and the "Rightist-Trotskiist bloc." Frinovskii testified in April 1939 that Ezhov complained to his colleagues that as soon as he entered his office, "he felt a metallic taste in his mouth"; blood appeared from his gums and his teeth got loose. He started repeating that he had been poisoned in his office and in this way, according to Frinovskii, "instilled the investigation to obtain the appropriate evidence."[42]

At his trial in February 1940, Ezhov denied the charge that he had ordered the fraudulent mercury poisoning affair; shortly after starting to work in the NKVD, he said, he began feeling bad and losing his teeth. The doctors diagnosed the flu, but he looked so ill that finally, during the spring of 1937, Zakovskii concluded he had probably been poisoned. The head of the GUGB Operative Department, N. G. Nikolaev-Zhurid, who was ordered to test the air of Ezhov's office, discovered mercury vapors in the air and came to the same conclusion.[43]

In June 1939, after arrest, Ezhov's former Kremlin doctor and personal physician, V. M. Pollachek, testified that in the spring of 1937 he had been summoned to Ezhov's office, together with his colleague Vinogradov. Ezhov complained about feeling bad and having a metallic taste in his mouth. An analysis of Ezhov's urine gave no results, but after ten or twelve days the doctors were summoned again and shown an analysis of Ezhov's urine from the clinic of the biochemist Professor B. I. Zbarskii, in which there were indications of mercury traces. Pollachek and Vinogradov then treated Ezhov until November 1937.[44] Years afterward, the same Zbarskii told the writer A. P. Shtein about how in 1937 Ezhov had confronted him with Iagoda's testimony that he (Iagoda) had instructed Zbarskii to poison Ezhov. The personnel had been ordered to spray Ezhov's office at night with a solution of a disinfecting preparation containing mercury (called "Zbarskii's bactericide"); the door curtains had to be sprayed with a special pulverizer and the windows and doors kept closed until the morning (mercury has no odor).[45]

During the rehabilitation campaign of the 1980s it was confirmed that Ezhov had himself staged the mercury poisoning affair. Nikolaev had rubbed mercury into the cloth and furniture of Ezhov's office and had then had them examined. An NKVD employee with access to the room was beaten up until he confessed to being responsible for the poisoning; a pot of mercury, which had been planted in his house, was duly discovered as "evidence."[46]

On 20 June 1937, with Stalin's approval, the first NKVD "conspirators" group was shot, among them Gai and S. V. Puzitskii, the head of the operational department of Dmitrov camp, or Dmitlag, charged with the construction of the Moscow-Volga canal, which had been opened in early May (Puzitskii had been arrested shortly after Stalin, Ezhov, and a number of colleagues visited the canal on 22 April, together with Dmitlag chief S. G. Firin and more than 200 other alleged participants in Iagoda's conspiracy).[47] In early June a commission of the NKVD and the Procuracy, or *dvoika*, was created for quick examination of such cases. During the following months a great number of former OGPU-NKVD leaders were shot: on 14 August Pauker, Prokof'ev, Shanin, and Firin; on 21 August former Foreign Department head A. Kh. Artuzov; on 2 September Piliar and S. A. Messing; on 9 October Molchanov; on 15 November Bokii and Sosnovskii; and on 27 November F. D. Medved' and V. A. Balitskii.

Half a year earlier, in May 1937, Balitskii had been appointed Far Eastern NKVD chief, replaced by T. D Deribas as Ukrainian Interior People's Commissar. But Deribas never went to Kiev, for on 7 June 1937 Ezhov sent a brigade under Frinovskii, Deribas, and the chief of the fifth GUGB department, I. M. Leplevskii, to the Ukraine in order to "expose and destroy the espionage, sabotage, diversion, and conspiratory Trotskiists and other counterrevolutionary groups" there, including some in the Red Army and the NKVD.[48] Now Leplevskii was officially appointed Ukrainian

Voroshilov, Molotov, Stalin, and Ezhov visiting the Moscow-Volga canal under construction near Iakhroma, 22 April 1937. The obvious brushed-in water and wall anticipate completion of the project. (RGAKFD collection)

Interior People's Commissar; Deribas returned to the Far East as NKVD chief, and Balitskii was dismissed. Balitskii was arrested on 7 July. Just over a month later, on 12 August, it was Deribas's turn to be arrested by his successor in the Far East, Liushkov.

All in all, almost all NKVD department heads, their deputies, and the regional chiefs were arrested and repressed, all on the basis of ridiculous charges. According to official NKVD statistics, from 1 October 1936 to 15 August 1938—that is, during the Ezhov purge—throughout the country 2,273 state security officers were arrested.[49]

Those arrested were, of course, replaced with Ezhov's own people—the investigation staff was nearly quadrupled—tempted with considerable salary increases and all kinds of other privileges.[50] "We must train Chekists now," Ezhov announced at a banquet on the occasion of the decorating of a group of Chekists, "so that this becomes a closely welded, closed sect that will unconditionally fulfill my orders."[51] The Party put quite a few of its people at the disposal of the NKVD.[52] So on 3 December 1936 Ezhov reported to an NKVD conference that he had made arrangements with the Central Committee about selecting 150 to 200 Party secretaries for work in the NKVD.[53] On 11 March 1937 he welcomed them with a pep talk:

> The title of Chekist is considered by our people the most honorary title. When the Party delegates people to work there, it considers this work to be the sharpest and most important battlefield. Therefore, a Chekist should wholeheartedly be devoted to our Party, to our Soviet people and system, and be prepared at any minute to sacrifice his life, no matter under what conditions he has to work.[54]

Military intelligence was purged as well. Since April 1935 the Red Army Intelligence Directorate (Razvedupr) had been headed by S. P. Uritskii. In January 1937, at Uritskii's insistence, his deputy, A. Kh. Artuzov, was dismissed by the Politburo and replaced by M. K. Aleksandrovskii (Artuzov was arrested on 13 May and shot on 21 August). But Uritskii himself felt uncomfortable and tried to put on a good face by practicing self-criticism. "We are rather bad intelligence officers," he said on 19 May 1937 at a Razvedupr Party meeting, but to no avail.[55]

Two days later, on 21 May, Stalin at the Kremlin, accompanied by Molotov, Kaganovich, Voroshilov, Ezhov, and Frinovskii, received NKVD Foreign Department chief A. A. Slutskii, the head of the Group for Special Tasks (which reported directly to the center and was charged with sabotage, abduction, and assassination operations on foreign soil), Ia. I. Serebrianskii, and Razvedupr leaders Uritskii, Aleksandrovskii, and A. M. Nikonov (another deputy of Uritskii's). They met for over two and a half hours.[56] Stalin announced that Razvedupr with its apparatus had "fallen into German hands" and demanded the disbandment of the agents network.[57] A fortnight later, on 8 June, the Politburo dismissed Uritskii as Razvedupr head and replaced him with Ian Berzin, who had headed military intelligence from 1924 to

1935.[58] (Uritskii was arrested in November and shot in August of the following year.)[59]

In July 1937 the real purging of Razvedupr started. Twenty people from the leading staff were arrested by the NKVD, among them Aleksandrovskii (he was later shot). On 19 July Berzin reported on the arrests at a Party bureau meeting.[60] A chain reaction followed. Having served less than two months, on 1 August Berzin himself was dismissed by the Politburo and replaced by Nikonov as temporary acting head of Razvedupr. Ezhov was empowered with its general supervision. He was charged with "studying the state of its work, taking urgent operational measures in agreement with the People's Commissar of Defense, revealing the shortcomings of Razvedupr, and reporting to the Central Committee within two weeks his proposals for the improvement of the Razvedupr work and its strengthening with fresh people."[61] In this way Ezhov also came to head military intelligence, strengthening it with "fresh people" from the NKVD.

Nikonov broke the record, being arrested only a few days after his appointment of 1 August (he was shot in October).[62] More and more arrests were carried out, and on 3 December Berzin's arrest was announced.[63] (He was shot in July 1938.) On 5 September 1937 the Politburo appointed Ezhov's protégé, the state security officer S. G. Gendin, as deputy head of Razvedupr; in fact, he headed it under Ezhov's direction. The Red Army officer A. G. Orlov became deputy head for foreign intelligence.[64] Gendin was arrested on 22 October 1938, and Orlov in the spring of the following year; they both dragged along their immediate subordinates. Not until September 1939 was a new Razvedupr head appointed, I. I. Proskurov. According to E. Gorbunov, the purge of Razvedupr from July 1937 to the beginning of 1938 brought about "a total paralysis of the central apparatus of military intelligence" that completely swept away the leadership and all department chiefs.[65] According to V. Kochik, between 1937 and 1940 hundreds of military intelligence officers were repressed, "approximately half the total intelligence staff."[66]

Ezhov eliminated some of Iagoda's people in a cunning way

in order not to provoke unnecessary commotion. Later, during interrogation, Frinovskii stated that in early 1938 Ezhov had thought it insufficient merely to arrest Foreign Department head Abram Slutskii, after Agranov and L. G. Mironov during their interrogation had called him a "participant in Iagoda's conspiracy"; if Slutskii was arrested, his testimony might harm Ezhov in Stalin's eyes, and furthermore, Slutskii's intelligence officers abroad could be induced not to return home, after the example of Reiss-Poretskii in 1937.[67] According to Frinovskii, Ezhov himself gave the order to "remove Slutskii without noise" and approved concrete plans in this respect; in February 1938, before leaving for the Ukraine, he ordered his deputy Frinovskii to liquidate Slutskii before his return.[68]

Some days later, on 17 February, Slutskii was summoned by Frinovskii (so the latter stated during interrogation); at the same time, M. S. Alekhin, head of the operational techniques department, hid in the adjoining room. While Slutskii reported, Zakovskii, another of Ezhov's deputies, entered Frinovskii's office, pretending to wait for the others to finish. Then suddenly Zakovskii "threw a mask with chloroform over Slutskii's face." After the victim had passed out, Alekhin entered the office and "injected poison into the muscle of his right arm, as a result of which Slutskii immediately died." Subsequently, Frinovskii summoned the doctor in duty, who certified Slutskii's death.[69]

The official NKVD report was that during his talk with Frinovskii Slutskii suffered a heart attack and died. The injected poison probably caused death that resembled a heart attack (no potassium cyanide was used, as has been stated by A. Orlov et al.). Allegedly, during his preliminary investigation Ezhov testified that he "had instructions from the leading organs not to arrest, but to eliminate" Slutskii.[70] So Stalin may have also approved of the murder. There is no reason to suspect Frinovskii of not telling the truth. Nevertheless, the post–Soviet Russian Foreign Intelligence Service (SVR) maintains the official point of view that Slutskii "suddenly died in office of a heart attack."[71]

After Slutskii's death, a successor was not immediately appointed; it seems his deputy, S. M. Shpigel'glaz, was requested to take over temporarily as acting Foreign Department chief. On 28 March 1938 the Politburo appointed Z. I. Passov as Foreign Department chief. He held the office until his arrest on 22 October of the same year, with Shpigel'glaz as deputy. Shpigel'glaz was arrested on 2 November 1938, one day after P. M. Fitin was appointed the new deputy, and a month later, on 2 December, Beriia appointed V. G. Dekanozov chief of the Foreign Department.

Meanwhile, a similar cleansing of the army command was under way. During the second half of 1936 the NKVD had started collecting evidence against high officers, and in early December at an NKVD conference Ezhov had stressed the need of strenghthening the NKVD work within the army: if there was sabotage in industry, why not also in the army? "The army offers rather more than less possibilities for it than industry."[72] On 6 May 1937 the former Red Army air defense chief, M. E. Medvedev, was arrested on Ezhov's orders. Later, during interrogation, the former Moscow NKVD deputy chief Radzivilovskii testified that Ezhov and Frinovskii had instructed him to interrogate Medvedev and "let him testify about the existence of a military conspiracy in the Red Army with as many participants as possible. . . . I should obtain the names of as large a number of leading military functionaries as possible." Radzivilovskii then elicited details of the existence of a military conspiracy, including the names of "a considerable number of major leading military functionaries."[73]

Later, during the same month, the Deputy People's Commissar of Defense, Marshal Mikhail Tukhachevskii, was arrested, together with a number of other "conspirators," and accused of conspiracy in collaboration with the Trotskiists, the Rightists, and the German intelligence service. They were tortured until they confessed. Later, during his own interrogation, Ezhov revealed that at the time there had been deliberations at the highest level about how to make Tukhachevskii confess, after Procurator Vyshinskii had insisted on using torture. Stalin's final words had been: "See for yourself, but Tukhachevskii should be forced to tell everything and to reveal his contacts. It is impossible that he acted on his own."[74] Indeed, analysis during the Khrushchev years showed that there were bloodstains on Tukhachevskii's testimony.[75] Ezhov directed the investigation and personally interrogated Tukhachevskii and others. Stalin supervised, read the examination records, and received Ezhov almost every day. On 11 June the Soviet press reported that the military tribunal in closed session had condemned Tukhachevskii to death for treason and espionage, together with seven army generals. During the following nine days, 980 high officers and political commissars were arrested as participants in a "military conspiracy." In connection with the case, Ezhov and a large number of NKVD officials were decorated.[76]

That was only the first act of the military purge. In November 1938 the People's Commissar of Defense, Voroshilov, declared that during 1937–38 more than 40,000 people had been purged from the Red Army.[77] A memorandum of September 1938 by Voroshilov's deputy, E. A. Shchadenko, gives precise figures. According to this source, during 1937–38, a total of 36,761 officers and political commissars were dismissed from the Red Army (some 10,000 of them being subsequently reinstated); 10,868 of them were also arrested, and 7,211 were condemned for counterrevolutionary crimes.[78] According to other more recently published official information, during the 1937–38 purge 33,947 (or 33,460) officers were dismissed, 7,280 (or 7,263) of whom were also arrested.[79]

Among Old Bolsheviks, the mood was extremely depressed. Shortly after Tukhachevskii's trial People's Commissar of Justice Nikolai Krylenko in a private conversation showed himself unbearably trapped by Ezhov's "hedgehog's gauntlets" (*ezhovy rukavitsy*): "Nowadays Leninists like me are not wanted; the fashionable ones are the Ezhovs and Vyshinskiis, parvenus with a lost conscience." Indignantly, he talked about the "chicken brain" and "sparrow short-sightedness" of Ezhov and his surroundings, so different from the old Leninists:

Intoxicated by power, they easily give in to misinformation and provocations of hostile intelligence services, seeking to destroy our functionaries and to weaken our successes. They believe the denunciations, inflate cases, pave the way for new accusations, misinform and delude the leadership of the Party and the government. In time the Party will figure it out and condemn the culprits. But now we are living through a terrible time.[80]

In half a year Krylenko was arrested, and in a year he was shot.

Ezhov was now one of the top Party leaders. On 23 January 1937 he replaced Iagoda as member of the Politburo Political-Judicial Commission (Komissiia po politicheskim (sudebnym) delam), overseeing judicial cases of political significance.[81] In the course of 1937 full power was transferred from the Politburo to a narrow circle of five, one of whom was Ezhov, even though he was not a Politburo member. On 14 April 1937, on Stalin's initiative, the Politburo set up a permanent commission to prepare and,

Ezhov, Kalinin, and Stalin leaving the Lenin Mausoleum, 1 May 1937. (RGAKFD collection)

if necessary, solve questions of secret nature, including foreign policy questions. Its members were Stalin, Molotov, Voroshilov, Kaganovich, and Ezhov.[82] In practice, the five became the working organ, in major questions supplanting the Politburo. The most secret and serious information of the political, punitive, and military departments was addressed to these five only. Moreover, on 27 April the Politburo set up a Defense Committee with Molotov (chairman), Stalin, Kaganovich, Voroshilov, Chubar', Rukhimovich, and Mezhlauk as members, and Gamarnik, Mikoian, Zhdanov, and Ezhov as candidates.[83]

The campaign against the former oppositionists had run basically from December 1934 to March 1937. Mass repressions within the Party started after the February–March Plenum of 1937. Now Central Committee members who had never belonged to any opposition were being arrested. In March and April, during the reelection campaign to local Party organs, Party conferences started at district and city level, during which, under the guise of "Party democracy," the rank and file were authorized to criticize and expel local Party leaders. In May and June, the same was repeated at the province level.[84] Expulsion often meant arrest. From 1 January to 1 July 1937, 20,500 members, mainly old Party cadres, were expelled.[85]

The purge of the Comintern Executive Committee apparatus also continued, Stalin in February 1937, during a conversation with Dimitrov, having expressed the suspicion that the Comintern worked into the hands of the enemy.[86] In addition to the Moskvin commission mentioned above, from now on another commission of the Comintern Executive Committee Secretariat checked foreign communists who had become VKP(b) members; it consisted of Manuil'skii, Moskvin-Trilisser, and Jan Anvelt.[87] On 1 April Manuil'skii sent Ezhov, Andreev, and Shkiriatov a letter proposing stricter regulations for foreign communists who wanted to be VKP(b) members.[88] In May a special control commission was instituted, including Dimitrov, Manuil'skii, and Moskvin-Trilisser.[89] On the twenty-sixth of that month Dimitrov noted in his diary that during the night he had visited Ezhov, who had claimed that "the greatest spies worked in the Comintern."[90] The following day, the commission started to verify the Comintern apparatus. By mid-June, 65 employees had been purged, among them representatives of the national parties in the Executive Committee. In July the commission suspended its work.[91]

Ezhov was particularly concerned about the need for vigilance against foreign intelligence services and their agents. On 3 December 1936 he told an NKVD conference: "Each year we draw nearer and nearer to a war. Foreign intelligence services get more active, develop a feverish activity on our territory."[92] Sensing a strengthening of the activity of the Gestapo and other German intelligence organizations on Soviet territory, the NKVD set about registering all likely intelligence sources, such as political émigrés, German citizens, and former German citizens who had received Soviet citizenship; the directive of 2 April 1937 also ordered surveillance of German diplomatic representatives, as well as people connected with them.[93] On 15 February Ezhov informed the Central Committee that "foreign intelligence services, especially the German one, for espionage and sabotage aims make use of representatives of German firms and specialists of foreign nationality, working in Western Siberian enterprises and institutions." This was followed on 13 March by a Politburo order not to renew residence permits of German, Japanese, Polish, and other foreign citizens staying in Western Siberia, and within a month, the NKVD instructed its regional organs in the course of six months to remove from the USSR all German citizens registered by the militia, as well as all foreign citizens who to some extent were suspected of espionage or counterrevolutionary activity; if necessary, German citizens were even to be arrested or deported. This did not involve German political émigrés, however; they were to be handled separately.[94] A commission of three was charged with deciding the question of renewing residence permits for foreign communists and political émigrés; the members were E. D. Stasova for the Central Committee, Agranov for the NKVD, and Moskvin-Trilisser for the Comintern.[95]

Another target was what remained of the non-Bolshevik political parties in the Soviet Union, who had long since suspended activity; those former activists who had not emigrated lived in inner-Soviet exile. In November 1936 Ezhov informed the regional NKVD chiefs of an "activization" of the former Socialist Revolutionaries (SRs), with a view to recovering their party and organizing a large-scale insurrectionary movement. All SR groups were to be tracked down and liquidated.[96] Arrests of former SRs started immediately. During the same month in Western Siberia, for example, a sabotage-espionage-terrorist organization, directed by a "Siberian Bureau of the PSR," was discovered and liquidated after being accused of working according to the instructions of an "All-Union United Center of the PSR."[97] Referring to alleged sabotage, agitation, and terrorism, in February 1937 Ezhov proposed to rearrest the SR former leadership; after approval by the Central Committee, the NKVD arrested some 600 people. During the same year a large-scale trial behind closed doors of exiled SRs was held in Ufa. Close relatives were also arrested.[98]

Nevertheless, on 17 January 1938 Stalin wrote to Ezhov that the policy with respect to the SRs had not yet been completed: "One should bear in mind that quite a few SRs have held out, both within and outside our army"; within two to three weeks he wanted to know how many of these (former) SRs had been registered by the NKVD.[99] The following day, Ezhov gave instructions for operational steps against former SRs, resulting in many arrests.[100] On 9 February he reported to Stalin about the execution of his orders to "rout the SR organization." At the time of Stalin's orders, the NKVD had registered 5,388 (former) SRs, including 1,014 VKP(b) members and 244 military men; as a result of Ezhov's instructions, 2,000 people had already been arrested, and the latest arrests had led to the discovery and liquidation of a number of SR organizations, including a "branched military anti-Soviet organization" that carried out subversive activity in the army.[101]

In April 1937 Ezhov signed an instruction with respect to the Mensheviks, accusing them of clandestine activity under the leadership of an "All-Union Menshevik Center"; contacts with the

Menshevik Foreign Delegation, the SRs, and the Communist Party opposition; and involvement in sabotage and terrorism. What was left of the Menshevik underground was to be immediately and fully rounded up.[102] On 14 February 1938 he gave new instructions for operational steps against former Mensheviks and Anarchists.[103]

Ezhov's greatest triumph came at the Central Committee Plenum of 23–29 June 1937. In the official information the main Plenum item was missing: Ezhov's report on the conspiracies revealed by the NKVD during the past three months. From the start it was presupposed that Ezhov's report would cause a sensation among the Central Committee members and that some of them might be arrested. Therefore, it appears, either from 23 to 26 June no shorthand report was made of the sessions, or it was not preserved.

In his report Ezhov sketched an all-embracing conspiracy against Stalin. Allegedly, already in 1933 on the initiative of various opposition groups a united "Center of Centers" had been created with Rykov, Tomskii, and Bukharin on behalf of the Rightists, SRs, and Mensheviks; Enukidze on behalf of the Red Army and NKVD conspirators; Kamenev and Sokol'nikov on behalf of the Zinov'evists; and Piatakov on behalf of the Trotskiists. The main task of the "Center of Centers" or "United Center" had been the overthrow of Soviet power and the restoration of capitalism in the USSR. Reportedly, the military conspirators led by Tukhachevskii, as well as Iagoda and his NKVD people, had also been subordinated to the Center. New in Ezhov's scheme was that in the leadership of every republic or province there were conspirators too. He mentioned the regional Party leaders Sheboldaev from Kursk, Razumov from Irkutsk, Kabakov from Sverdlovsk, and Rumiantsev from Smolensk—all of them Central Committee members who had already been arrested before the Plenum.[104]

All in all, Ezhov reported, after the February–March Plenum fourteen Central Committee members and twelve candidates had been arrested. He gave a detailed account of the wrecking in all economy branches, especially the People's Commissariats of Agriculture and State Farms, where the Second Five-Year Plan had been sabotaged with respect to high-quality crops, and the stock raising messed up. Indeed, the enemies "purposely spread epizootics among the cattle by means of the infection with foot-and-mouth disease, plague, malignant anthrax, etc.; castrated pedigree sheep; and wrecked the work of the artificial sowing points."[105] On the grounds of these accusations, on 3 August 1937 Stalin ordered the organization in each province of a number of show trials against agricultural saboteurs in order to mobilize the peasants in the struggle against wrecking.[106]

Ezhov also issued an ominous warning:

> At present, only the leadership and active members of the organization have been liquidated. It has been determined that the following sectors have been seized by its anti-Soviet work: the NKVD, the Red Army, its Intelligence Directorate, the Comintern apparatus (especially the Polish section of its Executive Committee), the People's Commissariat of Foreign Affairs, the defense industry, transport (particularly the strategic roads of the western war theater), agriculture.[107]

This implied that an even greater purge was still to come. According to Ezhov, the Polish intelligence service, by means of the "Polish Military Organization" (POV), had deeply infiltrated the Soviet intelligence and counterespionage services, massively exploiting people of Polish nationality. The Polish government had created a large-scale network of political agents in the USSR; under the guise of political émigrés, it had transferred a great number of spies and saboteurs there. The POV organization was headed by a center in Moscow with Unshlikht, Muklevich, Ol'skii, et al. The NKVD, the Red Army, Razvedupr, the Comintern apparatus, especially the Polish section of the Comintern, the People's Commissariat of Foreign Affairs, the defense industry, and transport had been seized by its anti-Soviet work. The POV top was also linked to the military conspirators (Tukhachevskii et al.)

and the Rightists. Unshlikht, Piliar, Sosnovskii, and other Polish spies had infiltrated the NKVD and seized all intelligence and counterespionage work with respect to Poland.[108]

After Ezhov's report, debates with further exposures unfolded at the Plenum. On the first Plenum day, fifteen Central Committee members (or candidates) were expelled "for treason to the Party and motherland and for active counterrevolutionary activities." Their cases had already been referred to the NKVD, practically all of them having been arrested in May–June—that is, before the Plenum. Seven other members (or candidates) were only expelled by the Central Committee, declaring its "lack of political confidence" in them. Moreover, during the Plenum, on 26 June, Central Committee candidate member and People's Commissar of Public Health Grigorii Kaminskii was expelled from the Central Committee and the Party for "not deserving confidence" and arrested. The same day, four Central Committee members were expelled "in view of incontrovertible facts concerning their belonging to a counterrevolutionary group." The last Plenum day, at Stalin's suggestion, four more members were expelled "in view of incontrovertible facts concerning their involvement in the criminal actions of the conspirators"; all four had already been arrested. All in all, during the June 1937 Plenum fifteen Central Committee members plus sixteen candidates were expelled. Before the Plenum, from 31 March to 1 June 1937, nine Central Committee members had already been expelled by referendum, among them Iagoda and Tukhachevskii.[109] Following the Plenum, on 7 July 1937, the former Secretary of the Comintern Executive Committee, Osip Piatnitskii, was also arrested (in July 1938 he was tried and shot).[110]

The June 1937 Plenum was an important turning point in the process of the increasing terror and the weakening position of the Party apparatus. The massive expelling of Central Committee members and candidates was unprecedented. No longer was expulsion limited to former oppositionists. Since the autumn of 1936, there had been an active policy to arrest Stalinists as well. In February 1934 some 139 people had been elected to the Central

Committee. In 1935 Enukidze had been expelled, in 1936 Sokol'-
nikov and Piatakov (Tomskii committed suicide). In 1937, during
the months before the June Plenum, another 11 people had been
expelled (excluding Gamarnik, who committed suicide). At the
June Plenum 31 members and candidates were expelled simultaneously. The Plenum may well have sanctioned the implementation of the mass operations that began in the following weeks.
Indeed, immediately after the Plenum, on 2 July, the Politburo
decided to start the operation against "anti-Soviet elements," implying the beginning of the "Great Terror."[111]

With the June 1937 Plenum, the scheme of a universal conspiracy was set by Ezhov and approved by Stalin. Arrests unfolded at all levels of the Party and state system. Ezhov directed
the NKVD officers to act in accordance with the scheme. When
on 19 July 1937 he sent Radzivilovskii as NKVD chief to Ivanovo,
he told him to prove that the provincial Party chief, I. P. Nosov,
who was trusted in the Central Committee, was connected with
the Rightist underground. He was to be arrested, and an operation in the textile industry was to be determined.[112] (Nosov was
dismissed in August and thereupon arrested; in November he was
shot.) So Ezhov showed initiative in organizing the arrest of a
Central Committee member, but it is unlikely that he did so without Stalin's consent.

4

The Great Terror

From 1937 on, Stalin was expecting war, and preparing for it.
Contrary to his usual custom, during the summer he did not take
a vacation in the south (a pattern he was to maintain during the
following years, until 1945), apparently because he felt that conditions demanded his constant presence at the nerve center. In
view of the danger, he wanted the purge of the Party and state
apparatus to coincide with a grand purge of society at large. The
potential "fifth column," in Stalin's perception, had to be deprived of its social base. Thus, the NKVD "mass operations for
subjecting anti-Soviet elements to repression," as they were officially termed, were conceived. Similar operations had already
been applied in 1930, during the campaign to deport the kulaks.
The first of the mass operations was the arrest and shooting of
"quotas" of former kulaks, criminals, and anti-Soviet elements,
as decided by NKVD troikas.

It may be assumed that the idea of large-scale arrests among
those categories of the population traditionally considered to be
hostile definitively ripened with Stalin during the Central Committee Plenum from 23 to 29 June 1937. Ezhov's Plenum report
on the enemies exposed by the NKVD during the previous months

had set forth a harmonious and consistent outline of an all-embracing "hostile conspiracy," but, Ezhov had ominously added, only the conspiracy leaders had been liquidated, whereas a whole range of institutions and sectors of the Soviet society and economy had been seized by the organization's anti-Soviet work. It was the run-up to a large-scale purge operation not only among the Party and economic executives, where in fact it was already going on, but at the lower level as well.

That such a plan was put on the agenda by Stalin as early as June 1937 is indirectly confirmed by the Politburo decision of 28 June (before the Plenum had finished its work) to form a troika in Western Siberia, consisting of the provincial NKVD chief (chairman), the procurator, and the first Party secretary. It was to review in a summary way the cases of "activists belonging to the counterrevolutionary insurrectionary organization among the deported kulaks" that had allegedly been uncovered, with a view to applying the death penalty.[1] Moreover, somewhat earlier, on 21 and 23 June, Ezhov's deputy, M. D. Berman, the Gulag chief, had urged the regional NKVD chiefs in good time to thin out the investigation prisons of convicts by transferring them to camps.[2] This adds to the evidence that mass arrests were being prepared.

The deported former kulaks had been considered a problem for some time. Ignoring instructions, more and more "special settlers" (*spetspereselentsy*) left their places of detainment, merging with free laborers. Others ran away and joined bands of social marginals around the cities. In many speeches at the February–March Plenum of 1937 the audience was alerted to the existence in the country of a large number of "anti-Soviet elements" and "offenders." According to Robert Eikhe, the Western Siberian Party chief, in his province there were a great number of exiled former kulaks, including "a not insignificant group of inveterate enemies." Turkmenian Party Chief Popok also pointed out the evident danger posed by former kulaks who had returned from imprisonment and exile and were making all kinds of demands. Other speakers brought up the existence of millions of believers.[3]

In early 1937, together with USSR Procurator Vyshinskii,

Ezhov addressed the Soviet government and the Central Committee about the question of the settlers' legal status. Because the new Soviet Constitution promulgated in 1936 declared them to be rehabilitated, Ezhov and Vyshinskii recommended that settlers who according to NKVD evidence were anti-Soviet should be sentenced to camp terms of three to five years by the NKVD Special Board. For the time being, settlers who had been rehabilitated should not be allowed to leave their places of detainment; only in 1939 should they be entitled to leave, though remaining within the bounds of the province, and in 1940 within the bounds of the entire country.[4] On 8 April 1937 in a letter Ezhov alerted Stalin to the dimensions criminality had assumed in the country, giving examples of the conduct of "incorrigible" criminals who "defy their unwillingness to work":

> The main contingent committing disruptive criminal offenses (robbery, brigandage, murder, aggravated theft) are people who have been convicted before, in most cases recently released from camps or places of detention. [This paragraph was marked in pencil by Stalin.] . . . Per month all over the Union more than 60,000 people are released from the camps and places of detainment after serving out their sentences; of these, no more than 6,000 to 7,000 (the shock workers) are placed in jobs by the NKVD organs, the others disperse over the Union, looking for work. . . . If left to themselves, those released from the camps are unable to find regular jobs and revert to the criminal path.

Ezhov went on to enumerate measures that in his opinion were necessary in the struggle against criminality. Most of them were rather traditional for the Soviet system, such as promoting the employment of former prisoners through the trade unions or exerting pressure on enterprises to make them employ criminals released from the camps. One point in Ezhov's proposals draws our special attention, however, especially in light of the decision a few months later about the execution of criminals. In April Ezhov did not yet go that far in his desire to finish with the criminal world; in point four of the letter he simply proposed with respect to recidivist, hooligans, recalcitrants—in short, all those who "have not reformed"—not to release them from the camps but to have them sentenced through the camp court or the NKVD troika to an additional term of three years at most (the maximum penalty these bodies could then impose).[5] Ezhov pointed out that his proposals had been submitted for Vyshinskii's approval, with the exception of point four. He probably feared that the "lawyer" Vyshinskii would criticize him for an antilegal attitude—that is, that prisoners who had not yet committed any offenses could be sentenced to an additional term only because of "bad" behavior in the camp. (Of course, Vyshinskii was not against repressions, but he preferred to have corresponding laws so as to observe the outward appearance of legality.) In the end, Stalin took far more radical measures then those proposed by Ezhov. The obsession with "kulak saboteurs infiltrating the enterprises" and "kulak bandits roaming the cities" explains why this "category" was designated for the first mass operation of the Great Terror.[6]

On 2 July, three days after the conclusion of the June Plenum, Stalin submitted a Politburo decision, "Concerning Anti-Soviet Elements," to the regional Party and NKVD chiefs. According to it, the "main instigators of all kinds of anti-Soviet and diversionary crimes" were the many former kulaks and criminals who had been deported and had returned home after their terms expired. The regional Party and NKVD chiefs were charged with "registering all kulaks and criminals who have returned home, in order that the most hostile among them be forthwith administratively arrested and shot by means of a troika"; within five days they were to present the composition of troikas and the number of those subject to the first category of punishment (execution) as well as the number of those subject to the second category of punishment (camps or prisons).[7]

Local officials responded by presenting estimates of numbers of kulaks and criminals to be confined or shot. During the following days, the Politburo approved the composition of "troikas for the verifying of anti-Soviet elements" and quantitative indices of the repressions, or "quotas," for each of the republics and provinces. From 5 to 31 July 1937, thirteen such decisions were taken, directly preceding the confirmation by the Politburo of order No. 00447 itself.[8] In early August, the Politburo continued confirming the personal composition of regional troikas, as a rule consisting of the NKVD chief (chairman), the first Party secretary, and the procurator. The troikas passed the requested information to the center. So on 8 July the NKVD chief and troika chairman of the Western Siberian province, S. N. Mironov, reported to Ezhov to having registered 25,944 people—10,924 of the first and 15,036 of the second category.[9] Two days later, the Moscow Party leader, N. S. Khrushchev, informed Stalin that 41,305 people had been registered in Moscow province—8,500 of the first and 32,805 of the second category.[10] Together with his deputy Frinovskii, Ezhov collected the data and streamlined the quotas.

By way of preparation for the forthcoming campaign of mass arrests, a briefing was held for regional NKVD chiefs. On 16 July, four days after having been invited,[11] the NKVD chiefs of the republics and provinces where the operation was to begin first (most of the RSFSR and the Ukraine) were summoned to Moscow for an "operational meeting" (in Central Asia, Kazakhstan, and the more distant part of Siberia the operation was to start somewhat later). There is no stenographic report of the conference, but we have information of Ezhov's words from the above-mentioned Mironov, testifying after his arrest in January 1939.

According to Mironov, Ezhov threatened those NKVD chiefs who showed "operational inertness," whereas at the same time others had already "fully started to disclose counterrevolutionary formations within and outside the Party." The laggardly chiefs (those of Omsk and Krasnoiarsk provinces, the mid-Volga region, and a few others) should be fired and called to account: "All should prepare for mass arrests among Harbin returnees, Poles, Germans, kulak and White Guardist groupings, as well as anti-Soviet groupings within the Party and in the state apparatus." A few days later, while the NKVD chiefs were still in Moscow, the four to six chiefs mentioned by Ezhov were arrested, according to Mironov's testimony. The others departed "in a very depressed mood."[12] According to M. P. Shreider, who himself did not attend but learned about it from his chief, A. P. Radzivilovskii, the Omsk NKVD chief, E. P. Salyn', who dared protest the quotas system, was even arrested right at the conference.[13]

Here again, discrepancies arise. Salyn' was arrested no earlier than 10 August, long after most participants to the conference had departed, though he was dismissed on 23 July and remained in Moscow. The others who were allegedly criticized—I. P. Popashenko (Kuibyshev, the former mid-Volga region) and F. A. Leoniuk (Krasnoiarsk)—were not arrested in 1937 at all; in the autumn of that year they were even promoted to the central NKVD apparatus. All the same, some regional NKVD chiefs were indeed arrested in mid-July: A. B. Rozanov (Voronezh, 11 July), I. M. Blat (Cheliabinsk, 13 July), Ia. S. Agranov (Saratov, 20 July), R. I. Austrin (Kirov, 22 July), and possibly P. G. Rud' (Tataria, shortly before the conference, since on 12 July his deputy was invited there). Of these, only Agranov and Austrin were arrested shortly after the conference.[14]

These arrests undoubtedly worried their colleagues, but the notion that the regional NKVD chiefs silently opposed Ezhov's plans and that Ezhov forced them to conduct mass operations under threats of arrest is contradicted by the testimony of another conference participant, the Orenburg NKVD chief, A. I. Uspenskii (given during investigation in April 1939). In his words, they "tried to surpass each other with reports about gigantic numbers of people arrested." Uspenskii is of course incorrect in speaking of "people arrested," since the conference dealt with quotas of *future* arrests in each region. According to him, Ezhov's instruction amounted to, "Beat, destroy without sorting out," and he quotes Ezhov as saying that in connection with the destroying of the enemies "a certain number of innocent people will be annihilated too," but this was "inevitable."[15] Two other sources offer similar wording: Ezhov announced that "if during this operation an extra thousand people will be shot, that is not such a big deal."[16] The style suggests that Ezhov was repeating Stalin's words. Stalin may indeed have spoken to Ezhov in such terms, explaining that the initial quotas for the regions could be rounded off, which inevitably led, as both Ezhov and Stalin well understood, to extending the repressions to people who had not been registered before—an "extra thousand."

During the conference, Ezhov and Frinovskii talked with each of the attending NKVD chiefs, discussing the quotas for arrest and execution put forward by them and giving instructions for the necessary measures in view of the preparation and the conduct of the operation. Mironov informed Ezhov about a "Rightist-Trotskiist bloc" that had been discovered within the Western Siberian leadership. When he called the evidence against some of those arrested unconvincing, Ezhov answered: "Why don't you arrest them? We are not going to work for you, imprison them, and then sort it out afterward, dropping those against whom there is no evidence. Act more boldly, I have already told you repeatedly." He added that in certain cases, with Mironov agreeing, department chiefs could also apply "physical methods of influencing."[17] When Uspenskii asked Ezhov what to do with prisoners older than age seventy, he ordered them to be shot.[18]

The unfolding correspondence of the center with the regional NKVD organs suggests an atmosphere much like that of the preparation of a wartime military operation. They were ordered to take into account all categories of "hostile" elements, to return from the judicial organs all cases of the "rural, kulak, rebel, and church counterrevolution" in order to pass them to the NKVD troikas for examination, and to continue registering "kulaks, White Guards, members of punitive expeditions [*karateli*], SRs, Mensheviks." Local functionaries were to be recalled from leave. The regional NKVD chiefs were ordered to summon all NKVD city and district chiefs to provincial instruction meetings.

An example is the "operational conference" of the heads of the "operational points," "operational sectors," city and district departments of the Western Siberian NKVD directorate on 25 July in Novosibirsk. Here the provincial NKVD chief, Mironov, explained that the operation was a state secret and that the divulging of any details was punishable. Straight after the meeting, the participants had to board the first train to their place of work in order on 28 July to begin arresting those belonging to the first category. Western Siberia had been given a quota of 10,800 for the first category, but Mironov assured the participants that they were allowed to surpass this figure and that if necessary they might just as well arrest 20,000 people; "I don't even pin you down on this figure." For they could be selected afterward— Mironov gave the operational workers a time of two and a half months. The task of an operational sector head was: "Finding a place where the sentences will be executed and a place where you can bury the corpses. If this is in a wood, a turf should be cut off beforehand so that for full secrecy's sake the place can be covered with this turf afterward." Even the apparatus was to know nothing about such details.[19]

The start of the "operation with respect to the first category" was planned for the end of July, as becomes clear also from a telegram Salyn' sent to his deputy in Omsk on 21 July (two days before he was replaced by G. F. Gorbach). He insisted on preparing orders for arrest, detaching the necessary number of Chekists to be sent to the districts, and leaving only 50 percent of them in the provincial center for the conduct of current affairs. The operation was to begin on 28 July, Salyn' added.[20] This explains the haste with which some of the North Caucasian NKVD chiefs, having returned home, began carrying out the operation without waiting for the appearance of order No. 00447. On 29 July, the Ordzhonikidze NKVD chief, Bulakh, informed Ezhov that the kulak operation had been started there prematurely; the next day, the NKVD chiefs of North-Ossetia, Checheno-Ingushetia, and Dagestan by wire justified their decision.[21] They all had attended the Moscow operational meeting and should have known that the operation was to start only after they received the order, but for some reason they were in a hurry. In all probability, the operation was initially planned for 28 July, and the remote regions had not been informed about the delay in time, and Ezhov himself, supposing the forthcoming order would soon be ready and confirmed by the Politburo, in this way had directed the participants of the meeting toward an earlier term.

Order No. 00447, "Concerning the Operation Aimed at the Subjecting to Repression of Former Kulaks, Criminals, and Other Anti-Soviet Elements," which Ezhov presented to the Politburo on 30 July, observed the existence in the country of a significant number of anti-Soviet elements: former kulaks who had escaped from camps or exile or had returned home after serving their time, priests, sectarians, SRs and members of other anti-Soviet parties, insurrectionists, White Guards, criminals, and others. Because not enough was being done to combat them, they could practice their criminal activities with impunity, but these anti-Soviet elements were the "main instigators" of all kinds of anti-Soviet and sabotage activities, and it was the NKVD's duty to annihilate them, in an "operation aimed at the subjecting to repression of former kulaks, active anti-Soviet elements, and criminals." The order split the target into two categories: the most hostile elements, the first category, were to be arrested immediately and shot, after consideration of their case by the troikas; the others, the second category, after arrest were to be confined in camps or prisons for a term ranging from eight to ten years, as determined by the troikas.

Subsequently, the order indicated the number of people subject to repression, split up in the first and the second category, according to data presented by the regional NKVD chiefs; this was done for each of the sixty-four listed republics and provinces, plus the Gulag. All in all, 268,950 people were to be arrested, 75,950 of them to be shot and 193,000 to be confined in camps. The indicated figures were tentative; regional NKVD chiefs desiring higher figures should submit a substantiated request. In specific circumstances, family members could also be confined or exiled. The operation was to start on 5 August and to be completed within four months. The first category should be dealt with first. In view of the operation, republics and provinces were divided into "operational sectors"; in each sector an "operational group" was created under the leadership of an NKVD executive, who had means of transport and communication and military and police units at his disposal. The operational group were charged with registering the candidates for arrest, with the investigation, with confirming the indictments, and with the execution of the troika sentences.

Incriminating facts should be collected for each person subject to repression on the basis of which lists for arrest were to be drawn up; these should be signed by the head of the operational group and sent to Ezhov and the regional NKVD chief for confirmation. On the basis of these lists, the head of the operational group should carry out the arrests. Then followed the investigation—in a swift and simplified manner, in which "all criminal connections of a prisoner are to be disclosed." Finally, the case was to be submitted for consideration to the troika, supplied with a short indictment. The order listed the approved troikas of all republics and provinces. The troika should pronounce the sentences, which were to be carried out under the direction of the head of the operational group. Ezhov's deputy, Frinovskii, was charged with the general direction of the operation, having at his disposal a special group for the purpose. Reports on the course and results of the operation were requested every five days.[22]

The next day, 31 July, the Politburo confirmed the order and directed that 75 million rubles from the reserve fund of the Soviet government were to be issued to the NKVD to cover expenses associated with the implementation of the operation, of which 25 million were to be earmarked for payment of railway fees for transport of those condemned to the camps. An advance of 10 million rubles from the same fund was issued to the Chief Directorate of the Camps, or Gulag, for the purpose of organizing camps. The prisoners were to be utilized on construction projects and forest works.[23] On 7 August, USSR Procurator Vyshinskii instructed the regional procurators to take note of order No. 00447 and to attend the troika meetings. "The observance of legal procedure and the preliminary approval of arrests are not demanded," he added. "I demand your active cooperation to the successful conduct of the operation."[24] (At the Novosibirsk instruction meeting of 25 July, the regional NKVD chief Mironov had urged the participants that it was not necessary to consult the procurators: only after the operation these should be sent the lists of people arrested, without mentioning whether they belonged to the first or the second category.)[25]

Within two weeks, more than 100,000 people had already been arrested.[26] The procedure first to complete the operation with respect to the first category was not maintained very long: on 4 September Ezhov allowed the regional NKVD authorities to begin work on the second category.[27] The figures quoted (268,950 people to be arrested, 75,950 of them to be shot) were known to be incomplete, and the regional authorities had the right—were even encouraged—to request enlargement of the quotas. So in October 1937 Ezhov told the new Smolensk NKVD chief, A. A. Nasedkin, that he could get any quotas he needed: "Purge your apparatus, and imprison whomever you should"; "better too far than not far enough."[28] Very soon many regions had used up their quotas. The Western Siberian province, for example, had been given a quota of 17,000, including 5,000 of the first category, but already in early October more than 25,000 people had been arrested and almost 14,000 of these had been sentenced to death by the troika.[29] Omsk province had been given a quota of 1,000 for the first and 2,500 for the second category. On 10 December the Omsk NKVD chief, Valukhin (Gorbach's successor), informed Ezhov that 11,050 people had been condemned in the first category and 5,004 in the second; he requested approval for the 50 people who surpassed the quota of the first category.[30]

In response to such requests, between 28 August and 15 December 1937 the Politburo sanctioned increasing the quotas for various regions by almost 22,500 in the first category and 16,800 in the second. On 31 January 1938, it allocated an additional 57,200 people, 48,000 of them for execution. The Politburo directed that the operation under order No. 00447 should be completed before 15 March (in the Far Eastern province, 1 April). However, although in many regions the operation was already completed during the winter of 1938, here and there it continued until the autumn of that year. Between 1 February and 29 August 1938 the Politburo sanctioned the repressing of almost 90,000 more (including quotas of 30,000 and 20,000, respectively, for the Ukraine and the Far East, confirmed on 17 February and 31 July). No categories were stipulated, most likely implying first category sentences.[31]

Thus, the operation, originally intended to take four months, extended over more than a year. As a result of the extra quotas allotted in the process of the implementation of order No. 00447, the total number of arrests almost tripled to 753,315.[32] The Politburo allotted extra quotas amounting to 183,750, including 150,500 of the first category. Indeed, in the regions executions sometimes exceeded those authorized by the center.[33] On the whole, however, this local initiative followed the policy of the center, which constantly encouraged the local authorities in that direction. Moreover, part of the allotted quotas (amounting to some 300,000) were approved by Ezhov himself without a formal Politburo decision. In these cases as well, there was always a request from the regional Party or NKVD leadership, supplied with arguments, to approve an additional quota—sent to Stalin directly or via Ezhov. Most likely, in these cases too, the approval came not from the Politburo but from Stalin's instructions, noted on incoming requests from regional authorities or by way of Stalin's oral instructions to Ezhov.[34]

For example, in September 1937 Stalin wired to the Far Eastern Party chief, I. M. Vareikis, who apparently had expressed doubts regarding the NKVD arrests: "Ezhov's orders for arrests in the Far Eastern province are usually made with the approval of the Central Committee."[35] See also Stalin's permission to extend the execution quota for Omsk province from 1,000 to 8,000, or his permission—together with Molotov's—to give Krasnoiarsk province an extra quota for the first category of 6,600.[36] Though Stalin's papers in the Presidential Archive are still inaccessible, it seems probable that Ezhov did not on his own make arbitrary decisions that allowed the increasing scale of the repressions. In any event, in the national operations there were no quotas at all, and the regional NKVD chiefs could arrest as many people as they wanted. All in all, in the operation with respect to order No. 00447, from August 1937 to November 1938, 767,397 people were condemned by the troikas, including 386,798 to the death penalty.

Hence, the current thesis that in 1937–38 NKVD authorities withdrew from the control of the Party is unfounded. On the contrary, the NKVD was in strict subordination to the center. "In the first place we are Bolsheviks, and for us all Central Committee decisions are the law," Ezhov had stressed in December 1936 in an NKVD conference speech; "and if our departmental laws go against the Party laws, nothing good can be expected of it."[37] If there was any spontaneity in the Party purges and repressions of the time, it is to be explained first of all by local Party politics, when district or provincial committees, or conferences, decided to carry out arrests of expelled Party functionaries, while at the same time the NKVD authorities now and then found no grounds to arrest those expelled.

Consider the objections raised at the time of the July 1937 Moscow conference by the Western Siberian NKVD chief, Mironov, to Ezhov against the First Party secretary, Robert Eikhe. Mironov reported to Ezhov—according to his testimony after arrest—that Eikhe "interfered in NKVD affairs." He had ordered the chiefs of the Kuzbass NKVD town branches to arrest Party members, although in most cases evidence was missing. Mironov thought his position difficult: either he had to liberate part of the prisoners and clash with Eikhe, or the NKVD organs were forced to "create fictitious cases." When Mironov suggested to orally instruct the NKVD organs concerned only to carry out orders approved by him, Ezhov answered: "Eikhe knows what he is doing. He is responsible for the Party organization; it is useless to fight with him. You better report to me the moot points arising, and I will settle them. . . . Comply with Eikhe's instructions, and don't strain your relations with him." Mironov added that it was Eikhe's habit to "suddenly come to the NKVD apparatus, attend interrogations, interfere in the investigation, and then exert pres-

sure in this or that direction, thereby muddling the investigation."
But Ezhov stuck to his opinion.[38]

This episode relates to the purge of the Party apparatus conducted since the February–March Plenum of 1937, which was a
quite different process from the mass operations that began in
July of the same year. In the documents it is often described as the
"Rightist-Trotskiist organization," tried by the Military Collegium of the Supreme Court and other judicial bodies, not by the
troikas. Another example of friction between provincial Party and
NKVD authorities is offered by Andreev in February 1938 reporting to Stalin on the situation in Kuibyshev province under the
Party chief Pavel Postyshev, who had been dismissed only a few
weeks before. According to Andreev, many arbitrary arrests had
taken place in the province, but "the NKVD organs offered a certain resistance to the arbitrariness, coming from the provincial
committee and secretaries of district committees who have now
been exposed as enemies of the people."[39]

Local Party politics gave the repressions some spontaneity. Expelling was the business of Party bureaus and conferences and
inevitably brought on arrest. As a result, the arrest of the Party
leadership was determined by the Party, with the NKVD only sup-
plying evidence. It would be wrong to think that in 1937–38 there
was no inner-Party life left and that there were only repressions
against the Party, organized by Stalin with the help of the NKVD.
The February–March Plenum of 1937 made the Party purge of
infiltrating "Rightist-Trotskiist" and other enemies the heart of
Party life—that is, by the Party itself, be it with the help of the
NKVD. Besides, however, traditional elements of Party life had
been preserved, although under the sauce of sharpened class
struggle and intensified political vigilance.

Another aspect of local initiative was a certain degree of "socialist competition" between regional NKVD departments with
respect to the number of arrests. So when the Chekists in Western
Siberia were told that in 1937 their province had reached the second place throughout the country in liquidating enemies of the
people, according to one of them, the mood "reached ecstasy."[40]

Kareliia showed "exceptional competition between NKVD departments and local organs to reach quotas."[41] But this sort of local initiative is inherent in any mass campaign. All in all, it did not change the general direction of the repressions. In some regions there may indeed have been cases of exceeding the bounds of the quotas established by Moscow, but these were exceptions. In most regions the extent of the repressions with respect to order No. 00447 strictly conformed to the alloted quotas.

Another target was that of the so-called "national contingents." In general, Soviet authorities aimed at not extending the residence permits of foreigners living in the USSR, who were seen as an "organizing source of espionage and sabotage."[42] Embassies and consulates of states that were considered dangerous (especially Germany, Japan, Italy, and Poland), as well as their employees, were placed under "continuous observation."[43] Specifically, an aspect of the Great Terror was the liquidation of the "potential intelligence base" of enemy states, the so-called "national operations" (terms used in NKVD orders and by Ezhov in his June 1937 Plenum report). The main victims were ethnic minorities, representing the nations of the "bourgeois-fascist" states bordering on the USSR, such as Germans, Finns, Estonians, Latvians, and Poles. The relevant people were arrested, their cases being examined regionally by so-called "dvoikas." After brief assessment and approval in Moscow, the sentences were executed by the regional authorities.

At the February–March Plenum of 1937 and at an enlarged session of the Military Council in June 1937, Stalin had dwelt upon the war preparations against the USSR by Germany, Poland, and Japan; he had insisted on precautionary measures against a possible "fifth column" and agents of foreign intelligence services. As we have seen, according to S. N. Mironov, already in mid-July, at the NKVD briefing, Ezhov had talked about forthcoming arrests of Harbin returnees, Poles, and Germans. Apparently, the national operations had been planned simultaneously with the kulak operation. Thus, from late July on NKVD orders appeared for repressions against "national contingents."

On 20 July, at Stalin's instigation, the Politburo instructed Ezhov to arrest all Germans employed in the defense industry and to deport part of them.[44] Five days later (that is, a few days before the issuing of order No. 00447) Ezhov signed operational order No. 00439, which stated that the Gestapo and German General Headquarters were using German citizens in main Soviet enterprises, especially the defense industry, for espionage and sabotage. Ezhov demanded lists of German citizens working (or having worked) in the defense industry and the railroads sector and ordered arrests starting 29 July, to be completed within five days. An exception was made for German political émigrés working in the defense industry, who were to be arrested only if they still held German citizenship. The order further stated that no later than 5 August a detailed memorandum with an exposition of the compromising materials was to be presented to Ezhov on each of the political émigrés who had accepted Soviet citizenship, in order to resolve the question of arrest. Those exposed as spies, saboteurs, or terrorists were to be arrested immediately.[45]

Although the order was originally intended for German citizens proper, from the autumn of 1937 on it was interpreted much more broadly. Now, Soviet citizens of German nationality were also arrested, as well as representatives of other nationalities who had ties with Germany or Germans: former German prisoners of war, political émigrés, deserters, inhabitants of German districts, former German citizens working in the defense industry, "consular contacts," Russians who had spent time in German captivity, former personnel of German firms, and so on. It had become a genuine "German operation," in accordance with the other national operations. It did not mean that all Germans were arrested, however; Germans in the autonomous republic of Volga Germans, for example, were not especially hit. All in all, in the German operation some 65,000–68,000 people were arrested; 55,000 of them were condemned, including 42,000 to the death penalty; only a little over one-third of those condemned were Germans.[46]

On 11 August 1937, two days after Politburo approval, Ezhov signed order No. 00485 for the liquidation of the "Polish diversionist and espionage groups and organizations of the Polish Military Organization (POV)."[47] This order stated that the investigation materials in the case of the POV "disclose the picture of a long-standing and relatively unpunished sabotage and espionage activity by the Polish intelligence service on the territory of the Soviet Union." Although the Moscow POV Center had been liquidated and many active members had been arrested, according to the order, the Polish intelligence service still maintained a sabotage network within the Soviet economy, especially defense objects. It was the duty of the state security organs to destroy this anti-Soviet activity and to "fully liquidate the large-scale sabotage and insurgent rank and file of the POV, untouched up to now, as well as the basic human contingents of the Polish intelligence service in the USSR."[48]

On this account it was decreed as of 20 August to start a "large-scale operation, directed at the full liquidation of the local POV organizations and, first of all, its sabotage-espionage and insurgent cadres in industry, transport, the sovkhozy, and kolkhozy." The operation was to be completed within three months—that is, before 20 November. Subject to arrest were prisoners of war from the Polish army who after the 1920 war had remained in the Soviet Union, deserters and political émigrés from Poland, former members of the Polish Socialist Party (PPS) and other anti-Soviet political parties, and inhabitants of Polish districts in border regions. The investigation was to be carried out by a special group of operational executives. Again, those arrested were divided into two categories: the first category was to be shot, the second to be confined in camps or prisons for five to ten years. For this purpose, lists were to be drawn up by regional dvoikas (the NKVD chief and the procurator) and sent to Moscow for confirmation. After confirmation by Ezhov and the USSR Procurator (Vyshinskii), "the sentence should be executed immediately."[49]

Together with the order, the regional NKVD chiefs received a detailed secret letter, also signed by Ezhov, "On the Fascist-Insurgent, Espionage, Sabotage, Defeatist, and Terrorist Activity of the Polish Intelligence Service in the USSR." The letter, which had been approved by the Politburo, together with order No. 00485, confirmed Ezhov's report at the June 1937 Plenum. It summed up the various accusations against the Poles: espionage, sabotage, terrorism, armed revolt, anti-Soviet agitation. For a long time, the letter said, POV agents had taken over the leadership of the Polish Communist Party and the Polish Comintern section and had penetrated all levels of the Soviet state apparatus, including the People's Commissariat of Foreign Affairs, the NKVD, and the Red Army; POV activity on Soviet territory was directed by a "Center" with Unshlikht, Muklevich, Ol'skii, et al.[50]

Later, during investigation, the Moscow NKVD executive A. O. Postel' testified that Ezhov's order aimed at the arrest of "absolutely all Poles, Polish émigrés, former prisoners of war, members of the Polish Communist Party, etc." The NKVD executives were told that "the Poles should be completely destroyed."[51] Ezhov subsequently added "consular contacts" to the Polish operation as yet another category for repression.[52] He had in mind persons connected with official Polish diplomatic representatives in the USSR. By analogy with the German operation, in this way the Polish operation, originally meant as an almost pure Polish matter, was transformed into an operation for the repression of all unreliable and suspicious people who were in any way linked to Poles and Poland.

Within a month, however, the Polish operation had clearly begun to stall, and Ezhov urged the regional NKVD chiefs to "speed up the termination of cases."[53] Even so, Stalin seemed to be very satisfied with the course of the operation, for on 14 September he noted on Ezhov's report: "Very good! Dig up and purge this Polish espionage mud in the future as well. Destroy it in the interest of the USSR."[54] On 2 October the NKVD decided to extend the Polish repressions also to family members of those arrested, in accordance with Ezhov's order No. 00486 of 15 August 1937.[55] As a result, their wives were arrested and their children under age fifteen were sent to children's homes.

Ezhov's order No. 00593 of 20 September 1937 (approved by the Politburo the previous day) decreed a "national operation" against returnees from Harbin. Almost 25,000 *kharbintsy* had been registered by the NKVD, mostly former personnel of the Eastern-Chinese Railway who had reemigrated from Manchuria to the USSR after the sale of the railway in 1935. According to the order, the overwhelming majority had turned out to be agents of the Japanese intelligence service, which had sent them to the Soviet Union for purposes of terrorist, diversionary, and spying activities. An operation for their liquidation was to be carried out from 1 October to 25 December. As in the Polish operation, the family members of those repressed should be treated according to order No. 00486.[56] But the stream of family members turned out to be much too large to handle so that in November the NKVD decided to restrict itself in the Polish and Harbin operations to exiling wives.[57] In addition to the German, Polish, and Harbin operations, there were other so-called "national operations" against Latvians, Estonians, Finns, Romanians, Greeks, Afghans, Iranians, and so on, though in these operations order No. 00486 was not applied (nor was it applied in the kulak operation, order No. 00447).[58]

The national operations used the so-called "album procedure." Every ten days the regional NKVD organs were to draw up lists with a "brief account of investigation and secret service materials, characterizing the degree of guilt of the prisoners," and send them for confirmation to Moscow in the form of albums. Those arrested were divided into categories by the regional NKVD chief, together with the regional procurator: the so-called dvoika. In Moscow their decision was assessed by the USSR NKVD chief and the Procurator—meaning by Ezhov (or his deputy Frinovskii) and Vyshinskii. After being confirmed, the sentence was carried out regionally.[59] In practice, this procedure led to large-scale delay; the decisions of the regional dvoikas some-times waited months for confirmation.

No quotas were set in the national operations; the regional NKVD chiefs were given free rein. As a result, people were ar-rested indiscriminately and on a large scale. In the words of the Krasnoiarsk province Party secretary, Sobolev: "Stop playing in-ternationalism, all these Poles, Koreans, Latvians, Germans, etc. should be beaten, these are all mercenary nations, subject to ter-mination . . . all nationals should be caught, forced to their knees, and exterminated like mad dogs." This may have been an exag-geration, but (after Ezhov's fall) he was accused of this by the Krasnoiarsk state security organs' Party organization: "By giving such instructions, Sobolev slandered the VKP(b) and comrade Sta-lin, in saying that he had such instructions from the Central Com-mittee and comrade Stalin personally."[60]

The Polish operation was to have been completed before 20 November, but early in November the regional NKVD organs were directed to speed up their work and finish before 10 Decem-ber.[61] When that, too, proved to be out of the question, the term was extended to 1 January 1938, and on 31 January the Politburo allowed the NKVD to extend the operation aimed at the destroy-ing of the saboteurs and spies among the Poles, as well as Latvi-ans, Germans, Estonians, Finns, Greeks, Iranians, Harbin return-ees, Chinese, and Romanians, to 15 April and at the same time ordered it to extend the operation to Bulgarians and Macedo-nians.[62] Again, the date had to be moved forward: on 26 May the Politburo allowed the NKVD to extend the operation with respect to all the above-mentioned nationalities, plus Afghans, to 1 Au-gust.[63] Two days later the NKVD passed the decision on to its regional organs, adding that the cases were to be examined in a simplified manner.[64] In this way the arrest and the extrajudicial procedure of the examination of cases with respect to the national operations continued until 1 August 1938. The album procedure was causing major delays, mainly owing to the inability of the Moscow NKVD center to cope with the stream, and on 15 September the Politburo decided to give jurisdiction to regional troikas (*osobye troiki*).[65]

The national operations were completed in mid-November 1938. All in all, almost 350,000 people went through these operations; 247,157 of them were condemned to death, 88,356 to camp or prison.[66] Almost 144,000 people were arrested in the Polish operation alone—more than 111,000 of whom were given the first category of punishment and almost 29,000 the second.[67] Nearly the entire Polish Comintern section was annihilated, and of the Polish Communist Party 46 members and 24 candidates of its Central Committee were executed.[68] In August 1938, the Polish Communist Party was even officially disbanded by the Comintern Executive Committee.[69] In the Greek, Finnish, and Estonian operations, the percentage of those sentenced to death was even higher, though in the Afghan and Iranian operations most of those arrested were deported.[70]

Indeed, the Great Terror years saw an extension to all border regions of deporting "unreliable elements." As early as April 1936 the Soviet government had decided on resettling by the NKVD to Kazakhstan some 45,000 Poles and Germans from the Ukrainian border region with Poland—over 35,000 Poles were deported.[71] In July 1937 it extended the new regime to territory bordering on Iran and Afghanistan; as a result, in 1937–38 over 1,000 Kurdish families and 2,000 Iranian families were deported. In November 1937 the Odessa provincial Party committee ordered the deportation of 5,000 German households.[72]

In August 1937, after the Japanese invasion of North China, the Soviet government deported all Koreans—theoretically if not actually still Japanese legals—from the Far Eastern province. A Central Committee and Soviet government decree of 21 August, signed by Stalin and Molotov, ordered regional Party and NKVD organs to begin deporting all Koreans from the Russian Far Eastern border regions at once and to finish before 1 January 1938. As a potential fifth column in the threatening war with Japan, they were deported to Kazakhstan and Uzbekistan; during transport many of them died. The operation, personally directed by the Far Eastern NKVD chief Liushkov (who had recently replaced Deribas), was completed within a few weeks. In late October Ezhov reported to Stalin that 171,781 Koreans had been resettled in Central Asia.[73] In addition, the NKVD arrested more than 2,500 Koreans.[74] Some 11,000 Chinese were also deported.[75]

On 5 July 1937 the Politburo approved an NKVD proposal to "confine all wives of the condemned traitors from the Rightist-Trotskiist espionage and sabotage organization in camps for 5–8 years." For this purpose special camps were to be organized in Narym province and Turgai district. Children under fifteen years should be taken under state protection.[76] Operational order No. 00486, of 15 August 1937, "on the repressing of the wives of the traitors from the Rightist-Trotskiist espionage and sabotage organizations who have been condemned by the Military Collegium and military tribunals," specified that wives as well as children above fifteen years who were "socially dangerous" should be arrested and sent to camps by the Special Board; children under fifteen years were to be sent to special children's homes (infants in arms accompanied their mothers).[77] (This was the order later applied in the Polish operation.) More than 18,000 wives of enemies of the people were arrested, and approximately 25,000 children were taken away.[78]

While the "mass operations" raged, the Party purge continued. During the summer of 1937 and after, Party leaders, including Stalin's adjutants Kaganovich, Molotov, Zhdanov, Andreev, Malenkov, Khrushchev, Mikoian, and Ezhov himself, made for the republics and provinces in order to accelerate the purge of the Party and state apparatus.[79] They gave instructions for arrests to the regional NKVD organs—that is, through them the Party directed the repressions and the NKVD, and not the other way around. As a result, in the regions one shift of old cadres was repressed after another. The Belorussian NKVD chief, B. D. Berman, complained to the republican Party secretary: "What can I do, it's beyond me? Ezhov has again sent an allocation of old communists. Where can I find them? There are no more left."[80] All too often, the executioners became victims themselves, resulting, for example, in a changed troika composition. During the second half of 1937, some 97,000 Party members were expelled, mainly old cadres. Now, expulsion often meant arrest.[81]

The purge of the Comintern also continued. In 1937, between January and September, 256 people were dismissed from its central apparatus; in general, dismissal resulted in arrest.[82] In October that year Dimitrov and Manuil'skii acknowledged that the NKVD had "discovered a broad espionage organization in the Comintern apparatus."[83] In November, Stalin told Dimitrov: "The Trotkiists [in the Comintern] should be persecuted, shot, destroyed. These are worldwide provocateurs, the most vicious agents of fascism."[84] Foreign communist parties residing in the Soviet Union were decimated.

The terror did not stop at the USSR borders. During the 1930s, Outer Mongolia, though a sovereign state, was treated as a Soviet republic; after mid-August 1937, S. N. Mironov, the former Western Siberian NKVD chief, was the USSR plenipotentiary there, at the same time representing the NKVD. Frinovskii accompanied him to Ulan-Bator, from where, on 13 September, he wired to Ezhov about plans to liquidate the lamas.[85] Six days later, the Politburo approved Frinovskii's proposal to institute a special troika for the examination of lama cases, consisting of the First Deputy Prime Minister Kh. Choibalsan, the Minister of Justice, and the Party chief.[86] On 18 October Mironov informed Frinovskii (who had returned to Moscow) about the disclosure of a "large-scale counterrevolutionary organization" within the Ministry of Internal Affairs; four months later (13 February 1938) he asked Ezhov's permission to arrest a new group of "conspirators" and urgently requested the sending of new NKVD instructors.[87] On 3 April Mironov reported to Frinovskii that 10,728 "conspirators" had been arrested, including 7,814 lamas, 322 feudal lords, 300 ministerial officials, 180 military leaders, 1,555 Buriats, and 408 Chinese; on 31 March, 6,311 of them had already been shot—3–4 percent of the male adult population of Mongolia. According to Mironov, the intention was to arrest over 7,000 more.[88]

The mass operations of 1937–38 were resisted only on a very small scale, mainly in the traditionally rebellious North Caucasus, where leading NKVD executives were attacked and murdered, convoyed people liberated, and so on. According to A. Avtorkhanov, thousands of Chechens and Ingush joined guerrilla groups, assassinating several local NKVD chiefs. Between February and December 1938, Chechen and Ingush insurgents carried out ninety-eight armed raids, killing Party and state officials and stealing 617,000 rubles' worth of property.[89] Therefore, on 13 July 1938, the First Party Secretary of Checheno-Ingushetiia asked Stalin and the Moscow leadership for permission to organize a Special Troika with exceptional powers during from four to five months in order to finally liquidate the insurgent elements.[90]

The simultaneous conducting of a purge of the Party and state apparatus and of mass arrests among the population was no coincidence. Precisely against the background of the exposure of highly placed leaders as "enemies, spies, conspirators, and wreckers" and the conducting of show trials against them with the accompanying stir and hysteria, it was possible to organize large-scale arrests among the population, even with mass approval. During the second half of 1937 Ezhov was master of the situation. The arrests carried out by his department knew no limits. With good reason Khlevniuk arrives at the conclusion that the mass terror of 1937–38 was "a purposeful operation, planned on a state scale." The purge was conducted "under control and on the initiative of the supreme leadership of the USSR." This "particular centralization" did not, however, exclude a certain "spontaneity" and "initiative" on the part of the local authorities, but these were "planned" and "followed the essence of the orders from the center."[91]

Some information on the scope of the terror was already available more than four decades ago. In 1956, in his "secret speech" to the Twentieth Party Congress, Khrushchev reported that, out of a total of 15, 5 Politburo members had been repressed: Chubar' and Kosior (full members), and Eikhe, Postyshev, and Rudzutak (candidates); of the 139 Central Committee members and candidates elected at the Seventeenth Party Congress in 1934, 98 had been arrested and shot; 1,108 of the 1,966 delegates to the same congress had been arrested.[92] Khrushchev further revealed that the NKVD drew up lists of leading Party, Soviet, Komsomol, military and economic functionaries, writers, artists, and others whose death or other sentences had been determined before trial. Ezhov sent the lists to Stalin and a few other Politburo members for approval. According to Khrushchev, in 1937–38 Stalin received 383 such lists, containing the names of over 44,000 people, 39,000 of whom were to be sentenced to death by the Military Collegium of the Supreme Court.[93] Between February 1937 and September 1938, Stalin and a few of his Politburo colleagues indeed approved the death sentence through the Military Collegium for 38,679 people, as had been proposed by the NKVD (16,606 in 1937, 22,073 in 1938), including 3,167 people on 12 September 1938 alone.[94] This extraordinary procedure, in which Stalin, together with a few adjutants, in fact acted as judge, concerned only the Party and state elite. By signing the lists, Stalin pronounced sentence.

In determining the total of the mass operations, we have at our disposal the act on the transfer of authority for the NKVD from Ezhov to Beriia in December 1938. According to this source, from 1 October 1936 to 1 November 1938, 1,565,041 people were arrested, including 365,805 in the "national operations" and 702,656 in the operation with respect to order No. 00447; during the same period, 1,336,863 people were condemned, including 668,305 to the first category of punishment (death).[95] According to more detailed information in the same source, during the same period 1,391,215 people were condemned in NKVD cases, including 668,305 to the death penalty. Of these, 36,906 were condemned by the Military Collegium of the Supreme Court (including 25,355 to the death penalty), 69,114 by the Special Board (no death penalties), 767,397 in the operation with respect to order No. 00447 (including 386,798 to the death penalty), 235,122 in the national operations (including 172,830 to the death penalty), 93,137 in the operation with respect to order No. 00606—that is, those national operations that after 15 September 1938 had been handed over to the special troikas (including 63,921 to the death penalty), 189,539 by military tribunals and special collegia of the republican and provincial courts (including 19,401 to the death penalty).[96]

Staggering though these figures are, the total should come out somewhat higher because the mass operations between 1 and 15/16 November 1938 (that is, until the end date) have not been taken into account. According to information from the Soviet Ministry of Internal Affairs of December 1953, during 1937–38, a total of 1,575,259 people were arrested (936,750 in 1937, 638,509 in 1938); 1,372,382 of them were arrested for counter-revolutionary crimes (779,056 in 1937, 593,326 in 1938); 1,344,923 of them were condemned (790,665 in 1937, 554,258 in 1938); 681,692 of them were condemned to death (353,074 in 1937, 328,618 in 1938).[97] However, these figures, too, are incomplete. All in all, during the "Ezhovshchina" probably some 1.5 million people were arrested, 700,000 of whom were shot.

These figures are confirmed by the increase in the number of prisoners in camps and other places of detention during 1937–38. According to information from the Soviet Ministry of Internal Affairs of 1960, on 1 January 1937 there were 1,196,369 people in the camps; on 1 January 1938, 1,881,570; and on 1 January 1939, 1,672,438, plus 352,508 in the prisons (together, 2,024,946 people).[98] This means that, from early 1937 to early 1939, the total number of prisoners was increased by approximately 800,000 people. If one adds the almost 700,000 people executed, a total figure of approximately 1.5 million people repressed during 1937–38 is reached again. During 1937–38, according to M. Wehner, some 160,000 people died in the camps, but this figure could include those executed as a consequence of order No. 00447—that is, they have already been counted among the almost 700,000 above.[99] Khlevniuk adds that it is unclear how, or even whether, those who perished during investigation have been counted.[100]

As concerns the repression of Party members, those condemned by the Military Collegium were mainly victims of the Party and state purge—nomenklatura victims, although there are some exceptions. According to the journal *Istochnik*, 779,056 people were repressed in 1937, including 55,428 Party members and candidates (7 percent); 593,336, including 61,457 Party members and candidates (10 percent), in 1938.[101] Thus, less than 10 percent were Party members, though one should keep in mind that those expelled during the Party purges of 1936 and before are not included in this figure.

Who were these people, and why were they repressed? The total purge unleashed by Stalin allowed him to strengthen his personal power, which considerably centralized the regime, and made it easier to run the country. It replaced the Old Bolsheviks and "bourgeois specialists" by a new, obedient bureaucracy, consisting of young "specialists" who had been educated in the Stalinist spirit of the 1930s and would execute any order by Stalin without protesting. In this way repetition of the problems with the verification campaign of 1935, having met passive opposition by the local Party leadership, should be prevented. A second aim was the elimination of all "socially dangerous elements," both "people of the past" (*byvshie*) and "spies." Consequently, the Great Terror meant the hunt for spies, meaning anyone who maintained any contacts with the world outside the USSR, and the liquidation of a potential and mythical "fifth column."[102] By isolating the country from foreign influence, an iron curtain was drawn up.

Decades later, a surviving member of Stalin's circle, Molotov, maintained that "1937 was necessary": "Enemies of various tendencies were left over, and in the face of the growing threat of fascist agression they might unite. Thanks to 1937 we had no fifth column during the war." According to him, "in the main it was the guilty who suffered, those who needed to be repressed to one degree or another." In the process errors were made and "innocent people were sometimes caught. Obviously one or two out of ten were wrongly caught, but the rest rightly. . . . Any delay was out of the question. War preparations were under way." In his words, Stalin's policy was, "better an innocent head less, than hesitations during the war."[103] Echoing Molotov, his colleague Kaganovich contended that, apart from a few innocent victims, the country had rightly been purged in order to defend the revolution from its enemies and to prevent the hostile activity during wartime of a "fifth column." The Trotskiists, Rightists, and so on may perhaps not have been "spies," but they had thought it possible to "come to an agreement against the people." Moreover, everything had been done in accordance with the law: "We did not break the law, did not sign just like that, at will. These are lies. Ul'rikh [chairman of the Military Collegium] gave reports. There was a court, an indictment, there were sentences: everything as it should be, everything according to the law."[104]

As a result, the main categories subject to repression were: Party and state functionaries, including Chekists and Red Army officers, that is, former oppositionists or loyal Stalinists refusing to break with them completely; "people of the past," that is, former tsarist functionaries, White Guards, SRs, Mensheviks, kulaks, priests, part of the old intelligentsia; and "spies," that is, foreigners or people with foreign contacts.

Why were these people repressed just at this time? Apart from the war scare, there was yet another element. The adoption in 1936 of a new USSR Constitution reinforced the Soviet leadership's fear of a possible activization of oppositionist elements. Already in October 1936 NKVD reports had been received about commotion among anti-Soviet circles, who wanted to take advantage of the new Constitution and the forthcoming elections.[105] During an NKVD conference in December 1936 Ezhov strongly contested that the new Constitution would result in more legality and freedoms: "Now, the question of the struggle against the counterrevolution stands sharper, and if you want to do the new Constitution a good turn, then your main task is to guard it against any encroachment by the counterrevolution with all strength and possibilities."[106] At the February–March Plenum of 1937, many orators stressed the danger arising from kulaks returning from exile, as well as the threat from believers and activists of Church organizations during the forthcoming elections.[107]

One should keep in mind that operations proceeding from order No. 00447 were supposed to have been completed within four months—that is, by early December 1937. This suggests a close connection between the campaign of mass arrests and the elections for the Supreme Soviet, set for 12 December. It is no coincidence that the question of the Supreme Soviet elections was discussed at the same June 1937 Plenum, where Stalin took the decision about the operation against "anti-Soviet elements." Whereas several categories of citizens had previously been deprived of suffrage, the new Constitution enfranchised the entire adult population, with the exception of those who had been sentenced and lunatics. In this way quite a lot of these "anti-Soviet elements" were given the vote. Moreover, a system of secret-ballot elections had been introduced, with multiple candidates campaigning for each seat.

Regional Party leaders feared that class enemies would take advantage of the freedom offered at the elections. At the June 1937 Plenum the Kazakh government leader, U. D. Isaev, warned: "We will clash here with a situation of direct class struggle. Even now, mullahs, Trotskiist, and every kind of other counterrevolutionary elements are preparing for the elections."[108] At the October 1937 Plenum the Moscow Party leader, A. I. Ugarov, again pointed to intensifying utterances of hostile activity. By now, however, his Western Siberian colleague R. I. Eikhe was able to establish that, on the contrary, thanks to the crushing of the organized counterrevolutionary base the situation had much improved. Stalin agreed: "People are glad to have freed themselves of the wreckers."[109] For safety's sake, during the same month it was decided to ban contested elections and introduce uncontested single candidacies.

Stalin himself later acknowledged one of the main reasons for order No. 00447. In March 1939, in his report to the Eighteenth Party Congress, he explained the succesful conduct of the elections to the USSR Supreme Soviet in December 1937 and to the Supreme Soviets of the republics in June 1938 with the timely conduct of the repressions.[110] Apart from these immediate, practical tasks, by means of the mass operations Stalin wanted to bring Soviet society in accord with the theoretical tenets of his report of 25 November 1936 on the Constitution project with respect to the erasing of class borders. He had added that former White Guardists, kulaks, priests, and so on, would no longer be deprived of suffrage.[111] Thus, they were given suffrage—but by means of order No. 00447 they were not given the chance to participate in the elections of 12 December 1937. By physically destroying the alien people whom it was impossible to reeducate in socialism, Stalin speeded up the process of erasing class borders. It is to be noted that the preamble to order No. 00447 set the state security organs the task "to put an end, once and for all" to the activities of anti-Soviet elements. It shows that Stalin indeed aimed at a "final solution" of the problem of anti-Soviet elements.

Legality was of no concern to Ezhov's NKVD. In January 1939, after his fall, a commission consisting of Andreev, Beriia, and Malenkov accused Ezhov of having used illegal investigation methods: "In a most flagrant way, investigation methods were distorted, mass beatings were indiscriminately applied to prisoners, in order to extort false testimony and 'confessions.' " During twenty-four hours an investigator often had to obtain several dozen confessions, and investigators kept each other informed about the the testimony obtained so that corresponding facts, circumstances, or names could be suggested to other prisoners. "As a result, this sort of investigation very often led to organized slander of totally innocent people." Very often, confessions were obtained by means of "straight provocation"; prisoners were persuaded to give false testimony about their "espionage activity" in order to help the Party and the government to "discredit foreign states" and in exchange for the promise of release. According to Andreev et al., "the NKVD leadership in the person of comrade Ezhov not only did not cut short such arbitrariness and excesses in arresting and conducting investigation, but sometimes themselves encouraged it." All opposition was suppressed.[112]

The functioning of the troikas was also sharply criticized. Andreev et al. reported that there had been "serious slips" in their work, as well as in that of the so-called Grand Collegium [*bol'-shaia kollegiia*], where during a single evening session from 600 to 2,000 cases were often examined. (They were referring to the examination in Moscow of albums in the national operations; before being signed by the People's Commissar of Internal Affairs and the Procurator, the albums were examined by a number of department chiefs of the central NKVD apparatus.) The work of the regional troikas was not controlled by the NKVD at all. Approximately 200,000 people were sentenced to two years by the so-called militia troikas, "the existence of which was not legal." The NKVD Special Board "did not meet in its legal composition even once."[113]

As an executive of the Tiumen' operational sector of the NKVD testified later, arrests were usually made arbitrarily—people were arrested for belonging to groups that did not actually exist—and the troika duly fell in line with the operational group: "At a troika meeting, the crimes of the defendants were not examined. In some days during an hour I reported to the troika cases involving 50–60 persons." In a later interview the Tiumen' executive gave a more detailed account of how the operational group carried out the troika's "first category" sentences. Those sentenced to death were executed in the basement in a special room with covered walls, with a shot in the back of the head, followed by a second shot in the temple. The corpses were then taken away to a cemetery outside town. In Tobol'sk, to which the person involved was transferred in 1938, they executed and buried right in prison; for lack of space, the corpses were piled up.[114] The assistant chief of the Saratov police administration gave similar testimony: "The basic instruction was to produce as many cases as possible, to formulate them as quickly as possible, with maximum simplification of investigation. As for the quota of cases, [the NKVD chief] demanded [the inclusion of] all those sentenced and all those that had been picked up, even if at the moment of their seizure they had not committed any sort of concrete crime.[115]

After arrest, Ezhov's deputy, Frinovskii, explained that the main NKVD investigators had been the "butchers" [*sledovateli-kolol'shchiki*], mainly selected from "conspirators or compromised people." "Unchecked, they applied beatings to prisoners, obtained 'testimony' in the shortest possible time." With Ezhov approving, it was the investigator rather than the prisoner who determined the testimony. Afterward, the protocols were "edited" by Ezhov and Frinovskii, usually without seeing the prisoner or only in passing. According to Frinovskii, Ezhov encouraged the use of physical force during interrogations: he personally supervised the interrogations and instructed the investigators to use "methods of physical influencing" if the results were unsatisfactory. During interrogations he was sometimes drunk.[116]

As one of the investigators later explained, if somebody was arrested on Ezhov's orders, they were convinced of his guilt in advance, even if all evidence was lacking. They "tried to obtain a confession from that individual using all possible means."[117] Under arrest, the former Moscow NKVD deputy chief A. P. Radzivilovskii quoted Ezhov as saying that if evidence was lacking, one should "beat the necessary testimony out of [the prisoners]." According to Radzivilovskii, testimony "as a rule was obtained as a result of the torturing of prisoners, which was widely practiced both in the central and the provincial NKVD apparatuses."[118]

After arrest both the chief of the Moscow Lefortovo investigation prison and his deputy testified that Ezhov had personally participated in beating prisoners during interrogation.[119] His deputy, Frinovskii, had done the same thing.[120] Shepilov recollects how after Stalin's death Khrushchev told his colleagues that one day, while visiting Ezhov's Central Committee office, he saw spots of clotted blood on the skirt and cuffs of Ezhov's blouse. When asked what was up, Ezhov answered, with a shade of ecstasy, that one might be proud of such spots, for it was the blood of enemies of the revolution.[121]

In this respect, however, Ezhov did not act on his own authority. During the 1950s the former Moscow NKVD executive A. O. Postel' tried to justify himself by stressing that the "physical methods of investigation" had "emanated directly from the People's Commissar Ezhov and the Party leader Stalin."[122] Ezhov indeed acted according to Stalin's instructions. In one such case Stalin ordered Ezhov to rake over the coals a prisoner who was not making the demanded confessions: "Isn't it time to squeeze this gentleman and force him to report on his dirty little business? Where is he: in a prison or a hotel?"[123] Besides signing Ezhov's lists, Stalin sometimes gave instructions concerning certain individuals; for instance, in December 1937 he added to M. I. Baranov's name, "beat, beat!"[124]

From the summer of 1937 on, beating and torturing were practiced on a broad scale, with the permission of the Party leadership. In early 1939, Stalin informed the regional Party and NKVD chiefs that "from 1937 on in NKVD practice the use of physical pressure [on prisoners] was permitted by the Central Committee." It was permitted ("exceptionally," according to Stalin), "only with respect to such overt enemies of the people who take advantage of humane interrogation methods in order to shamelessly refuse to give away conspirators, who for months don't testify and try to impede the unmasking of those conspirators who are still free." Stalin considered it a "totally correct and expedient method"—though later the practice had been soiled by scoundrels like Zakovskii, Litvin, and Uspenskii, Stalin added, after these NKVD executives had been liquidated themselves. They had turned it "from an exception into a rule," applying it to "accidentally arrested honest people."[125] Of course, the point is that they had acted on Stalin's instructions and had been dealt with only after they were no longer of use.

Stalin made no secret of his intentions. According to the Secretary General of the Comintern, Georgii Dimitrov, in November 1937, at a dinner on the anniversary of the October Revolution, Stalin proposed a toast to Politburo members and a few other leaders with the words: "We will destroy every enemy, even if he is an Old Bolshevik, we will destroy his kin, his family. Anyone who by his actions or thoughts encroaches on the unity of the socialist state, we shall destroy relentlessly."[126]

5

Apogee

On 17 July 1937 the Central Executive Committee (TsIK), in agreement with the Politburo, awarded Nikolai Ezhov the Lenin order "for his outstanding success in leading the NKVD organs in their fulfillment of government assignments."[1] Ten days later, with the preparations of the mass operations in full swing, TsIK President Mikhail Kalinin ceremonially handed over the order to him, as well as orders to some 120 other NKVD executives: Bel'skii, Berman, Dagin, Frinovskii, Gendin, Leplevskii, Litvin, Redens, Tsesarskii, Zakovskii, et al. Kalinin embraced him warmly, declaring that he had "introduced Party spirit, Bolshevism into the NKVD work" and calling him an example for the Chekists.[2]

A few days after that, *Izvestiia* published Boris Efimov's famous cartoon of Ezhov's "hedgehog's gauntlets" (*ezhovy rukavitsy*).* The cartoon showed an armored gauntlet crushing a reptile covered with the words "terror" and "espionage"; in the corner were Trotskii and his son, with frightened faces.[3] Later during the

---

*In Russia, the expression *derzhat' v ezhovykh rukavitsakh* means "to rule with an iron rod."

Kalinin handing over the Lenin order to Ezhov, 27 July 1937. (Memorial collection)

same year, a poster by Efimov was published with Ezhov himself depicted, with the same gauntlet squeezing a poisonous snake, personifying the "enemies of the people."[4] His influence had reached its apogee. On 12 October 1937, following Stalin's proposal, the Central Committee at its Plenum promoted him to candidate member of the Politburo (replacing Ian Rudzutak, already arrested, shot the following year).[5]

During the Supreme Soviet elections of December 1937 Ezhov was preceded only by Stalin, Molotov, and Voroshilov in the number of nominations.[6] The poster of his "hedgehog's gauntlets" was affixed everywhere.[7] He was ultimately nominated in Gor'kii, where, on 9 December, three days before the elections, he

СТАЛЬНЫЕ ЕЖОВЫ РУКАВИЦЫ

"Ezhov's hedgehog's gauntlets of steel" (*ezhovy rukavitsky*): poster by Boris Efimov, 1937. (Collection N. Petrov)

addressed a meeting attended by 75,000.[8] He praised the successes achieved during the socialist construction in the field of industrialization, the collectivization of agriculture, the conquering of unemployment, the increasing living standard, free education, equal rights of nations and of men and women. However, he stressed, these successes had not been achieved without struggle, and the struggle was not over. For the capitalists offered fierce resistance:

> . . . the stronger and richer we get, the more anger we provoke from the frenzied pack of the bourgeoisie, flirting with Fascism, preparing for war with us, and in the meantime sending us packs of spies, saboteurs, and wreckers. They inspire to struggle with the working people of the Soviet country those leftovers of the capitalist classes that have not yet been finished off, mobilizing under their Fascist banners the wretched remains of kulaks, criminals, and Trotskiist-Bukharinist degenerates. During their struggle, this whole disgusting bunch of Trotskiist-Bukharinist degenerates play the most dirty, fishy, monstrous tricks on us, in order somehow to call a halt to the triumphant advance of our people toward communism.
>
> Our further successes to a high degree will depend on our ability to identify these clever methods of the class enemy against us, on our will at last to cleanse the Soviet country of this vermin. . . . Much of our success must depend on the increasing of our revolutionary Bolshevist vigilance. . . . Our Soviet people will exterminate to a man all these despicable servants of the capitalist lords, vile enemies of all workers.[9]

He was of course elected to the Supreme Soviet, together with Frinovskii, Bel'skii, and sixty-two other NKVD executives; moreover, thirty-two of their colleagues were elected to the Nationalities Soviet.[10]

On 20 December 1937 the twentieth anniversary of the NKVD was celebrated all over the country, with articles in the press and meetings in factories and kolkhozes.[11] A ceremonial meeting was held in the Bol'shoi Theater, with in the Presidium

Andreev, Kaganovich, Khrushchev, Mikoian, Molotov, Voroshilov, Zhdanov, Frinovskii, Redens, et al. and in the middle, of course, Ezhov himself. In his speech Politburo member Anastas Mikoian praised him as a "gifted, faithful Stalin pupil": "He has smashed the vicious spy nests of Trotskiist-Bukharinist agents of the foreign intelligence services, cleansed our native land of many enemies of the people, who had sought to turn back the wheel of history." "Learn from comrade Ezhov the Stalinist style of working he has learned and is learning from comrade Stalin!" Mikoian added. Ezhov had "created within the NKVD a splendid backbone of Chekists, Soviet intelligence officers." He had taught the Chekists "an ardent love for Socialism and for our people, as well as hatred for all enemies": "Therefore today the whole NKVD and comrade Ezhov in the first place are the favorites of the Soviet people. . . . In our country every worker is an NKVDist!"[12] Ezhov and the NKVD were praised by the rest of the Party press as well—for example, by *Partiinoe stroitel'stvo*, edited by Malenkov, writing in December 1937: "The Soviet people love their intelligence service, because it defends the vital interests of the people and it is their flesh and blood."[13]

Ezhov's name was bestowed on everything from a Dal'stroi steamer, a factory in the Ukraine, the Dinamo stadium in Kiev, to a district in Sverdlovsk, the NKVD troops officers' school, the Krasnodar Higher Agricultural School, and hundreds of other educational institutions, kolkhozes, Pioneers' troops, and so on; on 15 July 1937 the Politburo voted to rename the city of Sulimov, capital of the Cherkess Autonomous Province in the Northern Caucasus, Ezhovo-Cherkessk.[14] (Early in 1938 Ezhov proposed that Moscow be renamed Stalinodar, but Stalin dismissed the idea.)[15]

Ezhov was even immortalized in poetry. On 10 December 1937, during the election campaign for the Supreme Soviet, *Ogonek* weekly published a long paean of praise by Kazakhstan's "national poet," Dzhambul Dzhabaev. The title was "Song of *Batyr* Ezhov," *batyr* being a local word for hero:

Stalin's faithful and devoted friend,
Before whom enemies tremble in fright.
He does not betray his love for the native land.
The country knows him as its best friend.
Spies and sworn enemies dream about him,
Always with a bare slicing sword.

. . . .
I praise the hero, who sees and hears
How the enemy, who creeps upon us in the dark, breathes.
I praise the courage and strength of the hero
Who strikes the enemies with an iron hand.
I praise *batyr* Ezhov, who
Dug up and wiped out the snakes' lairs,
Who stood up, threatening the winged enemies,
To guard the country and its harvest.
Be forever decorated with the Lenin order,
Our sharp-sighted guardian of factories and fields,
And let my song carry throughout the world
Universal glory to our native *batyr*.[16]

A week earlier, on 3 December, *Pravda* had published parts of another poem by the same Dzhambul, "People's Commissar Ezhov." During the next month, the literary journal *Novyi mir* published the complete text of this "Poem on People's Commissar Ezhov," again in a Russian translation from the Kazakh:

Make, dombra,* for the country's favorite
Eagle's screams with your strings.
Play, dombra, so that the nations will learn
About the knight of Stalin's strong rock.

. . . .
In flashing lightning we came to know
Sharp-sighted and intelligent People's Commissar Ezhov.
Great Lenin's wise words
Trained the hero Ezhov for battle.
Great Stalin's ardent call

---

*Dombra: a Kazakh stringed instrument.

Was heard by Ezhov with all his heart, all his blood.
When October's dawn began to shine,
He stormed the palace with courage in his eyes.
. . . .
With glittering sword he boldly leads
The people, dressed in greatcoat, into the attack.
He fights, while learning from the great *batyrs*,
Like Sergo [Ordzhonikidze], Voroshilov, and Kirov.
He is tender to fighters, severe to enemies,
Battle-hardened, brave Ezhov.

. . . .
Ezhov was sent to us [Kazakhs] by Lenin and Stalin.
Ezhov arrived, dispersed the mist,
And roused Kazakhstan to the battle for happiness,
United the *auls* under the banner of the Soviets,
Gave the strength and wisdom of the Kremlin decrees.
Leading the Kazakh people,
He led the advance against *bais* and *beks*.
The people followed Ezhov into the offensive.
The golden visions came true.
Ezhov drove the bloodsuckers over the mountains,
Liberating their herds.

. . . .
All love you here, comrade Ezhov!
Canals, ponds, the blue lakes
Look to you happily.

. . . .
The feather-grass sings its song about you,
Your breathing is in the movement of the wind.
More sonorous than waterfalls, more wonderful than canals,
The steppe bards [*akyny*] sing songs for you.

. . . .
They exulted, bringing us fetters,
But the beasts fell into Ezhov's trap.
Great Stalin's faithful friend,
Ezhov broke their traitorous circle.
The wicked enemy breed has been disclosed
By the eyes of Ezhov, the eyes of the people.
Ezhov has been on the watch for all poisonous snakes

And has smoked out the reptiles from their lairs and dens.
The whole scorpion breed has been routed
By the hands of Ezhov, the hands of the people.
And the Lenin order, all ablaze,
Has been given to you, faithful Stalinist People's Commissar.
You are a sword, quietly drawn and threatening,
A fire, scorching the snakes' nests.
. . . .
The clear word of millions of voices
Flies from the people to *batyr* Ezhov:
Thank you, Ezhov, that, raising the alarm,
You guard the country and the leader.[17]

In an article titled "My Happiness," Dzhambul recalled his visit to Ezhov in Moscow on 8 January 1938, on which occasion he sang his song. Ezhov called Dzhambul "our country's best poet" and declared: "I have been brought up by Stalin and the party of Lenin and Stalin. I have served it, do serve it, and will serve it until the end of my days."[18]

A grateful Dzhambul then produced a new work, "Wipe Them Out," which *Pravda* published on 7 March 1938 during the Bukharin trial. The poem pleads for "a dog's death for the dogs" and ends with another tribute to the hero:

Keep the country from the damned vipers,
Just as it is piously guarded by Stalin's friend
Who has been brought up for us by Lenin and Stalin,
Who is hard and severe, like cast steel,
Who is more courageous than the snow leopard
and more sharp-sighted than the eagle:
The country's favorite, vigilant Ezhov!

Probably in 1935, after being elected secretary of the Central Committee in February of that year, Ezhov and his wife, Evgeniia, moved from an apartment near Pushkin Square to the Kremlin.[19] They also had a luxurious dacha in Meshcherino, a picturesque place on the Pakhra River to the southeast of Moscow, just beyond Gorki Leninskie, where more Soviet leaders had their dachas.[20] During the 1930s Evgeniia directed the editing of the popular journal *USSR Under Construction* (*SSSR na stroike*); successive editors in chief were Uritskii, Piatakov, Mezhlauk, and Kosarev.[21] Ezhov seems to have had little interest in his wife's literary, musical, and other passions.[22] According to Babel', he never attended her salons, and as soon as the guests saw Ezhov arriving at the house (it was said that Stalin himself sometimes gave him a lift), they quickly departed.[23] Under arrest one of Ezhov's adjutants, I. Ia. Dagin, testified that the Ezhovs very regularly ordered packages abroad through the People's Commissariat's Secretariat, which had at its disposal foreign valuta especially for this purpose, and "in the course of two years, several thousand dollars were spent for Ezhov's wife."[24]

They had no children of their own, and—probably in the summer of 1936—adopted a little orphan named Natasha from a children's home near Moscow. At the dacha, Ezhov taught her to play tennis, skate, and ride a bicycle. He is remembered as a gentle, loving father, showering her with presents and playing with her in the evenings after returning from the Lubianka.[25] Ezhov's mother, Anna Antonovna, lived in their apartment, or at least was there very often.

After arrest, Ezhov testified to having provided all his relatives with apartments. Moreover, he got his brother Ivan work in a GUGB Department of Operational Techniques workshop.[26] In November 1938, in a letter to Stalin that was probably never sent, Ezhov had depicted his relationship with his brother in a more negative way. He wrote that until recently his brother had been employed "as a warden [*komendant*] in one of our works [*ob'ekt*]." He had repeatedly instructed Frinovskii to fire him, but his deputy was in no hurry; on the contrary, Ivan had even received an apartment.[27] In 1934 Ivan had married Zinaida Ivanova, but in 1937 they divorced; she said that he humiliated her by bringing home prostitutes.[28] Later, during interrogation, an acquaintance affirmed that Ivan "constantly drank heavily and indulged in debauchery and hooliganism. Repeatedly he was

Ezhov *en famille*. From left to right, Natasha, Ezhov, Evgeniia Solomonovna, Ordzhonikidze, Zinaida Ordzhonikidze, possibly Ordzhonikidze's assistant Semushkin, 1936. (Memorial collection)

detained by the police; once, being drunk, he even broke the head of a policeman. But he was always released as soon as his close relationship with comrade Ezhov came to light."[29] One highly improbable story describes a meeting of the two brothers in the apartment of an acquaintance, during which, after some drinks, the two began arguing; Ivan called Ezhov a "bloodsucker" who had drenched the country in blood, and after a few days he was arrested and disappeared without a trace.[30] Certainly it is possible that behind his back Ivan called Ezhov a bloodsucker—the two had after all never gotten along—but Ivan did not disappear but was arrested only after his brother's arrest.

Ezhov's sister, Evdokiia, had six children with, it seems, a man called Nikolai Babulin. From the early 1930s on she lived in Moscow, in one of Ezhov's former apartments, with her second husband, Egor Pimenov, apparently a tailor, and some of her children; her son Sergei Babulin, also a former tailor, got an NKVD job and the apartment of Iagoda's sister but was later fired.[31] During the second half of the 1920s, as related earlier, Liudmila and Anatolii Babulin had lived with their uncle; during the 1930s Anatolii, a mechanical engineer at the Central Scientific Research Institute for Aircraft Motor Building, again lived with Ezhov's family, as did also his brother Viktor.[32]

Ezhov and his wife both had their lovers. Evgeniia, it seems, continued her relationship with Babel'; she also had intimate relations with her chief, Uritskii.[33] In the spring of 1934 Ezhov made advances to an employee of the People's Commissariat of Foreign Trade, Tat'iana Petrova.[34] In 1935, Evgeniia's close friend Zinaida Glikina separated from her husband, and Evgeniia invited her to settle in their apartment. Later, after arrest, Ezhov testified that he had established intimate relations with his wife's friend (probably Glikina), as well as with her husband.[35] He also testified about his relationship with Evgeniia Podol'skaia, the wife of the Soviet plenipotentiary in Warsaw (born in 1903), whom he got to know well in 1931–33. Soon they began to "cohabit," which continued until her arrest on 1 November 1936, shortly after Ezhov was appointed NKVD chief. He ordered the Secret Political Department chief, V. M. Kurskii, to handle her interrogation personally so that she would not give compromising evidence against him.[36] A fifteen-year-old daughter was left behind alone because her father, Podol'skii, was unable to come from Warsaw, and she began to lead a dissolute life. Ezhov offered her protection on the condition that she also would "cohabit" with him. In his own words, he "inclined her to cohabitation in an active form"; it probably meant he could not keep his hands off her. But the girl refused.[37] On 10 March 1937 the Military Collegium condemned Evgeniia Podol'skaia to the death penalty for counterrevolutionary and terrorist activity; she was shot the same day.[38]

Ezhov continued to drink heavily. His relatives testified about his "drinking bouts" at home or the dacha together with friends and colleagues, many of whom were later "unmasked" as "enemies of the people." According to Anatolii Babulin, friendly relations were based on systematic drunken orgies.[39] Nor did he drink only at home. According to the testimony of Vasilii Efimov, Ezhov's bodyguard in 1937–38, Frinovskii and Shapiro, the chief of his Secretariat, also introduced "drinking bouts" in his office, ordering wine, brandy, and other drinks via the guard department. Efimov recalled how Ezhov and Litvin, having gotten "terribly drunk," at six or seven in the morning started to play at skittles (*gorodki*), making Efimov and other adjutants run to collect sticks and skittles (*riukhi*). Ezhov often got drunk at his residence on Gogol' Boulevard and would then go to Lefortovo prison to interrogate prisoners.[40] I. Ia. Dagin, in 1937–38 chief of the guard department, during interrogation confirmed that "there was not a single day that Ezhov did not drink hard" and that he drank in his office as well, where Shapiro took care of the brandy. Sometimes, after heavy drinking, Ezhov indeed left for Lefortovo prison. Frinovskii and Bel'skii were not up to the drinking bouts, but Ezhov forced them to continue.[41]

All the same, Ezhov worked very hard. During this period of his career, he had to be forced to take a holiday. On 1 December 1937 the Politburo decided that Ezhov should be forbidden to appear at work and should leave town for a week's rest; Stalin personally was instructed to see to it that his state security chief carried out the decision.[42]

At the October 1937 Central Committee Plenum, Stalin announced that since the June 1937 Plenum eight Central Committee members and sixteen candidates had been expelled and arrested as "enemies of the people."[43] Among them were Deribas, Gikalo, Khataevich, Nosov, Piatnitskii, and Vareikis. In December of the same year the Central Committee by referendum voted for the expulsion and arrest of ten other members and candidates, also "enemies of the people."[44] From 11 to 20 January 1938 another Central Committee Plenum was held, coinciding with the first session of the Supreme Soviet (12–19 January). There has been much speculation about this Plenum. Some authors have considered it the beginning of the end of the mass repressions; others have seen it as simply marking a break in the activity of the troikas.[45]

USSR Supreme Soviet, first session, January 1938. From left to right (first row): Ezhov, Zhdanov, Mikoian, Kaganovich, Molotov, and Stalin, together with deputies from the Belorussian SSR. (RGAKFD collection)

What happened at the Plenum was that on 14 January Malenkov, who since February 1936 had been Ezhov's successor as head of the Department of Leading Party Organizations, reported "on errors of Party organizations in expelling communists from the Party, on formal bureaucratic attitudes toward the appeals of those expelled from the VKP(b), and on measures to eliminate these shortcomings." According to the speaker, during 1937 some 100,000 Party members had been expelled, whereas during the same period no less than 65,000 appeals had been submitted that had not yet been examined by the Party organizations. An end should be put to this "formalistic and callously bureaucratic attitude" toward Party members; the Central Committee and Stalin had already repeatedly insisted on this. Some communists sought to "reinsure themselves through repressions against Party members." They should be unmasked and branded as careerists, for they were "cleverly disguised enemies who try to disguise their hostility with shouts about vigilance, in that way to maintain themselves in the Party ranks, who strive through repressive measures to beat up our Bolshevik cadres and to sow uncertainty and excess suspicion in our ranks."[46]

Suggestions that Malenkov's words were an expression of moderation, the veiled criticism by a "dove" on "hawks" like Ezhov, are unfounded. Stalin and Ezhov himself had made similar remarks. During the January 1938 Plenum, more leaders criticized excesses in the examination of personal cases of communists. Politburo candidate member Zhdanov demanded that people should not be accused without grounds and that accusations against every suspect should be investigated. Kalinin wanted people to be judged on the basis of their actions instead of their relations. Even Molotov thought that people who had erred should be distinguished from wreckers.[47]

First of all, the criticism was directed at some of the regional Party leaders, who in the opinion of the central leadership expelled too many Party members. The main target was the Kuibyshev Party chief, Pavel Postyshev. Already at the February–March Plenum of 1937, he had been criticized for publicly questioning the accusations against certain Party members he knew personally. Although he acknowledged his guilt, he was dismissed as Second Party Secretary of the Ukraine and as First Party Secretary of Kiev and Khar'kov and was then appointed First Party Secretary of Kuibyshev, for the time being retaining his Politburo candidate membership. Shortly before the Plenum, Malenkov had reported to Stalin that during the past three months Postyshev had disbanded thirty district committees and had proclaimed their leadership enemies of the people. Malenkov considered these actions "politically damaging" and in their consequences "manifestly provocatory."[48]

At the Plenum, none other than Ezhov himself, as well as Kaganovich and Molotov, blamed Postyshev for having disbanded so many district committees. Stalin proposed to expel him from the Central Committee.[49] He was replaced as Politburo candidate by Khrushchev, dismissed as Kuibyshev Party Secretary, and shortly after the Plenum expelled from the Party, also because of his contacts with Rightist-Trotskiist counterrevolutionaries. On 21 February 1938 he was arrested. About the same time, the First Deputy People's Commissar of Defense, Marshal Aleksandr Egorov, was expelled from the Central Committee (in March of the same year he was arrested).[50]

The original idea had been to send the Party organizations a secret letter on the errors in expelling Party members, but after the Plenum discussion it was resolved to approve the draft of the secret letter and publish it as a Plenum decision. Stalin probably turned to publication because he wanted to put an end to the uncontrolled expulsions from the Party and to improve the situation in the lower Party organizations; simultaneously, he wanted to extend the mass operations, not mainly directed against communists. So on 18 January the Central Committee Plenum adopted a resolution, "On Errors of Party Organizations in Expelling Communists from the Party, on Formal Bureaucratic Attitudes Toward the Appeals of Those Expelled from the VKP(b), and on Measures to Eliminate These Shortcomings." It was pointed out that during the purges Party organizations had committed "serious errors and perversions." On many occasions they had adopted a "completely incorrect approach" and expelled communists from the Party "in a criminally frivolous way." They had pursued their "formalistic and callously bureaucratic attitude toward the fate of individual Party members"; many Party members had been expelled without foundation. This was made possible by the fact that among communists

> there exist, still unrevealed and unmasked, certain careerist communists who are striving to become prominent and to be promoted by recommending expulsions from the Party, through the repression of Party members, who are striving to insure themselves against possible charges of inadequate vigilance through the indiscriminate repression of Party members.

These communists should be unmasked and branded as "careerists striving to curry favor by expelling others from the Party and to reinsure themselves through repressions against Party members." Both the expelling and the restoring to the rights of Party membership of those who had been incorrectly expelled should be done "on a careful individual basis." The Party organizations were directed "resolutely to end mass indiscriminate expulsions from the Party and to institute a genuinely individualized differentiated approach to questions of expulsion from the Party or of restoring expelled persons to the rights of Party membership."[51]

Indeed, the purge of the Party and state apparatus had negative consequences for the country's economic, cultural, and defense potential. All branches of the economy were affected, and the arrests of specialists and leaders at various levels disorganized economic life to a certain degree. The January Plenum ended this purge, but the "mass operations," on the contrary, were continued.

On 24–25 January 1938, right after the Plenum and the Supreme Soviet session, a conference of regional NKVD chiefs was held in Moscow. Most regional NKVD chiefs were Supreme Soviet deputies, and because they, along with a number of executives of the central NKVD apparatus, had attended the Plenum, one can infer that almost all conference participants were aware of the Party decision on errors by Party organizations in expelling communists.[52] The conference aimed in the same direction as the Plenum. Although the Plenum resolution had pointed out that expulsion of Party members should be taken under control, it had remained silent about the NKVD work and the repressions conducted; during the discussions nobody had condemned the repressive NKVD policy, nor had there been any criticism whatsoever of Ezhov. The terror against the Party was partially suspended and completely taken under control by the center, whereas the purge of society at large continued.

Stalin made a clear distinction between the Party purge and the mass operations—that is, the liquidation of the "national base of the intelligence services" and the "fifth column." He aptly combined both campaigns in time but, strategically, began the Party purge approximately half a year before the mass operations, from the February–March Plenum of 1937 on; the Party purge was a necessary preparation for the mass operations starting in July 1937. But by early 1938 Stalin had realized that in order to preserve overall control, the Party purge had to be brought under control—hence the decisions at the January Plenum. Those decisions, however, had no relation whatsoever to the mass operations. One has only to think of the following Politburo decisions of 31 January 1938 and after about the allotting of new quotas and the continuation and even broadening of the national operations.[53] These were all Stalin's decisions. But during the summer of 1938 the situation in the Party was already quite different from what it had been in late 1937.

During the first seven months of 1938, some 37,000 people were expelled from the Party—only half as many as were expelled during the last six months of 1937. During the rest of 1938, the number diminished further. In carrying through the examination of complaints, proclaimed by the Plenum, during 1938 some 77,000 people were restored to Party membership, compared with 46,000 during 1937. Moreover, the Party began admitting new members on a large scale, a process that had been interrupted during 1937. Whereas during 1937 only some 32,000 members and 34,000 candidates had been admitted, in 1938 these numbers were approximately 148,000 and 437,000, respectively. All this testifies to a gradual restoration of the traditional practice of the Party function and of a relative stabilization of its personnel.[54]

The Party had changed considerably, however, with much more discipline and strict subordination to the center; it was much more manageable. Nor was it particularly a matter of restoring the balance between the Party and the NKVD, as Khlevniuk writes, for the balance had never actually been disturbed and the NKVD had always been strictly subordinated to the center. For the arrest of any Party member, preliminary approval by the relevant Party committee was obligatory (for nomenklatura functionaries this meant approval by the Central Committee).[55] In other words, the NKVD executives could not arrest Party members on a whim but only after their expulsion from the Party or after approval by the relevant Party committee. In 1938, the number of arrests of communists grew, whereas the number of expulsions decreased. It is a normalization indeed when those who should be arrested (or have already been arrested) are expelled on purpose. As a matter of fact, many of those expelled in 1937 were not arrested.

When opening the NKVD conference, on 24 January 1938, Ezhov called upon those present to speak out "bluntly" and "pass criticism on themselves in a Bolshevik way." "It is better if we ourselves disclose our shortcomings, of which we have many," he explained:

> We have not become a genuine Soviet intelligence service yet. In any case, if we compare the tasks lying before Soviet intelligence and its present state, we are incredibly behind. There is an enormous gap between the tasks before us, the hope placed in us by the people and the instructions given by the Party on the one hand, and our practical work on the other.[56]

In this way Ezhov touched upon the question of continuing the purge of the NKVD apparatus. Having noted that in 1937 "we worked quite a lot and not badly," he added:

> Many comrades think that we have strongly purged around ourselves, that we have smashed all scum within our ranks. That is correct. We have solidly smashed them. If I were to give numbers of how many we have arrested, it should be said that in any case we did not lag behind other institutions, but that is not the point. It does not mean that among us there are no swine left. I assure you, that we have yet to purge.[57]

This was clearly a suggestion that between different Soviet institutions there was a feeling of competition with respect to the number of purged and arrested employees.

During their speeches following Ezhov's introductory speech, the regional NKVD chiefs stressed the necessity of continuing the mass operations and allotting additional quotas. Later, during investigation, Aleksei Nasedkin, the former Smolensk NKVD chief and from May 1938 on Interior People's Commissar of Belorussia, described the situation at the conference this way:

> Ezhov approved of the activity of those NKVD chiefs, who cited "astronomic" numbers of persons repressed, such as, for instance, the NKVD chief of Western Siberia, citing a number of 55,000 people arrested, Dmitriev of Sverdlovsk province—40,000, Berman of Belorussia—60,000, Uspenskii of Orenburg—40,000, Liushkov of the Far East—70,000, Redens of Moscow province—50,000. The Ukrainian NKVD chiefs each cited numbers of people arrested from 30,000 to 40,000. Having listened to the numbers, Ezhov in his concluding remarks praised those who had "excelled" and announced that, undoubtedly, excesses had taken place here and there, such as, for instance, in Kuibyshev, where on Postyshev's instruction Zhuravlev* had transplanted all active Party members of the province. But he immediately added that "in such a large-scale operation mistakes are inevitable."[58]

On 25 January, in his concluding remarks to the conference, Ezhov declared himself in favor of continuing the mass operations and keeping the troikas. But he also stressed the temporary character of the campaign and hinted that at some moment it would be ended. The troikas and the mass operation "should not exist outside of time and space": "someone has to be repressed, someone has to be shot; so the question is about quotas."[59] In his opinion, the "kulak operation" (order No. 00447) not only "went off brilliantly"—first of all it was supported by "the kolkhoznik, the muzhik"—but both mass operations should continue, the one concerning the "kulaks" as well as the "national" one: "Although

---

*V. P. Zhuravlev, Kuibyshev NKVD chief from September 1937 to February 1938.

these operations were limited by the terms of my orders, nonetheless I think that they can be conducted further."[60]

In most regions, it should be noted, the kulak operation was already ending. On 1 February 1938, as a result of order No. 00447, some 600,000 people had been condemned; after that date large additional quotas were given only to the Ukraine (30,000 on 17 February) and the Far East (20,000 on 31 July).[61] On the other hand, the realization of the "national" orders concerning the repression against Poles, Germans, Latvians, and so on increased. The shifting of attention to the "liquidation of the human basis of foreign intelligence services" followed from some of the theses in Ezhov's speech at the January NKVD conference; he especially insisted on the continuation of the repressions against Poles and deserters from Poland.[62]

Of course, Ezhov had to take some note of local "excesses," mainly concerning numerous complaints received by the Central Committee from the provinces. He mildly pointed to shortcomings of the Ordzhonikidze NKVD chief, P. F. Bulakh, who had been carried away in exposing nonexisting conspiracies. "This tendency to go too far" was "exhibited by many," Ezhov said, and it could lead to "unpleasant consequences"; but it was "the enemies" who were to blame, for they directed the terror for their provocative purposes, complicating the investigation and giving erroneous signals to the NKVD, while diligent and honest Chekists were under their thumbs here and there.[63] Only ten minutes earlier, however, he had praised Bulakh as an "excellent executive," and he criticized him in a friendly way, shifting all his mistakes on the "enemies" surrounding him. On the whole, the January 1938 NKVD conference did not imply that Ezhov and the NKVD leadership took aim at struggling against local excesses, as had happened in the Party. The mass operations developed according to their own logic, different from the Party purge.

At the conclusion of the conference, on 27 January in the Kremlin, a large group of regional NKVD chiefs were handed government decorations by the president of the Presidium of the Supreme Soviet, Mikhail Kalinin: among others, B. D. Berman,

D. M. Dmitriev, N. N. Fedorov, A. I. Uspenskii, K. N. Valukhin, and V. P. Zhuravlev.[64] After arrest, the former deputy NKVD chief of Tula, V. Ia. Zazulin, testified that his chief, S. I. Lebedev, after returning to Tula convened a conference of the provincial NKVD operational staff at which he urged the speeding up of arrests, saying that the NKVD orders with respect to the mass operations were still in force: "As for the number of arrests, Tula province lags behind, and the NKVD will not forgive us that we did not cleanse Tula, the USSR smithy, as we ought to, from all kinds of suspicious elements subject to the NKVD orders, especially the defense industry." Lebedev gave instructions for competition between the provincial NKVD departments with respect to the number of arrests.[65]

At the time of his arrival in Moscow for the conference Uspenskii was still the Orenburg NKVD chief. Later, after arrest, he testified to have been summoned by a drunk Ezhov, with a bottle of brandy at hand, who urged his unwilling subordinate to succeed I. M. Leplevskii as Ukrainian Interior People's Commissar.[66] He was appointed and left for Kiev, to return to Moscow in early February in order to pick personnel. After the Politburo had decided on new quotas and "national contingents" subject to repressions, between 11 and 19 February (on those days he visited Stalin), Ezhov went on a mission to the Ukraine, accompanied by Uspenskii and a group of executives from the central NKVD apparatus. In Kiev, the group carried out large-scale arrests, with Ezhov, never sober, approving without looking into the matter.[67] Uspenskii was astonished and alarmed by his drunken table talk. During the trip, Ezhov drank uninterruptedly, boasting to Uspenskii that he had the Politburo "in his hands" and could do literally anything, arrest anyone, including Politburo members.[68] His bodyguard later testified that during the trip Ezhov stayed in Uspenskii's home, where the two men "systematically, day after day drank heavily"; the drinking bouts continued until the morning. Even at a meeting of NKVD executives, conducted by Ezhov, they appeared drunk. At a banquet with Ukrainian NKVD executives, the day before Ezhov's return to Moscow, the two "got outrageously drunk. Ezhov was so drunk that we, his adjutants, in the presence of all officials, had to carry him away under his arms to sleep."[69] Whether or not rumors of such behavior reached Stalin is not known, but even hints of Ezhov's excesses could become a reason for Stalin's growing distrust.

To the Ukrainian Chekists, Ezhov stressed the need of intensifying the "national operations." At a conference of Ukrainian NKVD bosses in the presence of the new Ukrainian Party leader, N. S. Khrushchev, he noted the extremely unsatisfactory results of the mass operations in the Ukraine in 1937: "It turned out that we executed a good deal, but have not always seized those we should have," and "we are now entering a new operation, or rather, continuing this operation on a new basis." His point was that although a great many enemies had been shot, their leaders had not been exposed and the major counterrevolutionary organizations had not been disclosed. On the new direction of the terror he declared: "In one word, the cream, the big shots should be removed. It should be such a blow, that it will be really felt." Noting the specific character of the Ukraine, he stressed the priority of the "national operations": "For you such operations, like the Polish, the German, the Romanian, should be the center of your attention."[70] In this way, he helped Uspenskii lead a large-scale purge in the Ukraine, with the Politburo on 17 February permitting the latter to arrest an extra 30,000 people.[71] Khrushchev was also involved. In June 1938, he reported to the Ukrainian Party congress that almost the whole Party leadership had turned out to be hostile, until Ezhov arrived, "and the real crushing started."[72] The wave of repressions touched other places besides the Ukraine, as is made clear by the quotas sanctioned by the Politburo on 31 January 1938 and after. Excesses were straightened out only in Party cases.

After January 1938, the center of gravity of the repressions was transferred to the national operations. In accordance with the Plenum decisions of the same month, action was taken against some people who had distorted the policy and had tolerated excesses, mass expulsions from the Party, or mass arrests. Later, after arrest, Frinovskii gave testimony on the matter: according to him, it was established that in Ordzhonikidze and a number of other provinces, prisoners had been murdered during interrogation, after which things were settled as if they had been condemned to death by the troikas; outrages were also reported from the Urals, Belorussia, Orenburg, Leningrad, and the Ukraine. They had increased most noticeably after the order "to repress other nationalities, suspects of espionage or ties with foreign consulates, deserters." In Leningrad and Sverdlovsk provinces and the Belorussian and Ukrainian republics, they had started arresting "indigenous inhabitants" of the USSR, on charges of ties with foreigners, although evidence was often lacking. "In this operation the cases were examined in Moscow by an especially created troika, presided over by Tsesarskii and then Shapiro."* In early 1938, the Central Committee sent Shkiriatov to Ordzhonikidze to "investigate evidence that had come through about criminal perversions during the mass operations" committed by regional NKVD organs. So as to create the impression that he had reacted on the signals in good time, after Shkiriatov's return to Moscow Ezhov handed over to him an "order," allegedly issued by him about the NKVD excesses in Ordzhonikidze province. But in fact no such order was ever issued.[73]

On 20 January Redens was transferred as NKVD chief from Moscow to Kazakhstan. Five days later I. M. Leplevskii was dismissed as Ukrainian Interior People's Commissar, to become head of the NKVD Transport Department; on 26 April he was arrested on a charge of belonging to the "Iagoda conspiracy" (that is, not because of any excesses). On 31 January the Rostov NKVD chief, Ia. A. Deich, was dismissed; on 29 March he was arrested. On 17 March the Ordzhonikidze NKVD chief, Bulakh, was dismissed because of "excesses" that went beyond the fixed quota (on 25 April he was arrested). On 16 April L. M. Zakov-

---

*In the national operations, the albums sent from the provinces, before being approved by the central dvoika, i.e. Ezhov and Vyshinskii, were surveyed by the main department chiefs, or at least by the chief of the Registration Department, V. E. Tsesarskii, in late March 1938 succeeded by I. I. Shapiro.

skii, Deputy Interior People's Commissar since January, was fired by the Politburo; two weeks later he was arrested, also on a charge of belonging to the "Iagoda conspiracy." On 22 May another NKVD chief who, like Leplevskii, was said to have committed excesses, the Sverdlovsk chief D. M. Dmitriev, was transferred to the NKVD Highways Directorate; on 28 June he was arrested as a conspirator.[74]

In Ezhov's view, it appeared that after the January 1938 Plenum the enemies had used the NKVD repressions for their own purposes, in order to parry the blow and direct it toward "honest" citizens. This thesis, apparently rectifying the situation, permitted new arrests (including some NKVD executives), this time to search for "real enemies." In the Bolshevik world view the enemies were insidious to such a degree that they could even turn the struggle against themselves in their favor, escape repressions, and incite the discontent of the innocently suffering masses.

Thus, from early 1938 on, the national operations became the main direction of the NKVD activity, replacing the kulak operation, which had been central during the autumn and winter of 1937. But shortcomings resulting from the inadequacies of the operational registration and from the simplified methods clearly manifested themselves in the work of the regional NKVD organs. So in February 1938 the Sverdlovsk NKVD chief, Dmitriev, complained about the slow examination of albums in Moscow. On 21 March Frinovskii riposted that the more than 10,000 prisoners in the albums presented by Dmitriev in overwhelming majority did not belong to the nationalities of the relevant national operations. He drew the conclusion that "you have in essence not executed the operational orders of the People's Commissar."[75]

In this way, numerous albums from the provinces piled up for examination in Moscow. In addition to this, in the spirit of the decisions of the January 1938 Plenum, the fight was started against those who had "distorted the Party line" by committing excesses, mass expulsions from the Party, or arrests. Of course, it did not bring the NKVD terror to an end, but a punctual execution of the directions from the center was clearly demanded, without any local initiative. So in February 1938 Frinovskii complained to Dagin that some regional NKVD chiefs "broke free from the leadership, ran off, went too far."[76] After arrest, Dagin testified that there had been "intolerable irresponsibility" in the examination of cases in the mass operations. The albums were supposed to have been examined by the NKVD leadership, which should also pass sentences; in fact, "the whole business was entrusted to Tsesarskii and Shapiro, who decided on their own whether a death sentence was passed or another punishment." But this procedure did not last long either: "soon they started to shove the album information over to the departments, leaving the decision to the department chiefs or sometimes even their deputies."[77]

During the summer of 1938 it had become evident that the central NKVD apparatus was unable to digest the enormous quantity of albums from the provinces with lists of those arrested in the national operations, which contained the names of more than 100,000 people. As a result, the prisons were overcrowded, and another way out had to be found. At Ezhov's request, on 15 September the Politburo decided to abolish the album procedure and to create regional Special Troikas, consisting of the regional Party chief, the NKVD chief, and the procurator, in order to settle the cases with respect to the national contingents. The troikas were allowed to impose the death penalty and immediately execute it. The decision further stated that the examination of the cases should be completed within two months—that is, before 15 November. The decision was signed by Stalin.[78]

All albums relating to national operations that had not yet been processed were returned to the regional NKVD organs to be examined by the Special Troikas. This time, the term set by the Politburo was not extended. On 15 November a halt was called to the examination of cases by the Special Troikas, and two days later, on 17 November, the Central Committee and the Council of People's Commissars in a joint resolution suspended the mass operations. During the two months of their activity, the Special

Troikas examined the cases of almost 108,000 people who had been arrested in the national operations. Over 105,000 of them were condemned, including more than 72,000 to the death penalty; among them were over 21,000 Poles and over 15,000 Germans.[79]

6

Decline

In March 1938 the last of the three great Moscow show trials, that of the "Anti-Soviet Bloc of Rightists and Trotskiists," took place; in the dock were Bukharin and his associates, and Iagoda. It was supervised by Stalin personally; Ezhov, who had headed the investigation, was in the supervising commission. He promised the defendants that if they behaved well, their life would be spared—a promise that was not kept.[1] According to testimony given after arrest by I. Ia. Dagin, then GUGB First Department chief, Ezhov even attended the execution. He instructed Dagin to beat up his predecessor Iagoda before the execution: "Come on, hit him for all of us." On the other hand, the shooting of his drinking companion Bulanov upset him, and he ordered that he should be given brandy first.[2] The trial was the logical conclusion, as well as the ultimate proof, of the scheme Ezhov depicted at the June 1937 Plenum, confirming it all: the joining together of all hostile forces (the Right and Left Opposition in the first place), the "Center of Centers," the ramified network of conspirators and spies in all spheres of Soviet life. In this sense, it completed his job. The mass operations, however, continued, and in this respect his mission in Stalin's eyes was not at all complete.

Chubar' (effaced), Dimitrov, Ezhov, Andreev, Kalinin, Mikoian, Stalin, Molotov, and Kaganovich on their way to Red Square, 1 May 1938. (RGAKFD collection)

On 8 April 1938, after sharp criticism, the People's Commissar of Water Transportation, N. I. Pakhomov, was dismissed (later during the same month he was arrested, to be sentenced and shot afterward).[3] Ezhov was appointed his successor, remaining at the same time Interior People's Commissar.[4] By charging him with the extra job, Stalin killed two birds with one stone: Ezhov could correct the water transportation situation with tough Chekist methods, and his transfer to the terra incognita of economic tasks would leave him less time for the NKVD and weaken his position there, thus creating the possibility that in due course he could be removed from the leadership of the punitive apparatus and replaced by fresh people. After his fall, in a letter intended for Stalin but probably never sent, Ezhov indeed stated that after his appointment as People's Commissar of Water Transportation, he had dived completely into the new work; during two months he almost never went to the NKVD but left its management to his first deputy, Frinovskii.[5]

Shkiriatov, Ezhov, and Frinovskii on their way to Red Square, 1 May 1938. (Memorial collection)

It is possible that the idea may already have been ripening with Stalin to force Ezhov gradually out of the supreme leadership. For the time being, however, Ezhov remained in favor. Neither he nor his associates sensed any kind of dirty trick in the appointment. On the contrary, his influence seemed to be growing: his appointment represented a further extension of his commissariat's power.[6] Another sign that he enjoyed Stalin's confidence was that in May, during the election campaign for the Supreme Soviets of the republics, only Stalin and Molotov were nominated in more electoral districts.[7] In June, the Ukrainian Party leader, N. S. Khrushchev, in an election speech praised Ezhov, together with Stalin, for having unmasked the bourgeois nationalists: "We thank you and greet you, great Stalin, your best pupil Nikolai Ivanovich Ezhov, and all of you who by your Bolshevik actions have destroyed these vermin."[8]

The new People's Commissar started with a noisy campaign to eradicate "wrecking" in water transportation. Just over a week after his appointment, a lead article, "Root Out the Enemy Rabble to the End, Liquidate the Consequences of the Wrecking," appeared in the People's Commissariat's paper, *Vodnyi transport*, confirming that the "band of Trotskiist-Bukharinist thugs and spies, having forced their way to the top posts in the People's Commissariat, have tried to mess up water transportation."[9] With the Politburo's consent, Ezhov reinforced the personnel of the People's Commissariat of Water Transportation with approved Chekists, bringing his own people from the NKVD and placing them in important functions—Ia. M. Veinshtok (who became his deputy), D. M. Sokolinskii, N. T. Prikhod'ko, R. A. Listengurt, V. M. Lazebnyi, and A. I. Mikhel'son.[10] No fewer than an estimated twenty-five to thirty Chekists were transferred to the leadership of the People's Commissariat.[11] On 4 May Efim Evdokimov, dismissed as Party Secretary of Rostov province, was also appointed Deputy People's Commissar.

In his new job Ezhov used his customary NKVD methods. On 23 April the head of the Central Water Building Directorate, Lapisov, was arrested for "wrecking" management.[12] He introduced special forms to draw up orders, named "Joint Order of the USSR People's Commissariats of Internal Affairs and Water Transportation."[13] Notwithstanding his claim that after his new appointment for two months he only made it over to the NKVD on rare occasions, he continued to devote himself seriously to NKVD business. When in April–May the NKVD was being restructured, he could not stand aloof. On 28 May, two weeks after the suicide of Zakovskii's successor as Moscow NKVD chief, V. A. Karutskii, he attended a conference of Moscow NKVD executives, where his protégé V. E. Tsesarskii was appointed the new chief. There were many similar matters demanding his attention, the more so because he was not satisfied with the management of Frinovskii, who—as he wrote to Stalin—"never was a deputy of full value." Especially, Frinovskii tarried over further purging the NKVD apparatus:

> At one time, with Frinovskii and many others present, I was so irritated that I requested the personal files of the officers of what was then the Fourth Department, in order to deal with them myself. Of course, nothing came of it. Once again I was worn out by all kinds of routine business, and the personal files were just lying there. To be fair, I must say that even in those times I purged quite a bit. But I did not look after the investigation, and it turned out to be in the hands of traitors. . . . I started to become irritable, snatched at everything, bringing nothing to an end. I felt that you were dissatisfied with the NKVD work, which deteriorated my mood still further.[14]

Ezhov made serious efforts to promote NKVD officers to crucial functions in the state and Party apparatus.[15] In mid-1938, for example, a number of regional NKVD chiefs were promoted to regional Party leadership, including Omsk NKVD chief K. N. Valukhin (Sverdlovsk, 27 April) and Kirov NKVD chief L. P. Gazov (Krasnodar, May).[16] Other protégés were placed in state apparatus positions. All these appointments were, of course, made with Stalin's consent and approved by the Politburo. Under certain conditions, Stalin might have been worried, but for the time being he closed his eyes to what might be happening and did not question Ezhov's loyalty and devotion. However, only a trace of doubt had to creep into his mind to arouse his suspicions to the point of accusing Ezhov of deliberately promoting his own people in order to seize power.

In mid-June Ezhov was astounded to learn that the Far Eastern NKVD chief, G. S. Liushkov, fearing arrest, had defected to Japan on 13 June, crossing the Manchurian border on foot.[17] This former GUGB Secret Political Department deputy head had been appointed NKVD chief of the Azov–Black Sea province in August

1936 and in July of the following year had been transferred to the post of Far Eastern NKVD chief (of course, not without Stalin's knowledge—he had received him a few days before).[18] Ezhov, who had known Liushkov well since 1933–34, had reason to feel apprehensive, since he might be suspected of having protected him. Later, Frinovskii testified that during the summer of 1937 the Georgian NKVD had sent them T. I. Lordkipanidze's testimony that Liushkov belonged to the "conspirators around Iagoda," but Ezhov had not only withheld the evidence from the Central Committee but had also appointed Liushkov Far Eastern NKVD chief. He had instructed Frinovskii to reinterrogate Iagoda, thereby leaving Liushkov out of it. Understanding what was expected of him, Iagoda had testified that Liushkov was not involved in the conspiracy.[19]

Testimony by L. G. Mironov and others about Liushkov's conspiratorial activities was also withheld. Liushkov himself, however, was informed, and in January 1938, when he was in Moscow for the Supreme Soviet session, he agitatedly complained to Frinovskii that he was distrusted and was being shadowed. Frinovskii assured him that he and Ezhov "tried to keep him safe," though in fact, Frinovskii wanted Liushkov arrested. Ezhov did not agree, fearing that the deceit with respect to the evidence would come to light and instead ordered Frinovskii to tell Liushkov that if the situation became critical he should commit suicide. The signal was to be a telegram from Moscow about his dismissal or promotion to Moscow, or the sending of a commission.[20] In March or April, when reinterrogating Mironov, Ezhov induced him to retract his testimony against Liushkov. Around the same time, on 16 April, Liushkov's deputy, M. A. Kagan, was summoned to Moscow and arrested upon arrival. According to Frinovskii, this was meant to signal Liushkov to commit suicide, but he did not react. The Central Committee wanted him dismissed soon. A second signal was Ezhov's telegram to Liushkov of late May 1938 about his promotion to the central NKVD apparatus in Moscow. But Liushkov, instead of committing suicide, escaped to Japan.[21] (Later, at his trial, Ezhov stated that he had wanted to arrest Liushkov but that he had escaped in time.)[22]

According to Frinovskii, when Ezhov informed Stalin about Liushkov's defection, he made no mention of this telegram, or of the evidence he had against Liushkov.[23] As a consequence, after Liushkov's flight Ezhov's greatest concern was that his deceit would come to light. To Stalin, Liushkov's move was an extraordinary event, for there had never been any defectors at this level. Moreover, Liushkov knew a lot and might disclose state secrets. Ezhov also feared that discovery of the telegram would be taken as a signal for Liushkov to escape, which would incriminate Ezhov as being his accomplice. After resignation, in his letter to Stalin (probably never sent), Ezhov stated that as a result of Liushkov's desertion he "literally went mad":

> I asked Frinovskii to go with me so that we could report to you together. On my own I did not have the strength. I told him: Now they will surely punish us severely. For such an obvious and major intelligence failure, they naturally don't pat you on the back. At the same time it proved that in the NKVD apparatus there were still traitors. I understood that you would develop a suspicious attitude toward the NKVD work. And that was indeed the case.[24]

On the evening of 15 June, three days after Liushkov's defection, Frinovskii met with the Far Eastern army commander, Marshal V. K. Bliukher, in Ezhov's office. Bliukher wanted information about the mass operations and about Liushkov. He also wanted to find out what the attitude was toward himself, since he was under suspicion of being connected to the "military-fascist conspiracy." Before Ezhov was able to talk with them, he was summoned to the Central Committee. Frinovskii and Bliukher waited for him for a while and then were told that Ezhov would not return soon; Frinovskii, meanwhile, had told Bliukher that in two days he was going to the Far East.[25] By consequence, Frinovskii's trip had been decided before, so apparently either Ezhov had already visited Stalin at some point between Liushkov's flight and the evening of 15 June, or else the decision had been taken during a telephone conversation of the two. Indeed, on 17 June the Politburo sent Frinovskii on a commission to the Far East, along with the chief of the Red Army Political Directorate, Lev Mekhlis. They were granted wide powers for sorting out the details of Liushkov's flight and making large-scale arrests. Before leaving, they sent an instruction to the regional NKVD and army and navy Special Departments chiefs to prepare within a week "a mass operation for the removal of Rightist and Trotskiist military-fascist elements, agents of the Japanese and other intelligence services, former White Guards, anti-Soviet elements among the former partisans, clergy, and sectarians, all Germans, Poles, Koreans, Latvians, Finns, and Estonians suspect of espionage." On arrival, Frinovskii carried out mass arrests. In addition, he watched Bliukher closely and reported on him to Moscow; on 22 October 1938 Bliukher was arrested on Ezhov's order (in accordance with Beriia). Frinovskii returned to Moscow only after 22 August, when Beriia had already been appointed Ezhov's first deputy.[26]

Ezhov's authority was no longer unquestionable. On 12 June Gosplan head Nikolai Voznesenskii in a private conversation expressed doubts about Ezhov's excessive administrative gusto in the mass disclosing of conspiracies.[27] Shortly after 30 June, the People's Commissar of Defense, Voroshilov, was asked by his deputy, Ivan Fed'ko, to arrange a meeting for him with Ezhov in order to prove his innocence. Voroshilov advised against it, saying (according to his former adjutant Khmel'nitskii in 1961): "You should not go to Ezhov. . . . They will force you to write down all kinds of fables about yourself . . . there, everybody confesses." Within a week, Fed'ko was indeed arrested.[28] After his own arrest, Ezhov testified that around July 1938 Stalin and Molotov all of a sudden had started asking him about his suspicious contacts with F. M. Konar, who had been closely related to Ezhov through their work in the People's Commissariat of Agriculture until he was executed in 1933 as a "Polish spy." In 1937–38, Poland may indeed have been Stalin's greatest enemy, and contacts with a Polish spy were considered something unforgiveable. As a result, Ezhov "felt that Stalin distrusted him."[29]

Realizing that Stalin was beginning to display his discontent, Ezhov felt that the ground was sinking beneath him. And when, on 14 July, the NKVD resident in Spain, Aleksandr Orlov, having been summoned to Antwerp, failed to arrive there, Ezhov did not report the fact to Stalin immediately, fearing that it would be another count of his future indictment. He understood that the Party leader already somewhat suspected him of having warned Liushkov of danger; withholding information on Orlov's defection confirmed the picture. More and more Stalin had reason to distrust Ezhov.

In early August, the Ukrainian NKVD chief, A. I. Uspenskii, was in Moscow for the session of the Supreme Soviet commencing 10 August. As Uspenskii testified after arrest, in the Lubianka he

Party leaders on top of the Lenin Mausoleum viewing a gymnastic parade, 24 July 1938, with Stalin (third from left), Ezhov (fifth from right), Shkiriatov (fourth from right), and others. (RGAKFD collection)

was told by the head of the NKVD Secretariat, I. I. Shapiro, that "Ezhov is in great trouble, for he is distrusted in the Central Committee." According to Shapiro, it was rumored that "next to Ezhov there will come somebody . . . who should be feared"; Shapiro did not mention a name. He deemed it necessary to cover the tracks: within the next five days, one thousand people should be executed.[30] When Uspenskii met with Ezhov, Ezhov confirmed: "The tracks should be covered. All investigation cases should be finished in an accelerated procedure so that it will be impossible to make sense of it." Leningrad NKVD chief Litvin added that if they failed to cover it up and things looked bad, he would commit suicide. In such an event, Uspenskii himself planned to escape.[31]

The decision to appoint a new first deputy to Ezhov was already ripe in late July 1938. Stalin was probably dissatisfied with the state of NKVD affairs: investigations were taking too long and as a result the prisons were overcrowded and the mass operations were dragging. Perhaps reflecting his dissatisfaction with the delay, Stalin immediately confirmed the list of a large group of leading Soviet, military, and Party functionaries to be shot on 29 July. The arrest of people from Ezhov's close circle, like Bulakh, Leplevskii, and Zakovskii in April and Dmitriev in June, may also have resulted from Stalin's loss of confidence. Significantly, by 10 August there were rumors that a new deputy was to be appointed to Ezhov and that this boded ill for him. It was no accident that the largest group of prisoners was shot in a rush on 29 July; a month later, on 26 and 29 August, another group was shot, including Zakovskii, Salyn', and L. G. Mironov.[32] Ezhov was in a hurry to get rid of people who might testify against him.

In connection with the discussion by the Supreme Soviet of the new law "On the Judicial System of the USSR," in August, it was rumored that the mass operations might cease and "Soviet legality" return. The leading Chekists believed in these rumors, though on the whole it made no difference: the mass operations proceeded at high speed and reached their apogee after 15 September, when Special Troikas were created to examine what remained of the national contingents.[33] (The measurement of the dose of the terror, practiced by Stalin since the January 1938 Plenum, only related to the purge of the higher echelons of the state and the Party apparatus.)

In early August, even before Frinovskii had returned from the Far East, Stalin proposed him as People's Commissar of the Navy—apparently a promotion—and simultaneously blocked Ezhov's attempt to appoint his protégé M. I. Litvin, then the Leningrad NKVD chief, as Frinovskii's replacement.[34] That is why Shapiro was alarmed by the appointment of a new first deputy, although for the time being he did not know who it was going to be. In any case, Stalin appointed someone quite different from anybody Ezhov would have hoped for.

On 22 August 1938, the Georgian Party leader, Lavrentii Beriia, was made First Deputy People's Commissar of the Interior. Ezhov, it appears, had started collecting incriminating evidence against him, in connection with his growing influence.[35] According to one version of events, Ezhov had even signed an order for his arrest, but Beriia learned about it from Georgian NKVD chief Goglidze and immediately left for Moscow to be received by Stalin, the result of which was a long conversation ending in Beriia's appointment as Ezhov's first deputy.[36] The story overlooks the fact that, without Stalin's consent, Ezhov could not have any plans, and certainly no written order, to arrest Beriia, who was a member of the Central Committee and of the Presidium of the Supreme Soviet. If Stalin had consented, he would not have received Beriia, who would have been arrested right away. It seems more likely that Stalin talked with Beriia about his transfer to the NKVD as first deputy during the session of the Supreme Soviet starting on 10 August; as members of the Presidium of the Supreme Soviet, they met regularly. (Between 11 March and 13 September 1938 no visits by Beriia to Stalin's Kremlin office were registered, but the visitors' journal does not reflect all of Stalin's contacts.)[37]

The register of visits to the NKVD chief (preserved in the FSB archives) indicates that Beriia was immediately received by Ezhov on the evening of 22 August.[38] Shortly after, Beriia returned to Georgia for a few days to direct a Plenum of the Georgian Central Committee at which a new First Secretary was to be elected. The Plenum took place on 31 August in Tbilisi. During the stay Beriia may well have selected loyal people, personally talking with V. N. Merkulov, B. Z. Kobulov, V. G. Dekanozov, and other executives: in the course of the following weeks these men appeared in Moscow to occupy main positions in the central NKVD apparatus. In early September Beriia was back in Moscow and began his NKVD work. On 4 September he conferred with Ezhov in his NKVD office for the entire afternoon.[39]

Later, in the (probably unsent) letter to Stalin, Ezhov wrote that he was upset by Beriia's appointment, sensing "an element of distrust toward me," and thought it "the preparation for my dismissal," supposing Beriia "might occupy the post of People's Commissar."[40] Shortly after Beriia's appointment, probably in late August, Ezhov indeed assembled some of his protégés at his dacha and warned that they would be disposed of soon.[41] His close collaborators were, as he predicted, dismissed and arrested and replaced by Beriia's people from Georgia. The ease with which this happened showed the People's Commissar's impotence. But, encouraged by Frinovskii, he did not intend to surrender without a fight.

According to a number of testimonies, after Beriia's appointment Ezhov took to even heavier drinking, appearing for work at three or four in the afternoon.[42] Nevertheless, he made several attempts to isolate his new first deputy within the NKVD leadership. He intended to appoint the Kazakhstan NKVD chief, S. F. Redens, second deputy as a counterbalance, but when Redens thought it no longer served any useful purpose, he tried to reduce Beriia's influence by reanimating the NKVD Collegium.[43] This led nowhere either. The collecting of evidence compromising Beriia was intensified, and on Frinovskii's advice Ezhov handed it over to Stalin, but to no avail.[44] Beriia had obtained wide powers from Stalin and did not intend to share them with anybody, and to that end he secured the acceptance of a procedure by which a number of key documents emanating from the NKVD were valid only with his signature added to Ezhov's.[45] On 29 September Beriia was appointed GUGB chief, with Merkulov as deputy.[46]

Frinovskii had returned to Moscow on 25 August, just after Beriia's appointment, and he was invited straight to the NKVD and stayed with Ezhov for more than an hour. After arrest he testified: "I had never seen Ezhov in such a depressed state. 'Things are rotten,' he said, passing right away to the question that Beriia had been appointed contrary to his wish." On 27–28 August Frinovskii met with Evdokimov, who insisted that before Beriia arrived he must take care of any unfinished cases (*nedodelki*) that might compromise them. He told Frinovskii: "Check to see whether Zakovskii and all Iagoda people have been executed, because after Beriia's arrival the investigation of these cases may be renewed and they may turn against us." Frinovskii then ascertained that a group of Chekists, including Zakovskii and Mironov, had been shot on 26–27 August (actually they were shot on 29 August).[47] Ezhov, Frinovskii, and Evdokimov were with good reason concerned about Chekists who had been arrested on charges of conspiracy and might under Beriia's regime testify against Ezhov's circle, or even against Ezhov himself. It was no accident that the executions took place in a hurry in late August, while Beriia was away in Georgia.

Frinovskii did not need explanations: Beriia had obviously been appointed so that he could be moved to the post of Interior People's Commissar. Frinovskii sensed a new purge was approaching.[48] He stayed on as Ezhov's deputy until 8 September, when he was appointed People's Commissar of the Navy. Beriia immediately took over as chief of the NKVD First Directorate (state security); henceforth, NKVD documents were signed by Ezhov and Beriia together. Beriia also immediately initiated a change in the NKVD central apparatus structure; the Politburo considered the first plans on 13 September, and within ten days approved the new structure. Officially, Beriia took over the GUGB on 29 September, but one may safely conclude that from early September on, after Frinovskii's departure, Beriia had assumed absolute power in the NKVD. On 13 September A. P. Radzivilov-skii and M. S. Alekhin were arrested, on 15 September the Moscow NKVD chief, V. E. Tsesarskii, was demoted to chief of the Ukhta-Izhma camp, and on 24 September the former Belorussian NKVD chief (since May 1938 head of the NKVD Third Directorate) B. D. Berman was arrested.

One can only conjecture why Beriia was promoted and not somebody else. Stalin's choice was probably connected with the fact that Beriia was under threat of being persecuted by Ezhov. In 1938 their former friendship had fallen apart, when Ezhov investigated a number of signals received in Moscow with respect to Beriia. Stalin understood that under these circumstances Beriia and Ezhov had become rivals, and he could appoint Beriia as Ezhov's successor without having to fear a possible intrigue between the two. The new Interior People's Commissar had to be a Party functionary who was a Central Committee member and had a serious Cheka record. The only other candidate with such a background was M. D. Bagirov.

Already years before, Beriia had made a good impression on Stalin, as appears in a 1932 letter that Stalin wrote to Kaganovich. Beriia was "a good organizer, businesslike and capable," whereas Ia. I. Mamuliia, proposed as Georgian Party secretary by Ordzhonikidze, was "not worth the left foot of Beriia."[49] Stalin appreciated Beriia not merely as a Party secretary, who moreover had actively contributed to the work of the February–March Plenum of 1937; he also knew him to be a man of tough Chekist methods. In 1937–38, as the Georgian Party leader, he had personally taken part in the interrogating and beating of prisoners.[50] But it was Stalin's tactic not to appoint Beriia as Interior People's Commissar immediately but rather to put him in as first deputy only, thus, by degrees, paving the way for Ezhov's removal. This was Stalin's characteristic cunning, moving step by step, frightening Ezhov to make him toss about, and pushing him to disclose his weak spots.

*   *   *

There were no more mass arrests and persecutions of Party members in the summer of 1938 like those during the second half of 1937. After the January 1938 Central Committee Plenum, the NKVD terror against the Party was carefully monitored by Stalin and rigorously supervised by the Party organs.[51] During the summer and autumn of 1938, the arrests of leading Party functionaries of course continued, but they were always approved by Stalin. The regional Party leadership appreciated the "healthier" atmosphere. In June the third secretary of the Party committee of Rostov province, M. A. Suslov, reported to a Party conference that the situation in the province had improved compared with half a year ago: "The practice of indiscriminate expelling from the Party has ceased. An end has been put to impunity for a various number of slanderers. Gradually the situation of general suspiciousness is breaking down. The provincial committee leadership has thoroughly and attentively investigated the appeals of those expelled."[52]

Throughout 1937 E. G. Evdokimov had been First Party Secretary of Rostov province (before September 1937 part of Azov–Black Sea province), until in May 1938 he was dismissed and appointed Deputy People's Commissar of Water Transportation under Ezhov. In April 1939, after arrest, he testified that upon being transferred to Moscow he had asked Ezhov to have him "politically verified," for he supposed that his dismissal was connected with the recent arrests, such as that of his assistant Magnichkin, and with distrust toward him. Ezhov promised a verification. When later Evdokimov asked him about it, however, Ezhov repeatedly hedged on it: "During all talks he had with me, I felt he was sizing me up and studying me."[53]

It is interesting to realize that the writer Mikhail Sholokhov, living in Veshenskaia in Rostov province, had complained to Stalin personally about the terror reigning in his home region with respect to communists. He had also criticized the provincial Party committee, especially Evdokimov, and the provincial NKVD (which until July 1937 had been led by Liushkov). A commission with M. F. Shkiriatov of the Party Control Commission and V. E. Tsesarskii, then the GUGB Fourth Department chief, examined the case on the spot and on 23 May 1938 reported to Stalin and Ezhov that Sholokhov's accusations were founded only in part and that no drastic measures were necessary.[54] By then, however, Evdokimov had already been dismissed. During his trial, Ezhov claimed that the Rostov Party secretary was dismissed on account of his reports to the Central Committee.[55]

From mid-1938 on, Ezhov's activity as NKVD chief clearly diminished. Later, during investigation, the (by then, former) head of the NKVD Secretariat, I. I. Shapiro, demonstrated the remarkable change in this respect. Originally, Ezhov had been much interested in investigation work: he frequently visited Lefortovo prison and sent for prisoners, "made the round of the departments, where prisoners were interrogated, summoned executives conducting the investigation." But since August he "completely kept aloof from this business": "It was all transferred to the department heads, without any control, leadership, and supervision from above."[56] Dagin testified that Ezhov's somber mood started in May; he rushed about in his office and was irritable. His adjutants, like Shapiro, Litvin, and Tsesarskii, were also depressed: "they had lost their former arrogance and were upset by something." Dagin supposed it was connected with the fact that "in a number of provinces serious excesses and perversions in the NKVD work had come to light, particularly in the Ukraine under Leplevskii, Sverdlovsk under Dmitriev, Leningrad and Moscow under Zakovskii, the Northern Caucasus under Bulakh, Ivanovo under Radzivilovskii, and so on." Then, after Liushkov's desertion, Ezhov "completely lost heart"; starting to cry, he told Dagin, "Now I am done for."[57]

After Beriia was appointed first deputy, A. I. Uspenskii (according to his testimony of April 1939) witnessed an "unbelievable panic" among the executives of the central NKVD apparatus in connection with the arrests of colleagues taking place. Uspenskii himself also feared arrest and decided to escape; according to Frinovskii, Ezhov was in a state of panic and started to drink heavily.[58] Dagin described Ezhov as being totally upset by Beriia's appointment; the very next day, he fell ill—that is, he "took to drink at his dacha"—and he stayed "ill" for more than a week. Then he reappeared in the NKVD, in a somber mood just as before; "he refrained from all business and received almost nobody."⁵⁹ A subordinate who was summoned to his Lubianka office late one evening found him "sitting in his shirt sleeves on a sofa behind a table laden with bottles of vodka. His hair was ruffled and his eyes were swollen and inflamed: he was obviously drunk but he also seemed excited and alarmed." A few days later the subordinate was arrested.⁶⁰

After arrest, Ezhov was accused of having schemed against the Party leadership. He testified himself that after arrests began within the NKVD he, together with Frinovskii, Dagin, and Evdokimov, made plans to commit a "putsch" on 7 November, the October Revolution anniversary, during the demonstration in Red Square. The plan was to cause a commotion and then in the panic and confusion to "drop bombs and kill someone of the government members." Dagin, who was chief of the NKVD guard department, was to execute the plan, but on 5 November he was arrested, followed a few days later by Evdokimov. Ezhov alone could not prevent Beriia's initiative. "This way all our plans collapsed."⁶¹

All this really only amounted to drunken talk. It was true that Ezhov's acquaintance V. K. Konstantinov (according to his evidence) witnessed a conversation between Ezhov and Dagin on 3 or 4 November, which he understood to mean that Dagin was to organize something "with conspiratorial aims" on Ezhov's orders. Dagin was somewhat embarrassed by Konstantinov's presence, but Ezhov, who was very drunk, paid no attention; when he asked Dagin whether he had taken all necessary steps, Dagin—looking at Konstantinov uncomprehendingly—answered that he did not quite understand. Then Ezhov raised his voice and said: "Immediately remove all people posted in the Kremlin by Beriia, and replace them with reliable people. Don't forget, time does not wait: the sooner the better." Looking with bewilderment at Konstantinov, Dagin answered that it would be done.⁶²

The striking scene may indeed have taken place. During interrogation, Dagin confirmed that one night in late October or early November, when he was still at work in the Kremlin around six o'clock in the morning, he was called in by Ezhov, who had not yet gone to sleep either. His chief turned out to be "heavily drunk" and was accompanied by Konstantinov, who was also "rather drunk."[63] Imagine the scene: Ezhov is completely drunk and gives his fantasies free rein. Dagin realizes the state he is in and that an outsider is present but has to say yes. And of course he is no longer in the position to replace members of the Kremlin guard because these things are now being dealt with by Beriia.

Evdokimov gave similar evidence. According to him, in September he discussed the threatening situation after Beriia's appointment with Ezhov, Frinovskii, and Bel'skii. Allegedly, they agreed to prepare an attempt on Stalin and Molotov. Ezhov was also said to have had plans to murder Beriia.[64] Obviously, Ezhov's utterances with respect to terrorism were no more than drunken talk, the fantasizing of somebody who had become embittered toward Stalin and his adjutants. After his arrest, Beriia's investigation, not taking it too seriously, did not delve into it deeply.[65] According to Iu. K. Ivanov, an NKVD executive from Evdokimov's circle, as early as late July, after a visit to Ezhov, Evdokimov had alluded to terrorism against the Party leadership. Involved in the conspiracy first of all were people originating from North Caucasia (Evdokimov's home base), Dagin, Nikolaev-Zhurid, and others. But the action, planned for 7 November, did not take place because Dagin was arrested beforehand.[66]

According to Konstantinov, some time in mid-November Ezhov told him that his song was ended, thanks to Stalin and loyal Stalinists like his deputy Beriia: "If they could be removed, all would be different." He suggested that Konstantinov should kill Stalin, but without giving any concrete form to his plans.[67]

On 8 October the Politburo instructed a commission to prepare within ten days a draft decree by the Central Committee, the Council of People's Commissars, and the NKVD pertaining to a "new policy on the making of arrests, on the supervision by the procuracy, and on the conducting of investigations." Ezhov presided over the commission, which included Beriia, Malenkov, Vyshinskii, and People's Commissar of Justice N. M. Rychkov.[68]

According to his son, Malenkov played a main role in bringing down Ezhov. Malenkov had (since 1935) been Ezhov's deputy as head of the Central Committee Department of Leading Party Organizations. Malenkov's biographer says that their relations were "those of a chief and a subordinate, of a teacher and a pupil," and continued to be so after 1936, when Malenkov replaced Ezhov as head of the department. Its journal, *Partiinoe stroitel'-stvo*, edited by Malenkov, thus extolled Ezhov's teaching abilities: "Comrade Ezhov taught us how to reorganize the Party's work, how to raise organizational work to a higher level, and how to make this work more effective. . . . We strive to carry out these instructions."[69]

In 1937–38 Malenkov made an important contribution to the forming of the NKVD staff. As head of the Department of Leading Party Organizations he supervised the selection and assignment of nomenklatura personnel over the whole country and in all branches, including the NKVD. In his recollections, Vasilii Riasnoi describes how in February 1937 as a regional Party secretary he was summoned to Moscow and received by Malenkov; he found himself in a group of Party people who had been transferred to the central NKVD apparatus. Malenkov accompanied them to the Lubianka, to Ezhov, and at parting addressed them: "We are surrounded by enemies. They are everywhere, and you should guard the achievements of the revolution!" According to Riasnoi, Malenkov "more than anybody else" was engaged in the organization of things in the Lubianka.[70] In his memoirs Khrushchev claims that at an unspecified moment (probably late 1937 or early 1938) Ezhov asked Stalin to give him Malenkov as a deputy.[71] In the statement for Stalin he probably never sent, Ezhov wrote that he had been in urgent need of somebody dealing with personnel and had asked for such a person all the time.[72] Because Malenkov was specialized in this field and Ezhov knew him well and trusted him, it is likely that he did ask for his pupil as a deputy for personnel.

It is of particular interest in this connection that, according to Minister of the Interior N. P. Dudorov's words at the June 1957 Central Committee Plenum, after his arrest on Beriia's orders Ezhov was interrogated especially about Malenkov and that he wrote down almost twenty pages of evidence on him. Until his own arrest, in June 1953, Beriia kept this document with him; it was then passed on to Dudorov, who in February 1955 showed it to Malenkov. "Malenkov stated that everybody knew about this document, and took it 'to his apartment in order to destroy it.' That is how the document disappeared."[73]

In light of the role Malenkov played in the repressions of 1937–38 against Party people, both in Moscow and in the provinces, it is clear that he could have acted against Ezhov only at the instigation of Stalin.

The commission had to regulate the policy of repressions. It had been Stalin's decision to end the mass terror. With Beriia's support, Malenkov could now act openly against Ezhov. The commission went to work, initially at the Lubianka. According to the register of visitors, on the evening of 13 October Malenkov, Vyshinskii, and Rychkov were with Ezhov for some two hours; between 9 and 14 November Ezhov several times received Vyshinskii alone; and on 15 November Malenkov and Vyshinskii visited Ezhov for several hours. The commission members also had separate meetings with Beriia, without Ezhov. The result of all these conversations and agreements was the resolution of the Central Committee and the Council of People's Commissars, "On Arrests, the Supervision by the Procuracy, and the Conducting of Investigations," which put an end to the mass operations; on 17 November 1938 the resolution was approved by the Politburo. Thus, the commission did not by order of the Central Committee make an investigation into Ezhov's activities. On the contrary, Ezhov himself presided over the commission; it was he who had to work out measures to curb the terror and new principles for the punitive policy.

7

Fall

Dissatisfied with the May 1938 result of Shkiriatov's and Tsesar-skii's examination, Sholokhov turned to Stalin again with respect to the terror in Rostov province and succeeded in being received by him on 23 October for almost an hour; during part of the conversation, Ezhov was present.[1] Apparently, it concerned I. S. Pogorelov, who had been ordered by the NKVD to collect compromising evidence on Sholokhov in order to have him arrested. Probably Stalin instructed Ezhov to examine the case immediately and report on it.[2]

One week later, on 31 October, a meeting took place in Stalin's office lasting more than two hours, attended by Stalin, Molotov, Malenkov, Ezhov, Sholokhov, P. K. Lugovoi (secretary of the Veshenskaia district Party committee, a terror victim liberated through Sholokhov's intervention), Pogorelov, and four local NKVD executives.[3] According to Lugovoi's recollections, Sholokhov complained that he was being persecuted by the NKVD, which had concocted evidence in order to "prove" that he was an enemy of the people. Stalin then asked one of the NKVD executives whether he had been ordered to slander Sholokhov and had given such instructions to Pogorelov. The man answered that he had indeed received such orders and that Ezhov had agreed with them. Ezhov, however, objected that he had given no such instructions.[4] According to Pogorelov's recollections, Stalin added that he had twice been asked by Evdokimov to approve of Sholokhov's arrest, but he had dismissed the request because he thought it unwarranted.[5]

There were more signs that Ezhov's fall was drawing near. On 14 November Stalin ordered the regional Party committees to check the NKVD organs and purge them of all "hostile" people "not deserving political confidence"; they should be replaced by people who had been approved by the relevant Party authorities.[6] The next day the Politburo confirmed a directive by the Central Committee and the Council of People's Commissars, with immediate effect ordering "a halt to examination by the troikas, military tribunals, and the Military Collegium of the USSR Supreme Court of all cases sent for examination on the basis of special orders or another simplified procedure."[7] When on 15 September the Politburo had decided to transfer the "national contingents" to the special troikas, it had indeed fixed their term for two months, and that was exactly the result. Ezhov himself had participated in framing the directive.

Two days later, on 17 November, the Politburo approved the joint resolution of the Council of People's Commissars and the Central Committee, drafted by the commission of Ezhov, Beriia, Malenkov, et al. The one-month delay was explained by the fact that the mass operations first had to be concluded before they could be stopped.[8] In general, the resolution approved of the results of the mass operations carried out by the NKVD in 1937–38. However, "a simplified procedure of conducting investigations and trials" had led to "gross inadequacies and distortions" in the work of the NKVD and the Procuracy. Enemies of the people and foreign spies that had infiltrated the security police and the judicial system had "tried in all conceivable ways to confound investigative activities, deliberately perverted Soviet laws, carried out unfounded mass arrests, while at the same time rescuing their accomplices from destruction." They had "committed forgeries, falsified investigatory documents, instituted criminal proceedings and arrested on trivial grounds and even without any grounds whatsoever, instituted criminal cases against innocent people with provocatory aims." They had relied exclusively on extracting confessions. The resolution called off the mass operations, abolished the troikas, and placed all detention procedures under the control of the procuracy.[9]

The resolution was a mortal blow to the sitting NKVD leadership. Stalin wanted to shift the blame for the mass operations' excesses on the NKVD and Ezhov—that is to say, for the excesses and deviations, not for the purge itself. Neither in this resolution nor in any later decision by Stalin was the significance and necessity of the mass operations ever doubted. It does not alter the fact that, apart from the mistakes committed, in Stalin's opinion their main goal had not been reached, since they had not succeeded in "fully unmasking the arrested spies and saboteurs from foreign intelligence services and fully exposing all their criminal connections." Therefore, the resolution specifically stated that the "purging" of the USSR of "spies, terrorists, and saboteurs" had not been completed.[10] In Stalin's eyes, the NKVD executives were to blame, for they had not carried out the mass operations as they should.

Already before the commission had finished its work, it had become evident that Beriia would be the new NKVD chief. On 7 November, during the military parade and demonstration in Red Square, Ezhov, who had first appeared on the tribune of the Lenin Mausoleum alongside Stalin and the other leaders, was later replaced by Beriia, his head adorned by a blue service cap with a speckled band—that is to say, he wore the uniform of a state security commissar of the first class, a very high rank, only a fraction lower than Ezhov's.[11] Western correspondents drew the conclusion that he was to succeed Ezhov as NKVD chief.[12] The names of other possible successors were also being mentioned. According to information of Malenkov's, Chkalov's, and Mikoian's sons, Stalin offered the post of Interior People's Commissar to their fathers as well. Another name mentioned among Chekists

Two photographs of the Party leaders on top of the Lenin Mausoleum during the 7 November 1938 parade, with, in the first photograph, Stalin (left) and Ezhov (right), and in the second photograph, Stalin (left) and Beriia (right). In the course of the demonstration Ezhov's place was taken by Beriia, who appeared at the tribune for the first time here wearing the uniform of a state security commissar of the first class, something Western correspondents did not fail to notice. (RGAKFD collection)

was that of Khrushchev. [13] Because all these rumors were un-founded, Stalin may purposely have sent up trial balloons to heat up the situation.

On 19 November, two days after the issuing of the joint resolution calling a halt to examination by troikas, a crucial meeting took place in Stalin's Kremlin office. The subject was a statement on disorders in the NKVD that the Ivanovo NKVD chief, V. P. Zhuravlev, had sent to Stalin on 13 November. Two days before sending the document, Zhuravlev had visited Beriia and told him all about it; probably Beriia then urged him to write Stalin, in order to promote Ezhov's dismissal. In his statement, Zhuravlev criticized Ezhov's hand in selecting suspicious people for the central NKVD apparatus, like Radzivilovskii and especially his acquaintance M. I. Litvin, the NKVD chief in Leningrad, who had had "hostile contacts" with Postyshev. When Zhuravlev had reported on it to Ezhov, he had not paid proper attention. [14] Beriia apparently set to work at once, for on 12 November Litvin was summoned to Moscow. That morning, Ezhov had rung him up, and although he had said nothing directly about any danger, the tone of the conversation and veiled allusions were sufficient to tell Litvin that nothing good was awaiting him in Moscow, so he shot himself at home.

Litvin was, of course, another enemy who had gotten away, and Ezhov was involved. Stalin sent Zhuravlev's statement on to the main Politburo members, including Ezhov, noting that it should be discussed. [15] Then, a day later, on 14 November, another of Ezhov's protégés disappeared, the Ukrainian NKVD chief A. I. Uspenskii, also after having been summoned to Moscow. He had been called by Ezhov, who had told him that his doings would be sorted out and that it looked bad. "See for yourself, how and where you will go," he had added. [16] Expecting arrest, Uspenskii disappeared, leaving a message that they should look for his body in the Dnepr. On 22 November Stalin told Beriia, not Ezhov, that Uspenskii's disappearance could in no way be tolerated and instructed him "*at any price*" to catch the "scoundrel." [17] He had to suspect that Ezhov was involved in the disappearance. Khrushchev (then the Ukrainian Party chief) later recalled that Stalin had told him, by telephone, of the planned arrest; he also recalled that Stalin had later told him that Ezhov had evidently overheard their conversation and had warned Uspenskii.[18]

The meeting in Stalin's Kremlin office on 19 November with respect to Zhuravlev's statement lasted from eleven o'clock in the evening until four o'clock the next morning and turned into a slating of Ezhov. Ezhov himself was present, along with Stalin and Politburo members Andreev, Kaganovich, Mikoian, Molotov, Voroshilov, and Zhdanov and also Beriia, Frinovskii, Malenkov, and Shkiriatov.[19] Ezhov was charged with littering the investigation agencies with foreign spies but, most important, with neglecting the department for the guarding of Central Committee and Politburo members, where conspirators had allegedly entrenched themselves (concerned, obviously, was Dagin's testimony of 15 November).[20]

On the evening of 23 November Ezhov was summoned again, this time for a meeting with Stalin, Molotov, and Voroshilov. The meeting began at nine and went on until one. It was Ezhov's last visit to Stalin. The topic of discussion was evidently Ezhov's statement resigning his position as Interior People's Commissar and admitting guilt in having let too many "enemies of the people" get away.[21] In the (unsent) letter to Stalin Ezhov wrote that after the meeting on 23 November, he had left "more upset yet. I had not at all managed to express . . . to you in a coherent form either my mood or my sins. . . . I had the feeling that the distrust you totally legitimately conceived toward me had not vanished, had possibly even increased."[22]

Within hours, the Politburo accepted the resignation, also taking into consideration Ezhov's "state of ill health, making it impossible for him to simultaneously direct two major People's Commissariats." He retained his functions of Central Committee Secretary, chairman of the Party Control Commission, and People's Commissar of Water Transportation but lost his position among the five highest Party leaders. This is indirectly demonstrated by the Politburo resolution of 27 November on the distribution of duties among the Central Committee Secretaries, which mentioned only Zhdanov and Andreev. One day after Ezhov's resignation was accepted by the Politburo, on 25 November, Beriia was appointed the new Interior People's Commissar.[23] The same day, Stalin informed the regional Party secretaries about the change, pointing as an explanation to the facts in Zhuravlev's statement and to new facts concerning the appearance in the NKVD, after the rout of Iagoda's gang, of a new gang of traitors, including Liushkov and Uspenskii, who had deliberately tangled up investigation cases and had shielded notorious enemies of the people, with Ezhov doing little to oppose them.[24] The change was given no immediate publicity, however. Two weeks later, a six-line item appeared in *Pravda*, relegated to the bottom of the back page.[25]

The next day, 26 November, the new NKVD chief gave instructions on how the resolution of 17 November was to be carried out. The NKVD organs were to end the mass operations immediately, and all prior orders and instructions were rendered inoperative. Regional and local conferences of NKVD executives should be organized so that the resolution could be read out and explained.[26] Some regional NKVD chiefs did not immediately understand the significance of the change. The Crimean chief, L. T. Iakushev-Babkin, for example, was arrested in December 1938 on a charge of having continued the mass operations after the dissolution of the troikas; on 28–29 November 770 people were shot with the Crimean NKVD chief personally participating in the shooting of 553.[27]

Beriia had many of Ezhov's people arrested, including S. G. Gendin and Z. I. Passov (22 October), S. B. Zhukovskii (23 October), N. G. Nikolaev-Zhurid and M. A. Listengurt (25 October), S. M. Shpigel'glaz (2 November), Dagin (5 November), Evdokimov (9 November), Ia. I. Serebrianskii (10 November), I. I. Shapiro (13 November), N. N. Fedorov (20 November), S. F. Redens (22 November), M. A. Trilisser (23 November), and G. F. Gorbach (28 November). Some of the regional NKVD chiefs tried to avert the danger. On 12 November Litvin shot himself, to be replaced by Beriia's protégé S. A. Goglidze. Two days later Uspenskii disappeared. Beriia gave instructions to strengthen the border guard and to trace the fugitive; he was arrested only on 14 April 1939.[28]

The ending of the mass operations, as much as their beginning in June 1937, went quite according to plan. Both were initiated by the center, by Stalin.

Reportedly, Stalin and Beriia had first wanted to arrest Ezhov's wife as an "English spy" and have her testify against her husband.[29] Evgeniia was particularly vulnerable because of her many lovers. One of them must have been the writer Mikhail Sholokhov. According to the testimony of Zinaida Glikina, USA expert of the Writers' Union Foreign Commission and an intimate friend of Evgeniia who used to live with the Ezhovs from time to time, they had first met in the spring of 1938, when during a stay in Moscow Ezhov invited Sholokhov to his dacha. That summer, when Sholokhov was in Moscow again, he went to see Evgeniia at the editorial office of *USSR in Construction*, under the guise of a contribution to the journal, and accompanied her home. In August, again in Moscow, he and Fadeev visited Evgeniia at the editorial office, after which the three had dinner together in the National Hotel. The next day Sholokhov returned to Evgeniia's office, this time inviting her to his room in the same hotel, where she stayed for several hours.

The day following, after returning to the dacha late at night and drinking a lot, Ezhov in a state of noticeable intoxication and irritability drew a document from his briefcase and in a rage asked his wife, "Did you sleep with Sholokhov?" It was a stenographic report of what had happened in Sholokhov's hotel room during Evgeniia's stay: on Ezhov's orders, everything had been monitored. Glikina reported that Evgeniia became very agitated as she read it; then Ezhov showed the document to Glikina. She read fragments like "our love is difficult, Zhenia," "they kiss each other," "they lie down." Getting beside himself, Ezhov jumped up toward Evgeniia and, according to Glikina, "started to beat her

with his fists on her face, breast, and other parts of her body."
Apparently, the marital spat soon ended, for a few days later Evgeniia told Glikina that her husband had destroyed the report.[30]
(In October, Ezhov told Glikina that Sholokhov had complained
to Beriia about being shadowed by him, Ezhov, and that as a result Stalin himself examined the case.[31] As we have seen, the examination was actually concerned with Sholokhov's complaints
to Stalin about the terror reigning in his home region.)

It did not take long, however, before Ezhov deemed it necessary to divorce. On 18 September 1938 he informed Evgeniia
about his decision. She felt completely lost, and the next day
turned to Stalin for "help and protection." In her letter she wrote:
"From the fact that he [Ezhov] long questioned me about my en-
counters with various acquaintances I understood that his decision has not been caused by personal reasons, i.e. by a cooling off
toward me or by love for another woman. I felt it has been caused
by political considerations, by suspicion of me." She said she did
not know what had caused this suspicion, for she was a "fighting
comrade and friend" to her husband. She proclaimed her innocence, regretting that because of her, suspicion fell upon Ezhov.[32]
Stalin did not answer the letter. Soon, Evgeniia left for a holiday
in the Crimea, together with Glikina (whose husband, Zaidner,
had that spring been arrested on a charge of espionage).

Ezhov's files contained evidence on his wife's contacts.[33] Certainly he realized how dangerous they were, and perhaps he was
hoping to protect her from arrest—that would explain her note in
the file: "Kolia darling! I earnestly beg you to check up on my
whole life, everything about me. . . . I cannot reconcile myself to
the thought of being suspected of double-dealing, of certain non-
committed crimes."[34]

In July 1938, almost two years after being arrested, Evgeniia's
former husband, A. F. Gladun, was shot.[35] That same month, one
of Evgeniia's alleged lovers, Semen Uritskii, was arrested. He was
the former editor of *Krest'ianskaia gazeta*, where Evgeniia had
once worked, and later the director of the All-Union Book Cham-
ber. Without a doubt, Ezhov himself had organized his arrest. It

is striking that, unlike Gladun, Ezhov was not able to have him shot before Beriia's arrival at the NKVD, and Uritskii thus could offer interesting testimony about the Ezhovs. He revealed the information that Evgeniia had had intimate relations with Isaak Babel', which Ezhov had learned about when he found love letters from Babel' in his wife's belongings. He thereupon gave orders to collect evidence with respect to Babel', and within a few days, a large file lay on the People's Commissar's table.[36]

From the autumn of 1938 on, one after another, people around Evgeniia were arrested. Afterward, Ezhov's nephew and housemate, Anatolii Babulin, testified that in late October 1938 Frinovskii brought Ezhov a document at the dacha that made him very worried. The next day, Ezhov called his wife in the Crimea and asked her to return to Moscow at once. From that moment on, his mood swiftly deteriorated; he started to drink more than ever and became extremely irritable. He feared that he had fallen from favor, especially because of the arrests of Dagin and Shapiro (on 5 and 13 November).[37] According to Ezhov's sister, Evdokiia, in the autumn of 1938 Evgeniia received an anonymous letter accusing her of espionage and betraying secrets to foreign countries.[38]

After Evgeniia, and Glikina, returned from the Crimea Ezhov installed them in the dacha; he came to see them twice, saying almost nothing to Evgeniia and only talking in private with Glikina about something.[39] Very soon, on 29 October, Evgeniia was hospitalized for asthenic depression (cyclothymia) in the Vorovskii sanatorium, a small clinic on the outskirts of Moscow for people suffering from nervous disorders, where the best Moscow doctors treated her.[40] On 15 November Glikina was arrested, together with another bosom friend of Evgeniia's, Zinaida Koriman, technical editor of *USSR in Construction*. This had to be Beriia's work. Logically, Evgeniia herself was next in line.

After the arrest of the "two Zinas," Evgeniia in desperation wrote again to Stalin. We don't know exactly when she sent the letter, but it was received on 17 November. It read as follows:

I beg you, comrade Stalin, to read this letter. For a long time I could not decide whether to write to you, but I have no strength anymore. I am treated by professors, but what sense does it make, if I am burned by the thought that you distrust me. I swear to you on my old mother, whom I love, on Natasha [the adopted daughter], on all who are dear and close to me, that until the last two years I never uttered any word about politics to any enemy of the people whom I met with and that during the last two years like all honest Soviet people I cursed this whole vile gang, and they agreed. As regards the time I lived with the Arkus couple* (it was in 1927), I remember several people who can confirm that I lived with them for one and a half weeks and then went to a boardinghouse. If I had liked them, I would not have left. In fact, when I learned that the (former) wife of Arkus was sent abroad for work, I remembered the impression she had made on me and told Nikolai Ivanovich about it; he checked the facts and gave orders to take away her foreign passport.

I cannot presume on your attention, so instruct somebody of the comrades to talk with me. With facts from my life I will demonstrate my attitude to enemies of the people who had not yet been unmasked then.

Dear, beloved comrade Stalin, oh yes, I may be defamed, slandered, but you are dear and beloved to me, as you are for all people in whom you have faith. Let them take away my freedom, my life, I will accept it all, but I will not give up the right to love you, as everybody does who loves the country and the Party. Once again I swear to you on the life and happiness of those close and dear to me that I have never done anything that could discredit me politically. In my personal life there have been mistakes about which I could tell you, and all of it because of jealousy. But that is personal. How unbearably hard it is to me, comrade Stalin! What doctors can cure these nerves, strained after many years of insomnia, this sore brain, this deep mental pain you don't know how to escape from? But I don't have the

---

*Probably Grigorii Moiseevich Arkus and his wife. Arkus, who had been the State Bank deputy chairman, was arrested in July 1936; in September of the same year he was sentenced to the death penalty and shot. *Rasstrel'nye spiski*, vol. 1 (Moscow, 1993), p. 8.

right to die. So I live only on the idea that I am honest toward the country and you.

I feel like a living corpse. What am I to do?

Forgive me for my letter, written in bed.

Forgive me, I could not keep silence anymore.[41]

Again, Stalin left the letter unanswered. On 19 November Evgeniia became unconscious as a result of an overdose of Luminal; two days later she died, at thirty-four years of age.

During interrogation, V. K. Konstantinov testified that Ezhov, after receiving a letter from Evgeniia from the hospital, sent her a sleeping draught (so Konstantinov had been told by Dement'ev). Then he took a knickknack and ordered the maid to take it to her; soon after, she poisoned herself. Dement'ev thought the sending of the knickknack to be "an agreed signal that she should poison herself." When later Konstantinov asked Ezhov why Evgeniia had committed suicide, he answered that she had been a good wife but that "he had been compelled to sacrifice her in order to save himself."[42] Dement'ev in turn testified that on 8 November—little more than a week after Evgeniia was hospitalized—Ezhov had sent him to see her and to take her a statuette. After receiving the figurine, "she wept for a long time, and we did not succeed in calming her." Then she gave Dement'ev a letter for Ezhov, which he handed over the same day. After reading the first page, Ezhov there and then tore it into small pieces. Three days later, Glikina went to the dacha, where she got a strong sleeping draught for Evgeniia.[43]

One has to assume that Ezhov and his wife had agreed that she was to poison herself after receiving a signal. Ezhov gave such a signal on 8 November, but Evgeniia was in no hurry, and only Glikina's arrest incited her to action, since it clearly meant that Evgeniia would be next. (Glikina was indeed accused of having been recruited by Evgeniia and of having committed espionage together with her on behalf of foreign intelligence services.)[44] And with their arrest, the shadow of suspicion would fall upon Ezhov himself; in the course of Beriia's investigation they would be forced to talk. Since the autumn, Beriia had been arresting people acquainted with the Ezhovs, and in this situation Ezhov had to cut off his contacts. Ezhov did not poison his wife (as accused after his arrest); he only contributed to her voluntary decision.

After arrest Ezhov testified that Zinaida Ordzhonikidze, after a visit to the hospital, had brought him a letter by Evgeniia in which she informed him of her decision to commit suicide and asked him to send her a sleeping draught. He then sent her a statuette of a gnome—the agreed sign—and a great quantity of Luminal, which Dement'ev personally delivered to her. He brought back a note in which she said goodbye to him.[45]

On the evening of 23 November—the same evening that Ezhov was in conference with Stalin, Molotov, and Voroshilov—Anatolii Babulin heard from Ezhov's mother that Evgeniia had committed suicide and that the funeral had taken place that same day, in the Moscow Donskoi cemetery. Ezhov seems not to have been present. Late that night, Ezhov returned to the dacha, together with Dement'ev, and they got very drunk. When the next day Anatolii's brother asked him why Evgeniia had committed suicide, Ezhov answered, "Zhenia has done well to poison herself, otherwise worse would have happened to her."[46]

After his wife's death and on the eve of his inevitable arrest, Ezhov returned to the affections and habits of his youth. In his statement of 24 April 1939 about his homosexual relations, partly quoted in an earlier chapter, he wrote with respect to the period of November–December 1938:

> In 1938 there were two cases of a pederastic liaison with Dement'ev, with whom I already had had such a liaison . . . in 1924. It was in the autumn of 1938 in Moscow in my apartment, soon after my dismissal as Interior People's Commissar. Then during approximately two months Dement'ev lived with me.
>
> Somewhat later, also in 1938, there were two cases of pederasty between me and Konstantinov, whom I had known through the army since 1918. We worked together until 1921. After

1921 we almost never met. In 1938, on my invitation, he often stayed in my apartment and was at my dacha two or three times. Twice he brought his wife, the other visits were without women. He often stayed the night. As I have said earlier, we had two cases of pederasty then. The liaison was mutually active. I should add that one time, when he visited my apartment together with his wife, I had sexual intercourse with her as well.

All this as a rule was accompanied by drinking bouts. I present this information to the investigation organs as an additional trait, characteristic of my moral and social decay.[47]

Perhaps his psychological state dictated the need to oust the fear of what lay ahead by trying to get back to the feelings and impressions of his younger and more successful days. Excessive drinking, uninterruptedly, is also a way of solving problems that suddenly overwhelm one.

During these months, his old friend Ivan Dement'ev, assistant chief of the guard of the Svetoch factory in Leningrad, indeed stayed with Ezhov regularly. The first visit covered the second half of October, when Evgeniia was in the Crimea; he returned in the second week of November and stayed until approximately 11 December. According to Dagin, during his visits, "one long drinking bout took place." This was confirmed by the Babulin brothers.[48] According to Konstantinov, during one of the drinking bouts, Ezhov, fearing arrest and with his nerves in tatters, tried to shoot himself, but Dement'ev took the gun away.[49] Dement'ev himself testified that during his stay in Moscow he and Ezhov were "engaged in pederasty," or, as he also called it, "the most perverted forms of debauchery." Ezhov was glad that Dement'ev had not brought his dental plate and repeatedly forced him to take his member in his mouth. Apart from this, Ezhov asked him to join his bodyguard, preferring to be guarded by a confidant instead of by Beriia's people.[50]

Vladimir Konstantinov, a Red Army political worker with the rank of division commissar, also testified about this period. According to him, between October and December 1938 Ezhov regularly invited him to his Kremlin apartment to drink. One time, he asked him to bring along his wife, Katerina. He started to ply them with liquor. In the end, Konstantinov fell asleep on a couch, drunk. When around one or two at night he awoke, the house-keeper told him that his wife was in the bedroom with Ezhov; the door was closed. Soon after, she came out of the bedroom, in a disheveled state, and the two went home. There she cried and told him that Ezhov had behaved like a beast. After Konstantinov lay down, Ezhov started dancing the foxtrot with her; during the dancing, she said, "he forced her to hold his member in her hand." After the dancing they sat down at the table and Ezhov "pulled out his member" to show her. Then he "got her to drink and raped her, tearing her underclothes."[51]

The following evening, Ezhov again invited Konstantinov to drink with him, and on that occasion he told him that he had slept with his wife and that she "might be rather old, but was not a bad wife." This time, Ezhov got even drunker than usual. They listened to the gramophone, and after supper they went to sleep. Konstantinov had just undressed and got into bed when Ezhov "lies down at my side and proposes to commit pederasty." Konstantinov pushed him away, and Ezhov rolled on his bed. But when Konstantinov had just fallen asleep, he "felt something in my mouth. When I opened my eyes, I saw that Ezhov had shoved his member in my mouth." Konstantinov jumped up, cursed at him, and threw him off, but Ezhov again crept toward him "with foul proposals."[52] Ezhov's bodyguard, V. N. Efimov, confirmed that Konstantinov and his wife spent the night in Ezhov's apart-ment and that they drank heavily. The next morning, Ezhov or-dered his adjutants to show Konstantinov the Kremlin, and after that the drinking bout continued throughout the whole day.[53]

Ezhov's affairs with women also continued. From late 1938 on, his nephew Anatolii brought him "girls" to spend the night with: Tat'iana Petrova, an employee of the People's Commissariat of Foreign Trade to whom he had made advances back in 1934; Valentina Sharikova, an employee of the Ordzhonikidze machine-tool construction works; and Ekaterina Sycheva, an employee of the People's Commissariat of Water Transportation.[54]

On 5 December 1938 the Politburo ordered Ezhov to transfer authority for the NKVD to Beriia in the presence of Andreev and Malenkov; the process was to begin on 7 December and to be completed within a week.[55] An agonizing phase started for Ezhov. Every day the commission gathered at the Lubianka, heard the reports of the department heads of the central NKVD apparatus, and recorded all offenses. Ezhov had to attend but, according to Anatolii Babulin, systematically avoided the commission work, calling the Central Committee and Beriia with the message that he was too ill to come. Apart from his drinking, he was completely sound, but every time he had to go to the commission meetings, he "became irritable, used obscene language, delayed his departure, and in the end stayed at home, devoting all his time to drinking and debauchery with various women of easy virtue."[56]

The commission worked until 10 January, bringing to light many offenses and abuses. Gradually the evidence against Ezhov himself piled up. It became clear that, contrary to the standing order, he had gathered piles of compromising evidence but had not informed Stalin about them. While understanding that the blame for the mass operations' excesses would be fully shifted onto him, he had sought to put the NKVD files in order. As Evdokimov testified later, during interrogation, in conversations in his own circle Ezhov washed his hands and blamed the Party leadership for the mass arrests, referring to the instructions issued from there; in this connection he used to quote the saying "God's will—the Tsar's trial."[57] "God," of course, meant Stalin, and "the Tsar" Ezhov himself; but Ezhov did not wash his hands. He fully understood that, in spite of the fact that he had only been the diligent executor of the Party leadership's instructions, it was he, not Stalin, who would be blamed. Bringing the NKVD files in order, he paid particular attention to the so-called "Special Archive," which contained compromising evidence that for the present he did not want to use. Though these were mainly materials on Chekists, there was material on Party executives as well. In this way Ezhov had them under his thumb. Stalin was not always informed about these materials.

Dagin, sometime in late August 1938, had seen a card-index and a large number of files on Ezhov's table. After reading the documents, Ezhov tore them up and threw them in the wastebasket. Dagin understood that he destroyed "compromising facts on officials." It was a "cleaning and destruction of materials put by at one time in the Secretariat," and it continued for days on end. I. I. Shapiro, the head of the Secretariat, also gradually got rid of documents; some he forwarded to the operative departments, others he destroyed. But Beriia got hold of the inventory of the Special Archive and reported to Stalin that Ezhov had destroyed evidence relating to leading politicians. It was easy for Beriia to demonstrate that people in the NKVD on whom there was compromising evidence, such as, for instance, Liushkov, had not been arrested or dismissed but, on the contrary, had been shielded by Ezhov. In other words, he had saved "enemies" from exposure.[58]

On 27 November Ezhov had a parcel delivered to Stalin via his secretary Poskrebyshev, containing a description of the evidence kept in the NKVD Secretariat, as demanded by Stalin. According to a draft by Ezhov, kept in his papers, the evidence had been collected during the preceding August and September, but when he first saw it in September–October he realized that much of it had never been reported to him. He then gave orders to deposit most cases in the archive, but he kept aside materials relating to Andreev, Beriia, Frinovskii, Khrushchev, Malenkov, Poskrebyshev, and Vyshinskii. Added was a list with the names of more than a hundred political leaders, Chekists, and so on, with indications of the nature of the evidence against them (testimonies on suspicious contacts, for example, with arrested persons). Some of the evidence involved people such as Andreev, Bagirov, Beriia, Bulganin, Chubar', Frinovskii, Iaroslavskii, Kaganovich's brother Mikhail, Khrushchev, Kosarev, Litvinov, Malenkov, Mekhlis, Mikoian, Poskrebyshev, Postyshev, and Vyshinskii. According to

Ezhov, a large part of the evidence had been sent to the Central Committee.[59]

Stalin suspected Ezhov of collecting evidence even against himself.[60] Among the papers confiscated during Ezhov's arrest in April 1939, there was indeed a pre-1917 correspondence of thirty-five pages of the Tiflis gendarme with respect to the search for "Koba" (i.e., Stalin) and other members of the Transcaucasian RSDRP organization. Later, the correspondence could not be found in Ezhov's file; Beriia was rumored to have kept it.[61] In Ezhov's papers, however, the authors came across a dozen notices of the Turukhansk post office relating to remittances and parcels received by I. V. Dzhugashvili (Stalin), when he was exiled there in 1913–15.[62] About Ezhov's intentions, one can only speculate. Could he have collected evidence in order to prove, if necessary, that Stalin had been an Okhrana agent? Or there could be a quite simple explanation, that is, that he collected evidence on Stalin's prerevolutionary activity for a museum of the leader, for he was a specialist in this field and in 1935–36 had directed the organization of the Central Lenin Museum in Moscow.[63] It is not to be ruled out, however, that during the period of Stalin's cooling off toward him, since the summer of 1938, Ezhov was no longer completely loyal and was quietly collecting strength and evidence against Stalin.

On 1 February 1939 Andreev, Beriia, and Malenkov handed over to Stalin the act on the transfer of authority for the NKVD. In their conclusions they established "flagrant errors, perversions, and excesses" in the NKVD work: "Enemies of the people who have forced their way into the NKVD organs have deliberately perverted the punitive policy of the Soviet regime and carried out unfounded mass arrests of completely innocent people, while at the same time concealing real enemies of the people." Illegal investigation methods had been used and torture applied in order to obtain "confessions." The work of the troikas had been full of defects. Under Ezhov the guarding of Party and government leaders had been directed by Kurskii, Dagin, and other enemies: "The whole foreign agents and informants network of the NKVD was in the service of foreign intelligence services." Ezhov used to appear at his office very late and had abandoned himself to drink. He had concealed from the Central Committee "compromising evidence with respect to leading NKVD executives who have now been unmasked and arrested as conspirators." All these things "cause serious doubts with respect to comrade Ezhov's political honesty and reliability." The draft of the covering letter, dated 29 January, asked whether Ezhov could remain a Party member, but this passage had been crossed out and was not included in the final text.[64] The authors are inclined to think it was crossed out in accordance with Stalin.

On 10 January Ezhov was reprimanded by the chairman of the Council of People's Commissars, Molotov, for neglecting his work in the People's Commissariat of Water Transportation, systematically arriving no earlier than three to five o'clock in the afternoon.[65] According to Anatolii Babulin, Ezhov, in private, answered Molotov's address with "choice swear words."[66] One week later he lost his membership in the Politburo Political-Judicial Commission.[67] On 21 January the general public saw him for the last time, when he appeared among the other leaders in the Presidium at the mourning ceremonies in the Bol'shoi Theater in observance of the fifteenth anniversary of Lenin's death. Standing behind the table of the Presidium he found himself next to his NKVD successor, Beriia. In the photograph that appeared in *Pravda* and *Izvestiia*, in his modest Party jacket without the habitual marshal stars on the tabs, the small and frail Ezhov cuts a poor figure next to the complacent, large-faced Beriia robed in the uniform of a state security commissar of the first class.[68] On 29 January he attended his last Politburo meeting.[69]

Ezhov surely knew what future was in store for him. His close comrades-in-arms promoted by him to the People's Commissariat of Water Transportation vanished one by one. His deputy, Ia. M. Veinshtok, had already been arrested (21 September). In October Rafail Listengurt tried unsuccessfully to shoot himself when the same thing happened to him; on 9 November Efim Evdokimov was arrested, in December A. I. Mikhel'son, and in early 1939

D. M. Sokolinskii. Ezhov saw it all, understanding how it threatened him, but was unable to do anything.

Nonetheless, on 19 February 1939, during the run-up to the Eighteenth Party Congress, he was elected to the honorary Presidium of a Party conference of the Sverdlov district in Moscow. This was a fixed Party ritual; after all, he still held his Party functions. It seems it happened without his knowledge, however, for when his nephew Viktor Babulin, who had read about it in the paper (probably the provincial committee organ *Moskovskii Bol'shevik*), told him about it, "he was surprised, cursed embitteredly, and declared that he would not go to the conference, since there was nothing for him to do there." According to Babulin, when he was not elected as a delegate to the Party Congress, he reacted extraordinarily bitterly.[70]

The Eighteenth Party Congress opened on 10 March. Although not a delegate, Ezhov as a Central Committee member was entitled to attend, but since he had begun all-day drinking, he only attended the evening sessions. He was not elected to any Congress organ. Still, as he told Viktor Babulin, he prepared himself for a speech. But after returning from the third evening session, he told Babulin that he had not been allowed to speak, and he used "unprintable language about the Congress Presidium." From then on, he stopped visiting the Congress and "drank uninterruptedly."[71] The FSB archives contain a delegate questionnaire filled in by him, evidently confiscated when he was arrested; apparently, he had taken it home, which explains why he is not in the delegates lists of the published official stenographic Congress report.

But even then he had not quite given up. During the Congress, on 19 March, he wrote a penciled note to Stalin on a small piece of paper: "I strongly ask you to talk with me for only one minute. Give me the opportunity."[72] He may still have wanted to have it out with Stalin and to justify himself, or perhaps he merely wanted permission to speak, since it was the last Congress day on which speeches could be made. As far as we know, Stalin ignored the request. After their very close cooperation of 1937–38, Stalin now was inaccessible to Ezhov.

There was yet one more humiliation to come at the Congress. In his memoirs N. G. Kuznetsov, the future People's Commissar of the Navy, writes that during the Congress there was a meeting of the old Central Committee in order to discuss the composition of the new Central Committee, to be elected the following day, 21 March. At the meeting Stalin fell upon Ezhov, "pointing to his poor work; more than his exceeding his authority and the unfounded arrests, he stressed his hard drinking." After this Ezhov admitted his faults, asking him to "appoint him to less independent work, work that he could cope with."[73]

According to another testimony, Stalin summoned Ezhov to the fore, asking him what he himself thought of his candidature. Turning pale, the People's Commissar of Water Transportation answered in a broken voice that he had devoted his whole life to the Party and Stalin, loved Stalin more than his own life, and was unaware of any guilt. How about Frinovskii and his other arrested assistants then, Stalin asked. Ezhov declared that he had unmasked them himself. But according to Stalin he had done so only in order to save his own skin; after all, had Ezhov not prepared an attempt to murder him, Stalin? Stalin left it to the others to decide whether Ezhov could be reelected to the Central Committee, but he said he had his doubts. This was enough to make Ezhov disappear from the list.[74] This secondhand testimony also sounds rather plausible, although Frinovskii was arrested only in April. As we have seen, Ezhov was indeed accused of having prepared an attempt on Stalin's life on 7 November 1938.

Frinovskii was himself a delegate to the Party Congress. When at the opening not he, the People's Commissar of the Navy, was elected to the Presidium but the commander of the Pacific fleet, N. G. Kuznetsov, he was alarmed.[75] It was rumored that he would soon be dismissed.[76] He was not reelected to the Central Committee either. On 16 March he sent Stalin a request to dismiss him as People's Commissar of the Navy, in view of his "ignorance of naval affairs."[77] His request was not granted immediately. On 24

March, at a meeting of the Main Navy Council, Kuznetsov was appointed First Deputy People's Commissar; Frinovskii stayed on as People's Commissar in name only.[78] In fact, his fate had already been sealed. After former NKVD executives had testified against him, wishing to justify himself, he wrote a number of statements to Stalin and Voroshilov. He assured Stalin that he was not an enemy and asked him to look into the matter and give him the opportunity to confront those who had accused him.[79]

During the Central Committee Plenum following the Congress, Ezhov was stripped of all Party posts. He remained in only one function, that of People's Commissar of Water Transportation. On 29 March the Politburo set up a commission for the transfer of authority for the Central Committee Secretariat to Malenkov, his successor as secretary. He did not appear in public, and though he continued to work at the People's Commissariat of Water Transportation, he did not attend any serious meetings. Most likely, they simply were not held. His colleagues understood that he would soon be arrested and did not particularly seek to be received by him; neither did he try to draw attention to himself.

A strange situation arose. On 6 March the paper *Vodnyi transport* mentioned his name for the last time, in a report on the People's Commissar's order "on the payment of an initiative of the Stakhanov school leaders." The only exception to the subsequent suppression of his name was a note by the captain of the steamer *N. Ezhov* published on 2 April. Nevertheless, he was active and the paper reported about him, but only as "the People's Commissar of Water Transportation." During the second half of March 1939 *Vodnyi transport* published some sharp criticism of the water transport situation. On 27 March the Council of People's Commissars established that since 1936 the People's Commissariat of Water Transportation had not fulfilled the plan, and in early April the same People's Commissariat was also criticized in *Pravda*.[80]

8

Enemy of the People

Ezhov's time was clearly running out, but he continued to work. According to R. Medvedev, during meetings of the People's Commissariat of Water Transportation he did not utter a word, only folded paper airplanes, tossed them in the air, and then crawled under tables and chairs searching for them.[1] This story seems hardly justified. Although undoubtedly depressed and upset, he had not become senile. The orders and instructions signed by him up to his last working day bear witness to this.[2] Nor have we found any traces of folded airplanes in the papers of the People's Commissariat of Water Transportation. Medvedev's story is no more than embroidered fiction about a half-mad People's Commissar.

On 9 April 1939 Ezhov signed his last three orders.[3] It was his last working day. Obviously there was a Party meeting in the People's Commissariat of Water Transportation with "criticism without respect of persons." He was not dismissed; his People's Commissariat was simply abolished by splitting it into two, the People's Commissariats of the River Fleet and the Sea Fleet, with two new People's Commissars, Z. A. Shashkov and S. S. Dukel'skii.[4] The next day, 10 April, Ezhov was arrested. It seems he was summoned by Malenkov to his Central Committee office, to be arrested there, possibly by Beriia personally. The same day, his apartment, dacha, and office were searched.[5] In his apartment, his nephews Anatolii and Viktor Babulin were also arrested as unwanted witnesses.[6] The search of his office and apartment revealed traces of his alcoholism and distress. In his desk and bookshelves (filled to a large extent with the works of his victims) guns with cartridges and vodka bottles were found hidden here and there. In a drawer was a package with the bullets by which Kamenev, Zinov'ev, and other former leaders had been executed, each wound in paper with the name of the person involved.[7]

His arrest was painstakingly concealed, not only from the general public but also from most NKVD officers. Nonetheless, perspicacious readers could notice that the press was now calling Ezhov Dinamo Stadium in Kiev simply the Dinamo Stadium. In April the Sverdlovsk Provincial Party Committee "requested" one of the districts to be renamed from Ezhovsk to Molotovsk.[8] Very quietly without any stir, Ezhov's name disappeared from other institutions. The city of Ezhovo-Cherkessk was renamed Cherkessk only in mid-June, however, and the arrest appears to have been officially legalized with a warrant dated 10 June, indicating that for two months Ezhov was kept in prison secretly.[9] After legalization of the arrest by the Procuracy, though it was no longer a secret, it was not reported in the newspapers. It would not do to make a fuss about the arrest of "the leader's favorite," and Stalin had no desire to arouse public interest in NKVD activity and the circumstances of the conduct of the Great Terror.[10]

Ezhov was confined in the Sukhanovka prison, the special NKVD prison for "particularly dangerous enemies of the people" in Vidnoe, just outside Moscow, not far from Ezhov's dacha in Meshcherino (which after his arrest was turned over to the disposal of the Comintern leader Georgii Dimitrov).[11] The prison was quite close to Moscow's main execution place, Butovo. The facility had been opened only at the end of 1938. An eyewitness description of Sukhanovka shows it to have been a fairly grim place:

It was a row of prison cells on both sides of a corridor, without natural light, with dim bulbs under covered bars at the high ceiling. Each cell contained an iron bunk, a chair, and a table, all riveted to the floor, and a lavatory pan. An iron door with a hole for the observation of the prisoners and a small opening to pass food, also with the bolt on the outside. The prisoners were only allowed to use the bunk during the permitted time; by day it was drawn up to the wall and locked.[12]

After two weeks Ezhov sent Beriia a note declaring his unbounded devotion to the Party and Stalin. On 10 June 1939 he was officially incriminated for spying during many years on behalf of Poland, Germany, England, and Japan; directing a conspiracy within the NKVD; preparing a coup d'état; organizing a number of murders; having sexual intercourse with men ("sodomy"). He was interrogated by the infamous NKVD investigation department executives A. A. Esaulov and B. V. Rodos, as usual mainly at night. He could not bear torture and signed everything.[13]

He confessed to having been recruited as a spy for German intelligence in 1930, when by order of the People's Commissariat of Agriculture he had visited Königsberg for the purchase of agricultural machines and to having spied on behalf of Poland, Japan, and England, to having directed a conspiracy within the NKVD, and to having plotted against Stalin and other leaders.[14] On 24 April he wrote a statement for the NKVD investigation department concerning "my vice of long standing, pederasty," characterizing his "moral and social decay"; it has been amply quoted in earlier chapters.[15] For the investigation authorities these facts turned out to be of secondary importance only. When two days later his partner I. N. Dement'ev wanted to give evidence on their homosexual relations, the investigator reacted: "That is of little interest to us. You are concealing your main enemy activity that you have undertaken on Ezhov's instigation."[16] In the case file ridiculous confessions alternate with interesting evidence on the mass operations and their mechanism, although here also Ezhov talked about his conscious distortion of the Party directives and sabotage in the conduct of the mass terror. He understood that such were the rules. Now he was the enemy and had to take all upon himself and confess to everything.

He dragged many people along in his fall. Besides his nephews Anatolii and Viktor Babulin, who were also arrested on 10 April, a few weeks later, on 28 April, his brother Ivan, by then already having lost his job, was arrested in Moscow, accused of plans to murder Stalin and of counterrevolutionary and anti-Semitic utterances.[17] In addition, Ezhov confessed to having recruited him for the Polish intelligence service.[18] A few days before Ezhov's arrest, on 6 April, his former first deputy, Mikhail Frinovskii, had been arrested, soon to be followed by his wife, Nina, and his seventeen-year-old son, Oleg.[19] He too was confined in Sukhanovka prison. Five days after his arrest he issued a forty-three-page statement for Beriia, in which he confessed his crimes: "Only after arrest, after having been shown the charge, and after a conversation with you personally, I took the path of repentance, and I promise to tell the investigation the whole truth to the end."[20] Two days later, on 13 April, Beriia sent the statement on to Stalin, who made some notes in it.[21] Ezhov's interrogation seems to have been combined with the interrogation of Frinovskii, as well as that of his other close colleague, Efim Evdokimov, who had been arrested in November 1938 (together with his wife, Mariia, and son, Iurii) but had denied guilt for five months.[22] On 14 April he changed his attitude, promising to give truthful evidence about his counterrevolutionary activity, but he stubbornly kept refusing to confess, until on 6 June during a confrontation Ezhov and Frinovskii exposed him as their co-conspirator; after this he promised to give detailed evidence.[23]

Other people arrested from Ezhov's surroundings were, on 20 November 1938 his Central Committee assistant, Sergei Shvarts; on 17 December his personal secretary, Serafima Ryzhova; on 13 January 1939 his bodyguard, Vasilii Efimov. His sexual partners Ivan Dement'ev and Vladimir Konstantinov were arrested no later than April 1939, an earlier partner, Iakov Boiarskii, on 5 July 1939, and Evgeniia's brother Il'ia Feigenberg, on 18 June 1939.[24]

Evgeniia's first husband, Gladun, had already been executed; her second husband, Khaiutin, was also repressed.[25] Association with Evgeniia indeed could have unpleasant consequences as well. During interrogation Ezhov mentioned Isaak Babel', Mikhail Kol'tsov, People's Commissar of Foreign Affairs (until May 1939) Maksim Litvinov, the writer Ivan Kataev (who was shot on 2 May 1939), the actor Topchanov, and the polar explorer Otto Shmidt as suspicious persons his wife had associated with; he described Babel' and Shmidt as her lovers.[26] Viktor Babulin added Aleksandr Kosarev and a student of the Industrial Academy, Nikolai Baryshnikov, as persons she had had intimate relations with.[27] Former Komsomol leader Kosarev (who had been editor in chief of Evgeniia's *USSR in Construction*) had already been arrested on 28 November 1938 and was shot on 23 February of the following year. He was arrested as a participant in an alleged Komsomol conspiracy, however, and there is no evidence that his case was in any way intertwined with Ezhov's.[28]

As we have seen, Isaak Babel' may indeed have had an affair with Ezhov's wife. In any case, he had been a regular visitor to their apartment. He seems to have been fascinated by Ezhov, the opposite of his own intellectual milieu and somebody who could dispose of the life and death of others. Moreover, he was working on a novel about the state security organs. According to Il'ia Erenburg, Babel' "knew he should not go to Ezhov's house, but wanted to understand the solution of the riddle of our life and death."[29] In May 1939 Ezhov confessed that Babel' had committed espionage together with Evgeniia. Within a week the writer was arrested; during interrogation he in his turn testified against the Ezhovs.[30] Another writer, Mikhail Kol'tsov, had already been arrested on 14 December 1938. Ezhov testified that after his return in 1937 from Spain, Kol'tsov's friendship with Evgeniia had become much stronger. Asked by her husband what bound them so closely, she had answered that it was connected with her work, both literary and of other nature. "I understood that Ezhova was connected with Kol'tsov with respect to espionage work on behalf of England."[31]

*   *   *

Ezhov's physical condition had been bad for years. In late November 1938, in his (unsent) letter to Stalin, he had written: "The last two years of tense, highly strung work have to a high degree strained my whole nervous system. All perceptions became exacerbated, and hypochondria [*mnitel'nost'*] appeared."[32] In prison, his health deteriorated further. On 10 January 1940, Beriia informed Stalin that the day before his prisoner had fallen ill. He had complained about pain in his left shoulder blade and the doctors had diagnosed lobar pneumonia, with a pulse rate of 140 and a temperature of 39°C. He was placed under close medical observation.[33] Three days later, Beriia reported to Stalin that Ezhov's condition was worsening. The doctors had diagnosed "a creeping form of pneumonia, assuming an acute character owing to the fact that Ezhov N. I. has previously suffered consumption. The inflammation has spread also to the kidneys; a deterioration of the functioning of the heart is being expected. In order to ensure better care, prisoner Ezhov N. I. will today be transferred to Butyrki prison hospital."[34] Apparently, Beriia feared Ezhov would succumb before his forthcoming trial.

For a trial was imminent. Another three days later, on 16 January, continuing Ezhov's methods, Beriia for approval submitted to Stalin a list with the names of 457 "enemies of the Party and the Soviet regime, active participants in the counterrevolutionary, Rightist-Trotskiist conspiratorial and espionage organization," who were to be tried by the Military Collegium of the Supreme Court. Those 346 who according to Beriia's proposal were to be condemned to death included: Ezhov, together with his brother Ivan and his nephews Anatolii and Viktor Babulin; Evdokimov, together with his wife and son; Frinovskii, also together with his wife and son; Zinaida Glikina, Zinaida Koriman, Vladimir Konstantinov, Serafima Ryzhova, Sergei Shvarts, Semen Uritskii, Isaak Babel', and Mikhail Kol'tsov. The list also included the names of at least sixty leading NKVD officers.[35]

The next day the Politburo approved Beriia's proposal without emendations.[36] Hereafter, Ezhov was interrogated by the Dep-

uty Main Military Procurator, N. P. Afanas'ev, right in the Sukhanovka prison. In his memoirs Afanas'ev writes that Ezhov had
bags under his eyes and looked exhausted and shabby. He asked
whether Stalin had really decided to try him, since he had sent
him a statement. With respect to the charge he said, "It is indeed
true that I have been drinking, but the work was also devilish."
He asked why he had to take responsibility for Vyshinskii, "that
Menshevik bitch and whore": "If they now accuse me of violating
legality, let them first of all ask that bitch Vyshinskii. . . . For he
was the Union Procurator, not me. He had to take care of legality.
By the way, comrade Stalin knew all about it."[37]

Following the Politburo decision of 17 January, trials began
within a few days and continued into February. With respect to
Ezhov's case, on 1 February the investigation resulted in an indictment unmasking him as the leader of a conspiracy within the
NKVD; a spy on behalf of Poland, Germany, England, and Japan;
the plotter of a coup d'état, guilty of attempts on Stalin, Molotov,
and Beriia; and a saboteur. He was accused of having forged the
mercury poison affair and of having organized the murder of a
number of people, including his wife, who allegedly had been an
English spy since the mid-1920s.[38] He was not charged with pederasty or with large-scale violations of legality.[39] That same day
Ezhov was taken to Beriia's office in the Sukhanovka prison, to
be promised that his life would be spared if he would sincerely
confess.[40]

The next day, Friday, 2 February, he was tried within closed
doors by the Military Collegium chaired by Vasilii Ul'rikh, without prosecutor, defender, or witnesses.[41] By virtue of his office, the
Deputy Main Military Procurator, N. P. Afanas'ev, attended the
trial. It took place in the prison, in the office of its chief. Ul'rikh
forbade Ezhov to bring up Vyshinskii.[42] Ezhov was permitted a
closing address to the court, and he then denied being a spy, a
terrorist, or a conspirator, saying that his confessions had been
obtained under extreme torture. Referring to Beriia's promise the
previous day, he pointed out that he preferred death to telling lies.
He did confess other crimes, however: "I purged 14,000 Chekists,

but my enormous guilt lies in the fact that I purged so few of them. . . . All around me were enemies of the people, my enemies." He did not expect his life to be spared, but he asked that they shoot him "quietly, without torture" and that they not subject his nephews to punitive measures; he also asked them to take care of his mother (if she was still alive) and his daughter. His very last words were for Stalin: "Let Stalin know that I am a victim of circumstances and that it is not impossible that enemies of the people I have overlooked have had a hand in this. Let Stalin know that I shall die with his name on my lips."[43]

After the session, Ezhov was returned to his cell. Half an hour later, he was called back, to hear the death sentence pronounced. On hearing it, he became slack and started to fall sideways, but the escort caught him and under his arms took him out the door. A few minutes later, Procurator Afanas'ev came to his cell to point out to him that he had the right to apply to the Supreme Soviet for pardon and commutation of the death sentence. According to Afanas'ev, Ezhov "lay on his bunk, somehow dimly lowed, then leaped up and spoke rapidly, 'Yes, yes, comrade procurator, I want to appeal for pardon. Maybe comrade Stalin will do that.' " Because the cell was too dark, they went to the inquiry office, where Ezhov wrote a short statement with big scrawls (his hands trembled). Afanas'ev then handed the statement to Ul'rikh, who from the prison chief's office by telephone consulted the Kremlin; within half an hour he was back to announce that the appeal had been declined.[44]

Ezhov was shot some time that very night, in a special execution place that had been built according to his own instructions—probably the special accommodation the NKVD had on Varsanof'evskii Lane, not far from the Lubianka headquarters. According to Procurator Afanas'ev, who attended the execution, it was a low, squarish building, in the heart of a yard, with thick walls. It was Afanas'ev's task to make sure that it was indeed Ezhov who was shot. The execution took place in a large room with a sloping cement floor. The far wall was made of logs, and there were hoses for water. The execution was carried out precisely against this wall of logs. According to Afanas'ev, before the execution Ezhov behaved in a very cowardly fashion. When the Procurator told him that his appeal had been declined, "he became hysterical. He started to hiccup, weep, and when he was conveyed to 'the place,' they had to drag him by the hands along the floor. He struggled and screamed terribly.[45] The sentence must have been executed by the NKVD Commandant, V. M. Blokhin. Besides Afanas'ev and Blokhin, the head of the NKVD First Special Department, L. F. Bashtakov, must also have been a witness.

After the execution, Ezhov's body was put in an iron case and taken to the crematorium where it was burned, with Afanas'ev attending.[46] His incinerated remains were then thrown into a mass grave at Moscow Donskoi cemetery, where Babel's remains had ended up as well. Evgeniia is buried in the same cemetery, alongside her three brothers.[47] Neither the press nor the radio gave any information about Ezhov's trial and execution.

After Ezhov's arrest his adopted daughter, Natal'ia, some seven years old, was taken away from her nanny, Marfa Grigor'evna, who had taken care of her at the dacha since the death of Evgeniia Solomonovna, and put in a children's home in Penza. She was instructed to forget her family name and took an earlier name of her mother, Khaiutina. In 1958, after finishing school, she voluntarily settled in faraway Kolyma region, one of the most notorious Gulag regions, and became an accordion teacher in a school. Around the turn of the millennium, she was reported living on a miserable pension in a one-room flat in Ola, just below the port city of Magadan, having a daughter, Evgeniia (called after her foster mother), and seven grandchildren. Her life has been extremely difficult. "All my life I have lived in fear," she told an interviewer. Nonetheless, she remembers Ezhov as a gentle and loving father; even now, when more and more details of her father's bloody activity have become known, she is not prepared to renounce him.[48]

In 1995, she appealed to the Procuracy to apply the law "On the Rehabilitation of Victims of Political Repressions" of October

1991 to her father, for, according to the legislation applying at the time, Ezhov had not been a counterrevolutionary or saboteur. She argued:

> Ezhov was a product of the system of bloody dictatorship of the time. He is to blame for not having found in himself the power to refuse to slavishly serve Stalin, but his guilt toward the Soviet people is absolutely no greater than that of Stalin, Molotov, Kaganovich, Vyshinskii, Ul'rikh, Voroshilov, and the other Party and government leaders.[49]

After reexamining the case, the Main Military Procuracy concluded that the charges with respect to espionage on behalf of foreign intelligence services and the organization of his wife's murder should be excluded from Ezhov's sentence, since they had not been proved. But it saw no reason to exclude the other charges from the sentence—that is, "sabotage, the attempt of carrying out terrorist acts, and the participation in the organization of the carrying out of these crimes." The Procuracy alluded to the serious consequences of Ezhov's activity as NKVD chief and the casualties he inflicted upon the country—his responsibility for the organization of the mass repressions. Therefore, in the Procuracy's opinion, Ezhov was not subject to rehabilitation.[50]

On 4 June 1998 the Military Collegium of the Supreme Court decided that Ezhov indeed was not subject to rehabilitation. Its president, Nikolai Petukhov, argued that, in this way, justice had prevailed. In his opinion, the law of October 1991 had not been written for people like Ezhov. Former CPSU Politburo member and by now chairman of the Presidential Rehabilitation Commission, Aleksandr Iakovlev, even considered the reopening of Ezhov's case "undemocratic," "a dangerous signal of a return to the old times, and a rehabilitation of the crimes of the Stalin regime."[51] Nevertheless, Natal'ia Khaiutina is determined to go on fighting for a revision of the case.[52]

On 3 February 1940 Frinovskii was tried and condemned to death for participation in a conspiracy directed by Ezhov; five days later he was executed.[53] (His relatives, too, have made unsuccessful attempts to have him rehabilitated.)[54] On 2 February the Military Collegium sentenced Evdokimov to death, to be shot the next day; unlike Ezhov and Frinovskii, he has been rehabilitated (on 17 March 1956).[55]

As for the other people around Ezhov, on 19 January his bodyguard Vasilii Efimov was condemned to the death penalty by the Military Collegium and executed two days later.[56] On 20 January his brother, Ivan, and his nephew Anatolii Babulin were sentenced to death by the same court; both were shot the next day.[57] That is to say, when on 2 February before the Military Collegium Ezhov requested that his relatives be left in peace, the same Collegium had already sent them to their death. On 21 January Semen Uritskii was condemned to the death penalty and executed next day.[58] On 24 January Zinaida Koriman and Zinaida Glikina were condemned to the death penalty; the next day they were both executed.[59] On 26 January Isaak Babel' and Ezhov's secretary, Serafima Ryzhova, were sentenced to death; the next day they were shot.[60] On 1 February Kol'tsov was sentenced to death; he was shot the following day.[61] Boiarskii was also sentenced to death by the Military Collegium on 1 February and shot the next day.[62] On 2 February Il'ia Feigenberg was sentenced to death by the same court; he was shot the following day.[63] The charges were terrorism, espionage, conspiracy, counterrevolutionary activity. Filipp Goloshchekin was arrested on 15 October 1939 and shot in Kuibyshev on 28 October 1941.[64] Information about what happened to Ezhov's other homosexual partners, Ivan Dement'ev and Vladimir Konstantinov, as well as to Viktor Babulin, is missing. Their files could not be found in the execution lists of Moscow Memorial Society, which means that either they were not shot (in that case they may have been sentenced to imprisonment), or if they were shot they have not yet been rehabilitated. Ezhov's first wife, Antonina Titova, was never persecuted and died in 1988 in Moscow.[65] His sister, Evdokiia, also survived the Stalinist terror and died in 1958 in Moscow.[66] Neither was Ezhov's mother mentioned in Beriia's list of people to be shot. The nanny, Marfa Grigor'evna, also survived.[67]

After Ezhov's fall, hundreds of his direct accomplices and other NKVD officers were arrested. This goes for all of Ezhov's deputies and department heads. Almost all former NKVD chiefs of the Union and Autonomous Republics as well as the majority of the provincial NKVD chiefs and other leading executives were dismissed and convicted.[68] In the autumn of 1938, between September and December, 332 leading NKVD executives had already been arrested, 140 of them from the central apparatus and 192 from the provinces.[69] Arrests continued in 1939; during that year 1,364 NKVD executives were arrested, 937 of them state security officers.[70]

After Ezhov's dismissal as NKVD chief, many cases were reviewed.[71] Several tens of thousands of people who were under investigation were liberated and the charges dropped. The Gulag was emptied somewhat: during 1939, unprecedentedly, 327,400 prisoners were liberated from the camps and colonies. Although quite a few of them were political prisoners, there were almost no prominent Party or state functionaries among them.[72] On the other hand, on 28 October 1939 procurators of the USSR Procuracy complained to Zhdanov (the Politburo member in charge of the investigation of the cases of Ezhov and his NKVD accomplices) that the resolution of 17 November 1938, putting a ban on the flagrant violations of Soviet laws by the NKVD organs, was not being executed. According to them, Beriia and his associates succesfully undermined the Procuracy's desire to drop the charges.[73] So, during 1939, the procuracy of the Western Siberian province (Novosibirsk) received 31,473 complaints of people who had been sentenced by the troika and the NKVD Special Board, but the provincial Chekists obstructed the handling of the complaints by sending very little material to the procuracy, and with enormous delay.[74]

How far had the organizers of the Great Terror attained their objective? In any case, Stalin's idea to put a final end to the criminal world by means of order No. 00447 had utterly failed. Within a year, Moscow was again overcrowded with criminals. On 21 February 1940 Beriia wrote government chief Molotov that during 1939 and the first two months of 1940 the Moscow police had arrested 28,921 people for various crimes (robbery, theft, murder, hooliganism, violation of the passport regime). Moreover, the criminal investigation department in Moscow had registered 7,032 people who had previously been condemned for stealing, hooliganism, robbery, and other criminal offenses. Every day, the Moscow police detained on average 300 to 400 people, approximately half of them "people without a definite occupation and a permanent address." Beriia deemed it necessary to "cleanse Moscow" of bandits, professional thiefs, and other criminal elements, asking permission to arrest 5,000 to 7,000 criminal elements illegally living in Moscow (town and province) and have them sentenced to eight years at most by the Special Board; moreover, 300 professional bandits who had already been sentenced several times should be condemned to the death penalty by the Military Collegium. Molotov agreed, as did Voroshilov and Kaganovich; Stalin urged the execution of even twice as many people as Beriia had proposed.[75] So, in 1940, just as in 1937, the Soviet authorities condemned people to death on totally formal grounds, be it by a legal court instead of a troika; as a matter of fact, according to the rules, criminals were to be judged by ordinary courts, and only state criminals by the Military Collegium.

9

Concluding Remarks

We will destroy every enemy, even if he is an Old Bolshevik, we will destroy his kin, his family. Anyone who by his actions or thoughts encroaches on the unity of the socialist state, we shall destroy relentlessly.

—I. V. Stalin, November 1937

What kind of man was Nikolai Ezhov? At five feet tall, or 151 cm., he was extremely short.[1] In order to correct his small stature, he apparently used to wear high-heeled boots.[2] He is also reported to have had a slight limp. He was quite thin and frail. He had a small, rather expressionless face, with a sickly yellowish skin, and protruding ears.[3] His hair was dark, an irregular, shining crew cut. On his right cheek he had a scar, the result of an injury from the civil war time. He had bad, yellow teeth, which makes plausible indeed the report that after the alleged mercury affair they began falling out. More than anything, his eyes stuck in people's memory: they were "grey-green, fastening themselves upon his collocutor like gimlets, clever as the eyes of a cobra," wrote Dmitrii Shepilov.[4] Abdurakhman Avtorkhanov described them as "the greedy eyes of a hyena."[5] In general, however, Shepilov found him "shabby," "insignificant," when in the autumn of 1937 he talked with him in his Central Committee office. He was dressed simply, in army-issue trousers and blouse; his rather coarse boots were reddish from lack of care.[6] He seems to have had a "soft monotonous voice,"[7] a baritone, and he occasionally sang romances and

Russian folk songs rather well.[8] According to Fadeev, in his leisure time he loved to play the guitar and to sing and dance.

He was not notable for strong health. In the early 1930s he was diagnosed as suffering from tuberculosis of the lungs, myasthenia, neurasthenia, anemia, malnutrition, angina, and sciatica. In addition, he seems to have had psoriasis.[9] He had a long history of illnesses. In 1916 he was wounded and sent on leave for six months. Something similar happened during the civil war. In 1922, after falling ill from exhaustion, he was treated in the Kremlin hospital for colitis, anemia, and lung catarrh. Later in the

Before the fall: Ezhov on top of the Lenin Mausoleum, 1 May 1938. (Memorial collection)

same year he was granted a leave, for he was "worn out completely" and suffered from "almost seven illnesses"; he was treated in Kislovodsk. In the summer of 1927 he underwent a koumiss cure in the Urals. During the summer of 1934 the Politburo sent him abroad for medical treatment, and he was treated in a Vienna sanatorium for several weeks. In September 1935 he had become overworked again; on Stalin's instigation, the Politburo gave him a leave of two months and sent him abroad for treatment (from 1937 on, however, such trips abroad were no longer made). Shortly after his appointment as NKVD chief in September 1936, the mercury affair allegedly made him sick, and when in November 1938 he was dismissed, his "state of ill health" was taken into consideration. Indeed, after his dismissal he wrote that during the past two years his nervous system had been overstrained and he had started to suffer from hypochondria. After his arrest, in early 1940, he fell ill; the doctors diagnosed pneumonia, and he was transferred to a prison hospital. His consumptive condition did not promote good manners. During the talk with Shepilov, he "coughed heavily and strainedly": "He coughed and spit out straight on the luxurious carpet heavy clots of slime."[10]

His health was probably affected by his addiction to alcohol. After August 1938 it reportedly exceeded previous bounds, even the drinking bouts in the late 1920s together with Konar and Piatakov. By 1933–35 he was drinking heavily in a systematic way.[11] According to Serafima Ryzhova, his personal secretary for ten years, drinking bouts with his NKVD adjutants took a central place in his working day.[12] In early 1939 Andreev, Beriia, and Malenkov reported on having ascertained Ezhov's "constant drunkenness." He "systematically arrived at work no earlier than at four or five in the afternoon, adapting the whole NKVD apparatus to this."[13] At his trial, Ezhov did not deny that he "drank heavily," but he added that he "worked like a horse." "Where is my decay?" he objected.[14] Although he was able to work very hard indeed, at other periods as a result of his ill health and alcoholism he gave the impression of being a rather poor functionary.

One has only to think of the bad references after his service in the Mari province and the long periods of inactivity thereafter.

He seems to have been bisexual. He was married twice; the first marriage went wrong, and the second one was not without frictions either. With no registered children of his own, he had an adopted daughter, who in her diary describes him as a loving father, although she did not see him very often. Apart from affairs with other women, from the age of fifteen Ezhov must have had sexual relationships with men. One should, of course, approach this information with caution, since it comes from a Stalinist investigation, but Ezhov never denied his own confessions in this regard, in contrast to some of the other accusations.

Some authors stress his low intellectual level, emphasizing that he did not even finish primary education. Without wanting to demonstrate the opposite, we should add that before the revolution among co-workers he was known as "Nicky the booklover" and had the reputation of being well read. According to Fadeev, he loved reading and poetry and now and then scribbled a few lines himself. In a questionnaire of the early 1920s he answered that he was "literate (self taught)."[15] He also taught himself Marxism-Leninism. Fadeev describes how in the mid-1920s he used to sit over his books at night "in order to master the theory of Marx-Lenin-Stalin." In 1926–27 he followed the one-year Marxist-Leninist Courses of the Central Committee. According to people who knew him, however, even in high positions he remained an ignoramus.[16] Shepilov, for example, describes him as "a little cultured and in theoretical respect totally ignorant man."[17] His texts were crude, full of errors in syntax and grammar, and he was not much of an orator either and did not like to make speeches.

During the 1930s, Ezhov had offices in the Central Committee building on Staraia ploshchad' (fifth floor), in NKVD headquarters in the Lubianka, and, after April 1938, at the People's Commissariat of Water Transportation. He had an apartment in the Kremlin, plus a luxurious dacha in Meshcherino, just outside Moscow, with its own film theater, tennis court, nanny, and so on. There is evidence that several thousand dollars were spent on packages from abroad for Ezhov's wife. All this implies that—after the poverty of his youth and early career—he was not averse to "bourgeois" delights. Moreover, he seems to have been a collector. According to Lev Kassil', Ezhov once showed him "numerous models of yachts and ships, either made by himself, or gathered in a unique collection."[18] Rather macabre, on the other hand, was his collecting mania with respect to the bullets with which his more prominent victims had been executed.

Ideologically, he was a radical and a quibbler, to such a degree that he had sometimes deviated from the correct official line. During the early 1920s he had been at least a sympathizer of the Workers' Opposition, and in later years he had had contacts with different oppositionists, like Piatakov, Mar'iasin, and Konar. During the Mari episode, he made himself disliked by fighting "national chauvinism." In Kazakhstan, he vehemently opposed concessions to foreign capitalists. During the late 1920s he made a stand not just against the Rightists but against the "Party swamp" as well. He made a name for himself as a "Bolshevik Marat": a fanatic and bloodthirsty hangman, who did not know how to stop "purging," made countless victims, and spared nobody, not even his close acquaintances.[19] However, in this respect testimonies from the 1920s rather unanimously show him from quite a different side. At that time he seems to have been, on the contrary, well meaning, attentive, responsive, humane, gentle, tactful, free of arrogance and bureaucratic manners, helpful, modest, rather agreeable, quiet, somewhat shy.

By consequence, somewhere around 1930 he had changed, or another side of his character had emerged. From that time on he had the reputation of being fanatic, radical, cruel, immoral, ruthless, uncompromising. He saw enemies and conspiracies everywhere. He did not even spare those whom he had worked with and whose loyalty toward the Soviet regime he knew. He did not lift a finger for their acquittal or the mollification of their fate. For example, when in October 1937 the former chief of the Second Base of Radio-Telegraph Units—that is, his superior in 1919, A.T.

Uglov—was accused of espionage for Germany and arrested, his son asked Ezhov to stand up for his father. In response, Uglov's wife, whom Ezhov also knew well, was arrested as well, and in February 1938 Uglov was shot.[20] During the same year a number of former associates from the Mari province were executed, among them his former opponent as president of the Executive Committee, I. P. Petrov; one of the accusations was that they had hindered Ezhov when he was Party secretary in the Mari province and had plotted an attempt upon his life.[21]

In June 1937, according to Razgon, he confirmed the order to arrest his "godfather" Moskvin, together with his wife (who was accused of having planned an attempt on Ezhov); in November of the same year Moskvin was sentenced to death and shot; his wife was shot as well.[22] In March 1937 his former mistress Evgeniia Podol'skaia was shot. In early 1938 the Kremlin physician Dr. Lev Levin was arrested on a charge of deliberately having given Soviet leaders as well as Maksim Gor'kii incorrect medical treatment. After arrest, he was permitted to ring up Ezhov, who had been one of his patients. Ezhov answered that he did not know about it; Levin should formally submit, but he promised he would examine the case in the first instance. Instead, Levin's son was also arrested, and in March 1938 Levin was tried and shot.[23]

Ezhov's murderous suspicions were aimed at more people from his own circle, such as his drinking mate of old, Piatakov. According to Dagin, when in the autumn of 1937 Ezhov's former friend Iakovlev was shot, he witnessed the execution. Iakovlev turned to him, saying: "Nikolai Ivanovich! I see in your eyes that you feel sorry for me." Ezhov answered nothing but was noticeably flustered and gave the order to fire.[24] (It is not quite clear who is meant here by Dagin. It could have been Iakov Iakovlev, the USSR People's Commissar of Agriculture from 1929 to 1934, whose deputy Ezhov had been in 1929–30: he was arrested in October 1937 but shot only in July 1938, which is rather later than the autumn of 1937.[25] N. A. Iakovlev, deputy director of the Central Labor Institute, was shot in October 1937, but we are not aware of any connection between him and Ezhov.)

In December 1936, Ezhov's former colleague from the Central Committee apparatus, Lev Mar'iasin, was arrested; he had been a very close friend. Earlier that year, when Mar'iasin had given up his State Bank function, Ezhov had offered him a job in the People's Commissariat of Internal Trade or Heavy Industry, denying him a Party function.[26] In September 1937 he was sentenced to death by the Military Collegium, to be shot only almost a year later, on 22 August 1938.[27] For the period, this was an incredibly long delay. Ezhov took an exceptional interest in the case and personally directed the investigation. On his orders, Mar'iasin was terribly and continuously beaten. "I ordered to cut off his ear and nose, to put out his eyes, to cut him to pieces," Dagin was told by a drunken Ezhov.[28] According to Frinovskii's evidence, "other prisoners were only beaten until they confessed. But Mar'iasin was beaten even after the investigation had been completed and no evidence was requested from him anymore."[29] On the other hand, at night and in a drunken state Ezhov used to visit Lefortovo prison, where he had long private talks with Mar'iasin.[30] Might these have been cordial conversations with an old friend, whom Ezhov was unable to help? Fearing the possible consequences of his former friendship, Ezhov had him beaten heavily but spared his life for an exceptionally long time. On the day of Beriia's appointment, however, he promptly ordered to have him shot. Ezhov understood that in Beriia's hands such prisoners were dangerous, since they might testify against him. That is how Ezhov parted with old friends. His hatred of Poles, Germans—everything foreign—is the more striking if one considers that his own mother was Lithuanian (a fact naturally to be suppressed).

His victims ran to thousands—deliberately destroyed by means of "quotas," "contingents," and other bureaucratic expedients. "Better that ten innocent people should suffer than one spy get away," was his philosophy: "If during this operation an extra thousand people will be shot, that is not such a big deal," he stated in July 1937. Or, in January 1938: "In such a large-scale operation mistakes are inevitable." In accordance with Stalin's instructions, he ordered his subordinates to torture the prisoners so that they would "confess," sometimes attending the tortures himself.

He could not bear his own methods, though, and when he was handled in the same way as his victims, he confessed everything. This should not surprise us. What is striking is his naïveté in this respect. In common with many other Great Terror victims, he saw his own fall as a "coincidence." When Beriia promised to spare his life if at his trial he would sincerely confess, he indignantly rejected the proposal, perhaps forgetting that he had made the same hypocritical proposal to his own victims. In his (unsent) letter to Stalin of late November 1938, Ezhov complained that after his dismissal the comrades with whom he had made friends "suddenly turned their back upon me as if I were plague-stricken," but how many of his victims had not met with the same misfortune? He had come to the conclusion that he hardly knew people: "I never realized the depth of the meanness all these people could get to."[31] At the same time there was a sense of resignation. When interrogating Khristian Rakovskii, who was tried together with Bukharin in March 1938, he persuaded him to sign fantastic nonsense. "Sign, Khristian Georgievich, don't be shy!" he urged him (so Rakovskii told his fellow prisoner). "Today you, and tomorrow me."[32]

What had caused Ezhov's change? Some authors explain his abuse of power by pointing to an inferiority complex on account of his small size, simple origin, and scant education. Through Ezhov's career an anti-intellectualist thread is woven indeed. According to V. Topolianskii, his inferiority complex generated sadism, the particular cruelty of a spoiled, underdeveloped child who, as long as he is not punished, does not know when to stop tormenting weaker beings.[33] His "infantilism"—to use Topolianskii's word—may certainly have played a role, but it does not explain the change.[34] The same thing applies to the class hatred he allegedly developed during labor disputes before the revolution, when as a worker he faced the industrialists. Another explanation is Stalin's influence. While strengthening his power, the Soviet dictator could well use the ideal executor (as he was characterized by

Moskvin): a very energetic man of great organizational talents, a strong hand with an iron grasp. When Stalin provided him with power, Ezhov answered with an obedient, ultrazealous devotion in executing any of the leader's orders. In the eyes of anti-Stalinist historians he was above all a product of Stalin's totalitarian, terrorist, and bureaucratic system. In the present state of our knowledge this is indeed the most plausible explanation.

It is clear that Ezhov's advance on the hierarchical ladder was particularly pushed by Stalin. Originating from the Party apparatus, he was actually a stranger to the state security organs. It is possible that he had met with Stalin as early as 1922–23; in 1927 they were certainly acquainted, and by 1930 he belonged to Stalin's "inner circle." His rapid advance in key positions—head of the Distribution Department, Raspredotdel (1930), member of the Central Committee purging commission (1933), head of the Mandate Commission of the Seventeenth Party Congress, member of the Central Committee and the Orgburo and deputy head of the Party Control Commission (1934), Secretary of the Central Committee, head of the Control Commission, head of the Department of Leading Party Organizations and member of the Comintern Executive Committee (1935)—without a doubt was supported by Stalin. From 1930 on he was allowed to attend Politburo sessions and had access to the same information as Politburo members. From late 1934–early 1935 on, without being a Politburo member, he was in the supreme Party leadership, controlling personnel policy and state security.

After the Kirov murder in December 1934 Stalin charged him with the investigation of the case, instructing a reluctant state security chief Iagoda to carry out his orders. In fact, he was made Stalin's representative, supervising the NKVD. In May 1935 he provided Stalin with the "proof" that the former opposition in its struggle against the Party had resorted to terror; this was done in his text "From Factionism to Open Counterrevolution," that is, its first chapter, which Stalin himself edited. From the spring of 1935 until the autumn of 1936, he was engaged in a Party purge, inspired by Stalin, the verification and exchange of Party documents operations. The NKVD was involved in the conduct of the purge; enemies who had crept into the Party were unmasked and sometimes arrested. Ezhov's attack in June 1935 on the former TsIK Secretary Enukidze, also instigated by Stalin, shows that it was not a question only of former oppositionists but also of Stalinists who were thought insufficiently "vigilant." The ranks of the foreign communists and political émigrés to the USSR were purged as well, to root out the supposed "spies" among them. When in March 1936 Varga sought support against Ezhov's demands, Stalin sided with Ezhov.

Ezhov played a leading role in the organization of the great show trials. In July 1936 he supplied Stalin the text of a Central Committee instruction, "On the Terrorist Activity of the Trotskiist-Zinov'evist Counterrevolutionary Bloc," which, slightly edited, Stalin sent to the Party organizations. Evidently, however, Ezhov had not yet prepared an exact program of the Great Terror. As is clear from a draft of his letter to Stalin of September 1936, he was not yet convinced that the Rightists had really formed an organizational bloc with the Trotskiists and Zinov'evists. He wanted to punish them by only expelling them from the Central Committee and exiling them to remote places. After the trial of Zinov'ev et al. (August 1936), he was against further political trials; Piatakov, Radek, and Sokol'nikov also should be punished without trial. But he pleaded for the extrajudicial execution of "quite an impressive" number of prisoners, "in order to finish with this scum once and for all." In spite of this, in January 1937 Piatakov et al. and in March 1938 Bukharin et al. were tried in trials that had been organized by Ezhov on Stalin's orders. When Stalin appointed him state security chief in September 1936, the Party leader had clearly made him change his mind. Within the NKVD the newcomer was considered a representative of the Central Committee and Stalin. This enabled him to start a purge there of people connected to Iagoda; military intelligence was also thoroughly purged.

With Stalin's support, Ezhov now seriously went on the offensive against the Rightists, Bukharin and his colleagues. After the

February–March Plenum of 1937, mass repressions started within the Party. Under Stalin's supervision, Ezhov also carried out a purge of the Red Army command. At the June 1937 Central Committee Plenum he sketched an all-embracing conspiracy against the Party leadership, involving the Trotskiists, the Zinov'evists, the Rightists, people from the Comintern apparatus, Tukhachevskii and his accomplices from the Red Army, and Iagoda and his accomplices from the NKVD. According to Ezhov, the conspiracy extended to local levels. Because only the leaders had been liquidated, this implied the beginning of the great purge.

With this aim, from July 1937 on, "mass operations" were organized along "quotas" and "national contingents." It is beyond doubt that the Great Terror was thoroughly planned by Stalin and his staff. By order of Stalin and the Politburo, Ezhov drew up a plan aiming at the arrest of almost 270,000 people, some 76,000 of whom were immediately to be shot, their cases having been considered by troikas. For this purpose, the regional authorities were given quotas of arrests and executions. In return, they requested even higher quotas, with the central leadership encouraging them. The original term of four months was amply exceeded. During the following months, the Politburo approved the arrest of more than 180,000 additional people, including 150,000 who were to be shot. The arrest of some 300,000 more people was approved by Ezhov without formal Politburo decisions but apparently with Stalin's agreement. All in all, in the operation with respect to order No. 00447, from August 1937 to November 1938, 767,397 people were condemned by the troikas, including 386,798 to the death penalty.

Many thousands of other people were hit by the "national operations" against Poles, Germans, Harbin returnees, Latvians, Estonians, Finns, Romanians, Greeks, Afghans, Iranians, Chinese, Bulgarians, Macedonians, and related people of other nationalities. All in all, almost 350,000 people were involved in the national operations, including almost 250,000 who were condemned to death and 90,000 to imprisonment. Stalin signed 383 lists, sent by Ezhov, with the names of over 44,000 state and Party functionaries who were to be condemned, almost 39,000 of them to death. Another target was the Comintern apparatus and foreign communist parties. Over 7,000 army officers were condemned for counterrevolutionary crimes, and over 2,000 state security executives were arrested. From August through October 1937 more than 170,000 Koreans were deported from border regions in the Far East. Over 18,000 wives of "enemies of the people" were arrested and some 25,000 children taken away. Outside the Soviet borders, in Outer Mongolia, by orders of the Politburo in Moscow a troika up to March 1938 had almost 11,000 people arrested, including over 6,000 who were shot; yet another 7,000 people had been targeted. As a result, during 1937–38 more than 1.5 million people were arrested for counterrevolutionary and other crimes against the state, and nearly 700,000 of them were shot. By order of Ezhov, and with Ezhov personally participating, the prisoners were tortured in order to make them "confess"; the use of torture was approved of by Stalin and the Politburo.

In 1937 Ezhov's influence reached its apogee. In April, though not a Politburo member, he was included in the leading five who in practice had taken over from the Politburo. During the summer he was also empowered with supervising military intelligence. In October he was included in the Politburo as a candidate. In the spring of 1938 his decline started. In April of that year the People's Commissariat of Water Transportation was added to his functions. In June–July two major NKVD officers defected, Liushkov and Orlov; when Ezhov tarried over reporting it to Stalin, the latter's suspicion was aroused. In August Stalin appointed Lavrentii Beriia as Ezhov's deputy and intended successor. Apparently, by then the Party leader had decided to get rid of him. During the months September through November a number of his adjutants and other people surrounding him were arrested, and the net also closed around his wife, who in November committed suicide with Ezhov's cooperation.

After the Party purge was brought under control in January 1938, in mid-November of the same year Stalin signed a resolution criticizing the NKVD methods. An end was put to the mass operations. Within a week Ezhov sent Stalin a letter of resignation. It was accepted, and Beriia succeeded him as state security chief. After 23 November he was no longer admitted to Stalin. But Stalin let him dangle for a while. For the time being he stayed on as People's Commissar of Water Transportation, and on 21 January 1939 he still appeared on Stalin's side in a commemoration ceremony in honor of Lenin. In the draft act on the transfer of authority for the NKVD of 29 January, a passage questioning whether Ezhov could remain Party member was crossed out, probably in accordance with Stalin. The same day, he still attended a Politburo meeting, but it proved to be his last one. He was not elected a delegate to the Eighteenth Party Congress of March 1939 and was refused the floor there. After sharp criticism by Stalin, he was not reelected to the Central Committee. Following the Congress he was deprived of all Party posts. In April he was arrested. He could not bear torture and during interrogation confessed everything: spying, wrecking, conspiring, terrorism, sodomy. On 2 February 1940 he was tried behind closed doors and sentenced to death. During the investigation as well as at his trial he expressed his unbounded devotion to Stalin; he announced that he would die with Stalin's name on his lips. He was shot the following night.

Was Ezhov's role more or less independent, or was he merely Stalin's instrument? There is a great deal of documentary evidence that during the Great Terror Ezhov's work was thoroughly controlled and directed by Stalin. Stalin edited the principal documents, prepared by Ezhov, and supervised the investigation and the course of the political trials. For example, during the investigation of the Tukhachevskii case, Stalin received Ezhov almost daily. It is evident from the register of visitors that during 1937–38 Ezhov was received by Stalin in the Kremlin 278 times and altogether spent 834 hours with him. Only Molotov appeared in Stalin's office more often than Ezhov.[35] According to O. V. Khlevniuk,

Ezhov could hardly aspire to the role of organizer of the "Great Terror," an independent political figure who to any serious extent determined the scope and direction of the purge. He was the diligent executor of Stalin's wishes, and functioned within the framework of precise instructions "from above." We do not know of any single fact showing that he exceeded Stalin's control in any way. He was dismissed when Stalin himself thought it expedient.[36]

Indeed, there are no indications that Ezhov ever exceeded the role of Stalin's instrument. After his fall, contrary to the accepted order, he turned out to have gathered compromising evidence on many NKVD and Party executives, without informing Stalin about their existence. Among the papers confiscated during his arrest there was even evidence with respect to Stalin himself: pre-1917 correspondence of the Tiflis gendarme and notices of the Turukhansk post office. However, it is not necessarily the case that Ezhov was gathering evidence to prove that Stalin had been an Okhrana agent. It may simply have been intended for a Stalin museum.

For his part, Ezhov was boundlessly devoted to Stalin. When I. B. Zbarskii was summoned to his office in 1937, he saw a small, frail man with inquisitive eyes sitting behind a large desk in an enormous room. "On the wall behind his back hung a portrait of Stalin of impressive dimensions, on the desk were a bust of Stalin and yet another framed portrait of Stalin."[37] There is evidence that beginning in the summer of 1938, when Beriia was appointed his deputy and started arresting people from his circle, he became disillusioned with Stalin. A number of witnesses have testified that on several occasions after that he abused and insulted Stalin and other Party leaders. After arrest he himself confessed to having conspired against Stalin and having planned an attempt on him; this was confirmed by a number of accomplices and witnesses.[38] At his trial he revoked the confession, saying that it was made under torture. In all probability, it was simply drunken talk by one who had become embittered toward Stalin. It cannot be excluded that after falling into disgrace and with their relations interrupted, he was no longer completely loyal to Stalin and may have organized opposition and collected evidence against him, but it does not seem very probable, if only because he would not have wanted to risk the inevitable arrest.

Ezhov could not consult Stalin on every detail, and his role as Stalin's instrument had to involve a certain amount of autonomy, but with regard to the operations we know of, it is striking how closely Ezhov cooperated with his boss. We may recall that, being the ideal executor, according to Moskvin, he had one essential shortcoming: he did not know where to stop. Summed up in his own words, his logic was: "Better too far than not far enough." This method of working could not infinitely be prolonged without great danger even for the Stalinist system itself. So, during the spring of 1938, the first Party secretary of Karelia, N. I. Ivanov, who was also a troika member, declared that he was unable to imprison over a thousand enemies of the people because the prisons were overcrowded.[39] During the following months, the Novosibirsk NKVD chief, I. A. Mal'tsev, had to cancel a planned operation of his deputy to arrest some hundred priests because there was no place left for them in the overcrowded prisons. The Russian historian S. A. Papkov comments: "If there was nowhere to imprison a hundred priests, how could one handle thousands of other prisoners? It is clear that the Stalinists had reached such a scale of the terror that they lacked the means of maintaining it."[40]

Although Ezhov was chosen precisely because of his zeal, that zeal, which he carried to an excess, made it all the more easy for Stalin to dump him when he was no longer needed. It needs to be stressed, however, that the point of overzealousness was never touched upon during the investigation of his case and his trial. Some authors, incorrectly, tend to suppose that Stalin wanted Ezhov to bear responsibility for the excesses of the purges of 1937–38 and wanted him to be a scapegoat. If that had been the case, wouldn't he have publicly proclaimed him an enemy of the people and had him executed with a lot of noise? But there was no noise: Ezhov's disappearance went almost unnoted. The term *ezhovshchina* was invented only later, during the de-Stalinization campaign of the 1950s.[41] Only months after his fall, Stalin explained to the aircraft designer A. Iakovlev:

> Ezhov was a scoundrel! He ruined our best cadres. He had morally degenerated. You call him at the People's Commissariat, and you are told that he went out to the Central Committee. You call him at the Central Committee, and you are told that he went out for work. You send for him at home, and it turns out that he is lying in bed, dead drunk. He ruined many innocent people. That is why we have shot him.[42]

Because he especially referred to 1938, Stalin suggested that in his opinion in that year, unlike 1937, the terror had gotten out of control and endangered the country's stability.[43] At the end of his life, Stalin told his bodyguard that "the drunkard Ezhov" had been recommended for the NKVD by Malenkov: "While in a state of intoxication, he signed lists for the arrest of often innocent people that had been palmed off on him."[44]

In interviews in the 1970s, Molotov reasoned along similar lines. According to him, Ezhov had enjoyed a good reputation, until he "morally degenerated." Stalin had ordered him to "reinforce the pressure," and Ezhov "was given strong instructions." He "began to chop according to plan," but he "overdid it": "Stopping him was impossible." Extremely selective in his memory, Molotov gave the impression that Ezhov had fixed the quotas on his own and that therefore he had been shot. He did not agree that Ezhov had only carried out Stalin's instructions: "It is absurd to say that Stalin did not know about it, but of course it is also incorrect to say that he is responsible for it all."[45] Another former Stalin adjutant who justified the purges was Kaganovich. There *was* sabotage and all that, he admitted, and "to go against the public opinion was impossible then." Only Ezhov "overdid it"; he even "organized competitions to see who could unmask the most enemies of the people." As a result, "many innocent people perished, and nobody will justify this."[46]

In actual fact, Stalin himself bore full responsibility for the purge as well as its excesses. Just like its beginning, the end of the wave of terror went completely as planned. According to Avtorkhanov, in 1938, in Butyrki prison, Pavel Postyshev gave as his view:

Ezhov is a hunting dog on Stalin's rein, but a faithful and distinguished one, that following the will of his master destroys the Party and terrorizes the people. As soon as the dog finishes the hunt (and we won't be alive anymore by then), Stalin declares it mad and destroys it.[47]

Notes

Preface

1. N. S. Khrushchev, *Vremia. Liudi. Vlast'* (Moscow, 1999), 1: 173.

2. *Vostochnaia Evropa v dokumentakh rossiiskikh arkhivov 1944–1953*, vol. 2 (Moscow-Novosibirsk, 1998), p. 194.

3. A. Iakovlev, *Tsel' zhizni*, 2d. ed. (Moscow, 1970), p. 509.

4. *Istoriia Vsesoiuznoi Kommunisticheskoi Partii (bol'shevikov): Kratkii kurs* (Moscow, 1938), pp. 234, 313.

5. See V. Rogovin, *Partiia rasstreliannykh* (Moscow, 1997), pp. 274, 465.

6. *Revelations from the Russian Archives* (Washington, D.C., 1997), p. 176.

7. See variously, R. Conquest, *The Great Terror: A Reassessment* (London, 1990), p. 14; O. F. Suvenirov, *Tragediia RKKA 1937–1938* (Moscow, 1998), p. 23; S. Konstantinov, "Malen'kii chelovek," *Nezavisimaia gazeta*, 13 April 2000; also D. Volkogonov, *Triumf i tragediia* (Moscow, 1990), 1: 484, and D. Shepilov, "Vospominaniia," *Voprosy istorii* 1998, no. 4: 3–25, esp. p. 5.

Chapter 1

1. TsA FSB, f. 3-os, op. 6, d. 2, ll. 109–58; TsKhSD, f. 5, op. 98, d. 148732 (Ezhov's *lichnoe delo*), l. 9; B. Piliatskin, " 'Vrag naroda' Ezhov ostaetsia vragom naroda," *Izvestiia*, 4 and 5 June 1998.

2. TsA FSB, f. 3-os, op. 6, d. 2, ll. 109–58; TsKhSD, f. 5, op. 98, d. 148732, ll. 7, 9; Piliatskin, " 'Vrag naroda.' "

3. Execution lists, Memorial archives, No. 23D-848.

4. TsA FSB, f. 3-os, op. 6, d. 2, ll. 109–59.

5. APRF, f. 57, op. 1, d. 265, ll. 16–26-ob. The passage on the younger Ezhov in E. Skriabina's autobiography probably refers not to Nikolai but to Ivan: see A. Polianskii, *Ezhov: Istoriia "zheleznogo" stalinskogo narkoma* (Moscow, 2001), p. 42.

6. TsKhSD, f. 5, op. 98, d. 148732, ll. 7, 7-ob.

7. Ibid., l. 20; B. Sultanbekov, *Stalin i "Tatarskii sled"* (Kazan', 1995), p. 188. In his later writings Ezhov sometimes used the pseudonym "N. Knizhnik": see B. B. Briukhanov and E. N. Shoshkov, *Opravdaniiu ne podlezhit: Ezhov i ezhovshchina 1936–1938 gg.* (St. Petersburg, 1998), p. 21.

8. APRF, f. 57, op. 1, d. 266, l. 80.

9. Ibid., l. 30.

10. Testimony of I. Dement'ev of 22 April 1939, ibid., f. 3, op. 24, d. 375, l. 118.

11. See "Marshal sovetskoi razvedki," *Sovetskaia Belorussiia*, 14 June 1938; *Kratkii kurs istorii VKP(b)* (Moscow, 1938), p. 197.

12. V. Ivanov, *Zvezda* 1992, no. 1, cited in Briukhanov and Shoshkov, p. 6.

13. A. Fadeev, "Nikolai Ivanovich Ezhov: Syn nuzhdy i bor'by," RTsKhIDNI, f. 671, op. 1, d. 270, ll. 69–86. Hereafter, no specific citation.

14. APRF, f. 57, op. 1, d. 270, ll. 1–11.

15. A. Drizul, "Boevye stranitsy proshlogo," ibid., ll. 51–65.

16. Briukhanov and Shoshkov, p. 9.

17. R. W. Thurston, *Life and Terror in Stalin's Russia* (New Haven, Conn., 1996), p. 27. See also, V. Kovalev, *Dva stalinskikh narkoma* (Moscow, 1995), p. 177.

18. O. V. Khlevniuk, *Politbiuro: Mekhanizmy politicheskoi vlasti v 1930-e gody* (Moscow, 1996), pp. 200–201.

19. S. Konstantinov, "Malen'kii chelovek," *Nezavisimaia gazeta,* 13 April 2000.

20. APRF, f. 57, op. 1, d. 266, l. 78.

21. Ibid., d. 270, ll. 12, 33; L. H. Haimson, ed., *The Mensheviks: From the Revolution of 1917 to the Second World War* (Chicago, 1974), p. 11.

22. It was later rumored in the Gulag that in 1917–18 Ezhov engaged in banditry and robbery in the woods of Belorussia: A. Avtorkhanov, *Memuary* (Frankfurt am Main, 1983), p. 553.

23. APRF, f. 57, op. 1, d. 266, l. 80; TsKhSD, f. 5, op. 98, d. 148732, ll. 7-7-ob. In another source, the Cossacks are specified as the Khoper Cossack Division: N. V. Petrov and K. V. Skorkin, *Kto rukovodil NKVD, 1934–1941: Spravochnik* (Moscow, 1999), p. 185.

24. Briukhanov and Shoshkov, *Opravdaniiu,* p. 9.

25. See Kovalev, *Dva stalinskikh narkoma,* p. 177.

26. TsA FSB, f. 3-os, op. 6, d. 3, 1. 246.

27. Fadeev, "Nikolai Ivanovich Ezhov."

28. Sultanbekov, *Stalin i "Tatarskii sled,"* p. 181; Briukhanov and Shoshkov, p. 14. See also, G. Tsitriniak, "Rasstrel'noe delo Ezhova: Shtrikhi k portretu palacha," *Literaturnaia gazeta* 1992, no. 7.

29. TsA FSB, Archival investigation case of Frinovskii, N-15301, t. 10, l. 127.

30. TsKhSD, registration form on Ezhov of 1936; "Poslednee slovo Nikolaia Ezhova," *Moskovskie novosti* 1994, no. 5; see also Ezhov's testimony of April 1939, TsA FSB, f. 3-os, op. 6, d. 1, ll. 317–20.

31. APRF, f. 57, op. 1, d. 266, ll. 88–89; TsKhSD, f. 5, op. 98, d. 148732, ll. 7, 7-ob., 12-ob., 60.

32. TsKhSD, f. 5, op. 98, d. 148732, ll. 54, 55, 67; also ll. 59, 62, 63.

33. Sultanbekov, p. 183. In 1917 Kaganovich had worked for the Party in Gomel' and Mogilev provinces of Belorussia, and Khataevich had been a Party functionary in Gomel'. Ezhov seems to have met Kaganovich in November 1917, when the latter addressed a meeting of soldiers and railway workers in Vitebsk: Polianskii, *Ezhov,* p. 71.

34. TsKhSD, f. 5, op. 98, d. 148732, l. 22.

35. Ibid., ll. 1–2; Briukhanov and Shoshkov, pp. 21–23.

36. V. Iantemir, "Preliudiia k 'ezhovshchine,' " *Ioshkar-Ola,* 28 November 1996; TsKhSD, f. 5, op. 98, d. 148732, ll. 65, 68.

37. RTsKhIDNI, f. 671, op. 1, d. 267, ll. 7-ob., 8–11.

38. Briukhanov and Shoshkov, p. 24, mention the photograph, but unfortunately the authors have been unable to find it. *Lenin, Sobranie fotografii i kinokadrov* (Moscow, 1970), 1: 417–18, shows a photograph of Lenin during the CEC session, but the surrounding group has apparently been cut off.

39. RTsKhIDNI, f. 671, op. 1, d. 267, ll. 12–14 and 6-6-ob.

40. TsKhSD, f. 5, op. 98, d. 148732, l. 30.

41. Ibid., l. 23; Sultanbekov, p. 184.

42. TsKhSD, f. 5, op. 98, d. 148732, ll. 32, 33, 36.

43. RTsKhIDNI, f. 671, op. 1, d. 267, ll. 18–19.

44. Ibid., l. 20.

45. TsKhSD, f. 5, op. 98, d. 148732, l. 17.

46. Ibid., l. 64.

47. Briukhanov and Shoshkov, p. 26.

48. Fadeev, "Nikolai Ivanovich Ezhov."

49. *Trinadtsatyi s'ezd RKP(b): Stenograficheskii otchet* (Moscow, 1963), p. 722.

50. TsKhSD, f. 5, op. 98, d. 148732, ll. 1–2, 41, 42.

51. E. Gnedin, *Vykhod iz labirinta* (Moscow, 1994), p. 59.

52. Fadeev, "Nikolai Ivanovich Ezhov."

53. TsKhSD, f. 5, op. 98, d. 148732, l. 8.

54. Ibid., ll. 44, 53.

55. TsA FSB, f. 3-os, op. 6, d. 3, l. 81; Iu. Rubtsov, *Alter ego Stalina: Stranitsy politicheskoi biografii L. Z. Mekhlisa* (Moscow, 1999), p. 53.

56. Briukhanov and Shoshkov, p. 160.

57. TsKhSD, f. 5, op. 98, d. 148732, ll. 49–50. During the cure he became acquainted with Galina Egorova, wife of the later marshal A. I. Egorov: TsA FSB, f. 3-os, op. 6, d. 1, l. 321.

58. TsKhSD, f. 5, op. 98, d. 148732, l. 52.

59. Ibid., l. 24.

60. Briukhanov and Shoshkov, p. 30; *Sovetskoe rukovodstvo. Perepiska. 1928–1941 gg.* (Moscow, 1999), pp. 31, 477.

61. L. Razgon, *Plen v svoem otechestve* (Moscow, 1994), p. 50.

62. TsKhSD, f. 5, op. 98, d. 148732, l. 69.

63. *Piatnadtsatyi s'ezd VKP(b): Stenograficheskii otchet* (Moscow, 1962), 2: 1522; *Shestnadtsataia konferentsiia VKP(b): Stenograficheskii otchet* (Moscow, 1962), p. 697.

64. Briukhanov and Shoshkov, p. 32.

65. N. Ezhov, L. Mekhlis, and P. Pospelov, "Pravyi uklon v prakticheskoi rabote i partiinoe boloto," *Bol'shevik* 1929, no. 16: 39–62.

66. TsKhSD, f. 5, op. 98, d. 148732, l. 25.

67. *XVI s'ezd Vsesoiuznoi Kommunisticheskoi Partii (b): Stenograficheskii otchet* (Moscow, 1930), p. 771.

68. N. Ezhov, "Gorod—na pomoshch' derevne," *Sputnik agitatora (dlia derevni)*, no. 8 (March 1930): 4–9.

69. N. I. Ezhov, "Kondrat'evshchina v bor'be za kadry," *Sotsialisticheskaia rekonstruktsiia sel'skogo khoziastva* 1930, no. 9–10: 1–12.

70. N. Ezhov, "Nekotorye voprosy podgotovki i rasstanovki kadrov," *Pravda*, 17 and 20 March 1932.

71. TsKhSD, f. 5, op. 98, d. 148732, l. 69.

72. *Istoricheskii arkhiv* 1994, no. 6: 25. The visit lasted half an hour. On 29 November he was received again, this time for an hour and a half: ibid.

73. TsKhSD, f. 5, op. 98, d. 148732; *Stalinskoe Politbiuro v 30-e gody* (Moscow, 1995), pp. 20, 178; Khlevniuk, *Politbiuro*, p. 200. Ezhov's first attendance at a Politburo session was registered only in February 1934: *Stalinskoe Politbiuro*, p. 232.

74. *Istoricheskii arkhiv* 1994, no. 6: 39–40.

75. *Vozvrashchenie pamiati: Istoriko-arkhivnyi al'manakh*, no. 3 (Novosibirsk, 1997): 164–75.

76. RTsKhIDNI, f. 671, op. 1, d. 267, ll. 22–25.

77. Ibid., f. 17, op. 120, d. 45, l. 19.

78. Ibid., l. 55.

79. See TsKhSD, f. 5, op. 98, d. 148732, l. 9; Briukhanov and Shoshkov, pp. 16–18, 26, 32–35. From 1927 on the Ezhovs lived at no. 10/16 Molochnyi Lane, Apt. 20 (near Ostozhenka).

80. See V. Chentalinski, *La parole ressuscitée: Dans les archives littéraires du K.G.B.* (Paris, 1993), pp. 62–65; S. Povartsov, *Prichina smerti—rasstrel: Khronika poslednikh dnei Isaaka Babelia* (Moscow, 1996), pp. 39, 149–51; Briukhanov and Shoshkov, pp. 33–34, 47, 160; A. Vaksberg, *The Prosecutor and the Prey: Vyshinsky and the 1930s' Moscow Trials* (London, 1990), p. 199; G. Zhavoronkov, "I snitsia noch'iu den'," *Sintaksis*, no. 32 (1992): 46–65, esp. pp. 47, 51–52; interview with A. N. Pirozhkova, *Nezavisimaia gazeta*, 16 January 1998. In the late 1920s and early 1930s Ezhov lived at no. 1 Ostozhenka

Street, Apt. 21, without Titova: GARF, f. 1235, op. 14, d. 46, l. 65; Briukhanov and Shoshkov, p. 32, 34. Later he seems to have lived at no. 1 Neopalimovskii Lane, Apt. 3, and then on Mamonovskii Lane: APRF, f. 3, op. 24, d. 375, l. 63; d. 376, ll. 82–83.

81. TsA FSB, f. 3-os, op. 6, d. 3, ll. 420–23. In a later chapter the statement will be continued and commented on.

82. V. Shentalinskii, "Okhota v revzapovednike," *Novyi mir* 1998, no. 12: 170–96, esp. p. 179.

83. TsA FSB, f. 3-os, op. 6, d. 1, l. 323.

84. *Izvestiia,* 5 March 1933; *Rasstrel'nye spiski,* no. 2 (Moscow, 1995).

85. TsA FSB, Archival investigation case of Frinovskii, N-15301, t. 12, ll. 83–84.

86. "Poslednee slovo."

87. See R. Medvedev, *Let History Judge: The Origins and Consequences of Stalinism,* rev. ed. (Oxford, 1989), pp. 358–59; *Literaturnaia gazeta,* 22 August 1990; A. Larina (Bukharina), *Nezabyvaemoe* (Moscow, 1989), pp. 269–70; N. Mandelstam, *Hope Against Hope: A Memoir* (New York, 1970), pp. 113, 322–25; Thurston, *Life and Terror in Stalin's Russia,* p. 28; Sultanbekov, *Stalin i "Tatarskii sled,"* p. 216.

88. Razgon, *Plen v svoem otechestve,* pp. 50–51. Ezhov ceased to visit Moskvin's apartment after he took over Moskvin's Central Committee seat in early 1934; their relation was disturbed.

89. D. Shepilov, "Vospominaniia," *Voprosy istorii* 1998, no. 4: 3–25, esp. p. 6; F. Chuev, *Sto sorok besed s Molotovym* (Moscow, 1991), p. 400.

90. Shepilov, p. 6.

91. Medvedev, *Let History Judge,* pp. 358–59.

Chapter 2

1. In the 1921 purge, 156,900 out of 585,000 Party members were expelled: R. G. Suny, *The Soviet Experiment* (New York, 1998), p. 254. According to Ezhov et al., from 1921 until June 1928, as a result of the 1921 purge and subsequent verifications, as well as the work of control commissions, 435,075 people were expelled from the Party or left its ranks: N. Ezhov, L. Mekhlis, and P. Pospelov, "Pravyi uklon v prakticheskoi rabote i partiinoe boloto," *Bol'shevik* 1929, no. 16: 39–62,

esp. p. 56. The 1929 purge resulted in some 170,000 expulsions, about 11 percent of the current membership; but subsequent rehabilitations reduced this figure to 133,000: T. H. Rigby, *Communist Party Membership in the U.S.S.R. 1917–1967* (Princeton, N.J., 1968), pp. 178–79.

2. According to T. H. Rigby (*Communist Party Membership*, p. 204), during the 1933–34 purge 22 percent of Party members were expelled; actually, membership fell by 33 percent, or 1.2 million. J. A. Getty and O. V. Naumov give a figure of 18 percent of the Party membership (2 million members and 1.2 million candidates) for the purge: see Getty and Naumov, *The Road to Terror: Stalin and the Self-Destruction of the Bolsheviks, 1932–1939* (New Haven, Conn., 1999), pp. 126, 128.

3. J. A. Getty, *Origins of the Great Purges: The Soviet Communist Party Reconsidered, 1933–1938* (Cambridge, Eng., 1985), pp. 50–51; R. C. Tucker, *Stalin in Power: The Revolution from Above, 1928–1941* (New York, 1990), p. 221. For two examples of Ezhov's activity (the 1933 expulsion of Tseitlin and Shliapnikov), see *Izvestiia TsK KPSS* 1989, no. 10: 69–70; 1990, no. 1: 50.

4. *XVII s'ezd Vsesoiuznoi Kommunisticheskoi Partii (b): Stenograficheskii otchet* (Moscow, 1934), pp. 7, 302–4.

5. Ibid., pp. 652–53; *Revelations from the Russian Archives* (Washington, D.C., 1997), pp. 65–66.

6. A. G. Solov'ev, "Tetradi krasnogo professora (1912–1941 gg.)," *Neizvestnaia Rossiia, xx vek*, no. 4 (Moscow, 1993): 140–228, esp. p. 174.

7. O. V. Khlevniuk, *Politbiuro: Mekhanizmy politicheskoi vlasti v 1930-e gody* (Moscow, 1996), p. 201.

8. B. B. Briukhanov and E. N. Shoshkov, *Opravdaniiu ne podlezhit: Ezhov i ezhovshchina 1936–1938 gg.* (St. Petersburg, 1998), p. 160.

9. *Stalinskoe Politbiuro v 30-e gody* (Moscow, 1995), p. 232.

10. APRF, f. 3, op. 58, d. 4, l. 2; Getty and Naumov, *The Road to Terror*, p. 121.

11. Getty and Naumov, p. 159.

12. Ibid., p. 123; F. Benvenuti, "The 'Reform' of the NKVD, 1934," *Europe-Asia Studies* 1997, no. 6: 1037–56, esp. pp. 1041, 1043; *Svobodnaia mysl'* 1998, no. 8: 109.

13. *Izvestiia*, 11 July 1934; "Ob obrazovanii obshchesoiuznogo Narodnogo Komissariata vnutrennikh del: Postanovlenie TsIK SSSR 10

iiulia 1934 g. (Izvlechenie)," *Sbornik zakonodatel'nykh i normativnykh aktov o repressiiakh i reabilitatsii zhertv politicheskoi repressii* (Moscow, 1993), pp. 61–62; "Ob Osobom soveshchanii pri Narodnom Komissare vnutrennikh del Soiuza SSR: Postanovlenie TsIK i SNK SSSR 5 noiabria 1934 g.," ibid., pp. 62–63; Getty and Naumov, p. 123.

14. "O vnesudebnykh organakh," *Izvestiia TsK KPSS* 1989, no. 10: 80–82.

15. Getty and Naumov, p. 158.

16. TsA FSB, f. 3-os, op. 6, d. 3, ll. 280–81.

17. APRF, f. 45, op. 1, d. 51, l. 13; d. 729, l. 19.

18. See R. Medvedev, *Let History Judge: The Origins and Consequences of Stalinism*, rev. ed. (Oxford, 1989), p. 339; B. Briukhanov and E. Shoshkov, " 'Ezhovye rukavitsy' tridtsatykh godov," *Molodaia gvardiia* 1997, no. 12: 106–33, esp. p. 111.

19. *Istoricheskii arkhiv* 1995, no. 3: 144.

20. *Vestnik Verkhovnogo Suda SSSR* 1991, no. 6: 21.

21. Getty and Naumov, pp. 140–41.

22. Testimony of S. F. Redens of 26 May 1939, TsA FSB, f. 3-os, op. 6, d. 4, l. 342.

23. *Genrikh Iagoda: Narkom vnutrennikh del SSSR, General'nyi komissar gosudarstvennoi bezopasnosti: Sbornik dokumentov* (Kazan', 1997), pp. 159–60.

24. TsA FSB, f. 3-os, op. 4, d. 6, l. 22.

25. Khlevniuk, *Politbiuro*, pp. 201–2; *Reabilitatsiia: Politicheskie protsessy 30–50-kh godov* (Moscow, 1991), pp. 153–54, 184; "Materialy fevral'sko-martovskogo plenuma TsK VKP(b) 1937 goda," *Voprosy istorii* 1995, no. 2: 16–17; D. Likhanov and V. Nikonov, "Ia pochistil OGPU," *Sovershenno sekretno* 1992, no. 4; "Poslednee slovo Nikolaia Ezhova," *Moskovskie novosti* 1994, no. 5.

26. Getty and Naumov, p. 147; see also, APRF, f. 57, op. 1, d. 158.

27. APRF, f. 57, op. 1, d. 128 and d. 139.

28. APRF, f. 57, op. 1, d. 118, ll. 1–2, 25–39, 44–46.

29. APRF, f. 57, op. 1, d. 5.

30. Khlevniuk, *Politbiuro*, p. 161.

31. APRF, f. 57, op. 1, d. 57; see also, *Istochnik* 1995, no. 5: 160.

32. D. Shepilov, "Vospominaniia," *Voprosy istorii* 1998, no. 4: 3–25, esp. p. 7.

33. Getty and Naumov, pp. 159–60.

34. Khlevniuk, p. 160.
35. M. Ebon, *Malenkov* (London, 1953), pp. 37–38.
36. Khlevniuk, p. 160; TsKhSD, f. 5, op. 98, d. 148732.
37. RTsKhIDNI, f. 17, op. 3, d. 961, ll. 61, 64–65.
38. Khlevniuk, p. 161.
39. Solov'ev, "Tetradi krasnogo professora," p. 178.
40. See A. Uralov, *The Reign of Stalin* (Westport, Conn., 1975; repr. of the original 1953 ed.), pp. 32, 42; R. Conquest, *Inside Stalin's Secret Police: NKVD Politics, 1936–39* (London, 1985), p. 22; Tucker, *Stalin in Power*, pp. 310–11, 647; A. Vaksberg, *The Prosecutor and the Prey: Vyshinsky and the 1930s' Moscow Trials* (London, 1990), p. 70; Briukhanov and Shoshkov, *Opravdaniiu,* pp. 46–47, 55 (these authors refer to a commission with Malenkov and Shkiriatov). According to Avtorkhanov in an account published in 1953, within less than two years the commission presented the following plan. The population was to be subjected to a secret political investigation by the NKVD and for this purpose was to be divided into categories—intellectuals, industrial workers, peasants. In each category, a predetermined percentage of persons was to be liquidated; "indices of guilt" were to be defined in advance. Exact dates were to be set for the purging of each category, by social groups and regions. During 1935–36, all questionable persons were secretly examined by the NKVD, under the direction of the commission; millions of people were involved. Therefore, it was resolved to set up a Special Board within the NKVD and regional troikas in order to judge the suspects *in absentia*. Agents of the commission were sent to the regions, provided with special orders vesting them with extraordinary powers; the regional NKVD bodies were to furnish them with lists based on the indices of guilt for all categories of persons aimed at. This account has no verifiable documentary base: Uralov, pp. 30, 31, 33.
41. A. Kolpakidi, "Val'ter Krivitskii: Vokrug pravdy i vymysla," in V. Krivitskii, *Ia byl agentom Stalina* (Moscow, 1996), pp. 343–73, esp. pp. 348–49.
42. N. V. Petrov, " 'Pervyi predsedatel' KGB general Ivan Serov," *Otechestvennaia istoriia* 1997, no. 5: 23–43, esp. p. 24.
43. Khlevniuk, pp. 143–44.
44. RTsKhIDNI, f. 17, op. 3, d. 963, l. 3.
45. Ibid., ll. 38–43.
46. Ezhov at the December 1935 Central Committee Plenum, ibid., op. 2, d. 561, ll. 127–33.

47. Ibid., f. 71, op. 10, d. 130, ll. 29–30.

48. *VKP(b) v rezoliutsiiakh i resheniiakh s'ezdov, konferentsii i ple-numov TsK*, izd. 6-e (Moscow, 1941), 2: 635.

49. Khlevniuk, pp. 161–62.

50. APRF, f. 57, op. 1, d. 273, l. 1.

51. Ibid., ll. 80, 798-b.

52. Ibid., ll. 2–82.

53. Ibid., ll. 798–902.

54. Iu. N. Zhukov, "Tainy 'Kremlevskogo dela' 1935 goda i sud'ba Avelia Enukidze," *Voprosy istorii* 2000, no. 9: 83–113, esp. p. 91.

55. RTsKhIDNI, f. 17, op. 2, d. 547, l. 66.

56. Ibid., op. 3, d. 960, l. 25.

57. Zhukov, pp. 94–95.

58. Ibid., p. 97.

59. Ibid., p. 98; RTsKhIDNI, f. 17, op. 2, d. 547, l. 66; op. 3, d. 963, l. 37.

60. APRF, f. 45, op. 1, d. 729, l. 20.

61. RTsKhIDNI, f. 17, op. 2, d. 547, ll. 49–56.

62. Ibid., l. 68.

63. Ibid., ll. 68–70.

64. Ibid., l. 73. It is interesting to note that the June 1936 Plenum decided that Enukidze had the right to be readmitted to the Party: Getty and Naumov, *The Road to Terror,* p. 178; Zhukov, p. 105. In February 1937 he was arrested, in August of the same year tried and executed: Zhukov, p. 106.

65. *Izvestiia TsK KPSS* 1989, no. 7: 86–93.

66. Zhukov, p. 104.

67. RTsKhIDNI, f. 671, op. 1, d. 28, ll. 184–85.

68. Ibid., f. 17, op. 3, d. 966, ll. 22–26; d. 970, ll. 152–57.

69. Ibid., f. 57, op. 1, d. 28, ll. 174–83.

70. *Partiinoe stroitel'stvo* 1935, no. 17: 79–80.

71. Getty and Naumov, pp. 190–92.

72. Khlevniuk, *Politbiuro,* p. 203.

73. RTsKhIDNI, f. 17, op. 3, d. 971, l. 49.

74. APRF, f. 45, op. 1, d. 729, ll. 71–72.

75. A. Polianskii, *Ezhov: Istoriia "zheleznogo" stalinskogo nar-koma* (Moscow, 2001), pp. 250–55.

76. *Istoricheskii arkhiv* 1995, no. 3: 177.

77. RTsKhIDNI, f. 17, op. 2, d. 561, ll. 127–33. Another source (Getty and Naumov, p. 275) states that during the 1935 verification operation 263,885 people were expelled, that is, 11.1 percent of the Party membership.

78. RTsKhIDNI, f. 17, op. 2, d. 561, l. 164.

79. *KPSS v rezoliutsiiakh i resheniiakh s'ezdov, konferentsii i plenumov TsK*, vol. 5 (Moscow, 1971), pp. 243–52; English transl.: *Resolutions and Decisions of the Communist Party of the Soviet Union*, vol. 3 (Toronto, 1974), pp. 160–67.

80. RTsKhIDNI, f. 17, op. 120, d. 240, ll. 21–22.

81. "Poslednee slovo."

82. Solov'ev, "Tetradi krasnogo professora," p. 178.

83. Ibid., pp. 181–82.

84. Ibid., pp. 185–86. Two years later, in March 1938, in a letter to Stalin, Varga dared to protest against the mass arrests of political émigrés: RTsKhIDNI, f. 495, op. 73, d. 48, ll. 96–99. Nevertheless, he survived the terror of the 1930s and only during the 1940s was criticized for his economic opinions and forced to self-criticism.

85. F. I. Firsov, "Stalin i Komintern," *Voprosy istorii* 1989, no. 9: 3–19, esp. p. 14.

86. A. Paczkowski, "Pologne, la 'nation-ennemi,' " in S. Courtois et al., *Le livre noir du communisme: Crimes, terreur et répression* (Paris, 1997), pp. 397–428, esp. pp. 398–400.

87. RTsKhIDNI, f. 671, op. 1, d. 70, ll. 2–8. Unfortunately, the authors were not allowed to see the document.

88. Getty and Naumov, pp. 200–201.

89. *KPSS v rezoliutsiiakh i resheniiakh s'ezdov, konferentsii i plenumov TsK*, vol. 6 (Moscow, 1985), p. 297.

90. A. Vatlin, "Kaderpolitik und Säuberungen in der Komintern," in H. Weber and U. Mählert, eds., *Terror: Stalinistische Parteisäuberungen 1936–1953* (Paderborn, 1998), pp. 33–119, esp. pp. 65, 99–101 (in the document 3 January is indicated as date). See also, V. N. Khaustov, "Iz predistorii massovykh repressii poliakov, seredina 1930-kh gg.," in *Repressii protiv poliakov i pol'skikh grazhdan* (Moscow, 1997), pp. 10–21, esp. p. 13.

91. F. I. Firsov, "Dimitroff, Komintern und Stalinsche Repressalien," paper for workshop "Stalinistischer Terror, Massenrepressalien, GULag," February 1998, Hamburger Institut für Sozialforschung, p. 8.

92. Khaustov, p. 13.

93. Ibid.; Firsov, "Dimitroff," p. 8.

94. Khaustov, pp. 13–14.

95. Ibid., p. 14.

96. *Revelations from the Russian Archives*, p. 90.

97. Khaustov, p. 15; V. Khaustov, "Repressii protiv sovetskikh nemtsev do nachala massovoi operatsii 1937 g.," in *Repressii protiv rossiiskikh nemtsev: Nakazannyi narod* (Moscow, 1999), pp. 75–83, esp. p. 83.

98. Vatlin, "Kaderpolitik," p. 75.

99. APRF, f. 57, op. 1, d. 70, ll. 62–77.

100. Vatlin, p. 66; S. Courtois and J.-L. Panné, "Le Komintern à l'action," in Courtois et al., *Le livre noir*, pp. 299–364, esp. p. 321.

101. Firsov, "Dimitroff," p. 8.

102. Ibid.

103. RTsKhIDNI, f. 17, op. 2, d. 572, ll. 67–73.

104. Getty and Naumov, p. 231.

105. Benvenuti, "The 'Reform' of the NKVD, 1934," p. 1051.

106. *Resolutions and Decisions*, 3: 189.

107. I. V. Stalin, *Sochineniia*, vol. 1 (XIV) (Stanford, Calif., 1967), p. 373.

108. RTsKhIDNI, f. 17, op. 3, d. 976.

109. TsA FSB, f. 3-os, op. 6, d. 4, ll. 1–29. Malenkov's son relates in a memoir of his father that in 1936 Ezhov was sent to Germany "for treatment for pederasty": A. Malenkov, *O moem ottse Georgii Malenkove* (Moscow, 1992), p. 35. This is complete nonsense. Ezhov's problem began to be discussed only following his testimony after arrest. Before, it was a problem neither for Ezhov nor for the Party. The later accusation that during his trip to Germany he had studied or copied Gestapo methods is also nonsense; when important leaders traveled abroad for medical treatment, this was more or less their private business; such trips never had an official character, nor could there have been any "exchange of experience" under the conditions of the relations between the USSR and Germany at that time.

110. *Genrikh Iagoda*, p. 163.

111. Khlevniuk, *Politbiuro*, p. 203.

112. *Reabilitatsiia*, p. 216; "Materialy," *Voprosy istorii* 1994, no. 12: 16–17; APRF, f. 57, op. 1, d. 28, l. 177; Getty and Naumov, pp. 200–201.

113. In 1932 Trotskii's son Sedov, with Trotskii's approval, had indeed formed what they called a "bloc" with oppositionists inside the USSR. It did not mean much, nor did it have any violent intentions, as far as can be judged; moreover, the bloc probably never really functioned. In June–July 1936, via a Soviet agent abroad, information about the bloc reached Stalin. Among other things, the correspondence showed that Ivan Smirnov had proposed to Trotskii's son to form inside the Soviet Union a united opposition of Trotskiists, Zinov'evists, and so on. See P. Broué, "Trotsky et le bloc des oppositions de 1932," *Les Cahiers Léon Trotsky* 1980 (January–March): 5–37; R. W. Thurston, *Life and Terror in Stalin's Russia* (New Haven, Conn., 1996), pp. 25–26; Getty and Naumov, p. 257.

114. "Materialy," *Voprosy istorii* 1994, no. 10: 22–23, 26; *Reabilitatsiia*, pp. 179–80.

115. *Reabilitatsiia*, p. 176; Briukhanov and Shoshkov, *Opravdaniiu*, p. 51.

116. *Izvestiia TsK KPSS* 1989, no. 8: 83–84.

117. *Reabilitatsiia*, p. 218.

118. Ibid., pp. 177, 186.

119. Getty and Naumov, pp. 250–55.

120. APRF, f. 57, op. 1, d. 189.

121. Ibid., d. 172, ll. 1–540.

122. *Reabilitatsiia*, pp. 182–83.

123. *Izvestiia TsK KPSS* 1989, no. 9: 36–37; Getty and Naumov, pp. 282–83.

124. "Materialy," *Voprosy istorii* 1994, no. 12: 18.

125. *Izvestiia TsK KPSS* 1989, no. 5: 70.

126. *Rodina* 1996, no. 2: 91.

127. APRF, f. 45, op. 1, d. 729, ll. 83–84; B. A. Starkov, quoting the part of the letter dealing with the Rightists, incorrectly supposes that it was written ten days after Ezhov took up the post of NKVD chief, that is, in early October: B. A. Starkov, "Narkom Ezhov," in J. A. Getty and R. T. Manning, eds., *Stalinist Terror: New Perspectives* (Cambridge, Eng., 1993), pp. 21–39, esp. pp. 28–29.

128. Quoted in Khlevniuk, p. 205.

129. APRF, f. 45, op. 1, d. 729, l. 85.

130. Quoted in Khlevniuk, pp. 205–6.

131. Ibid., pp. 205–6.

132. *Izvestiia*, 10 September 1936.

Chapter 3

1. APRF, f. 57, op. 1, d. 27, ll. 1–14.

2. Ibid., ll. 15–22; ibid., f. 45, op. 1, d. 729, ll. 86–89.

3. Ibid., f. 57, op. 1, d. 27, ll. 23–26.

4. Ibid., f. 45, op. 1, d. 94, l. 123. See also, *Reabilitatsiia: Politicheskie protsessy 30–50-kh godov* (Moscow, 1991), p. 221; D. Volkogonov, *Triumf i tragediia* (Moscow, 1990), 1: 468.

5. See "Materialy fevral'sko-martovskogo plenuma TsK VKP(b) 1937 goda," *Voprosy istorii* 1994, no. 10: 22–23; *Izvestiia TsK KPSS* 1989, no. 8: 83–84.

6. *Stalinskoe Politbiuro v 30-e gody* (Moscow, 1995), p. 150. Decision of VTsIK Presidium of 26 September to appoint Ezhov People's Commissar of Internal Affairs: *Izvestiia*, 27 September 1936.

7. V. Rogovin, *Partiia rasstreliannykh* (Moscow, 1997), p. 179.

8. TsA FSB, examination record of Pauker.

9. Ibid., Archival investigation case of Frinovskii, N-15301, t. 13, ll. 1–27. After arrest, during interrogation, Iagoda stated that in September 1936 on his instructions an assistant had tapped phone calls of Stalin with Ezhov, and the assistant had reported to Iagoda that "Stalin summons Ezhov to his presence in Sochi": *Genrikh Iagoda: Narkom vnutrennikh del SSSR, General'nyi komissar gosudarstvennoi bezopasnosti: Sbornik dokumentov* (Kazan', 1997), p. 147.

10. B. A. Starkov, "Narkom Ezhov," in J. A. Getty and R. T. Manning, eds., *Stalinist Terror: New Perspectives* (Cambridge, Eng., 1993), pp. 21–39, esp. p. 28.

11. *Stalinskoe Politbiuro*, pp. 148, 152.

12. TsA FSB, f. 3-os, op. 6, d. 3, ll. 81–82.

13. Ibid., Archival investigation case of Frinovskii, N-15301, t. 7, ll. 179–81; t. 13, ll. 1–27. On Litvin, see B. B. Briukhanov and E.N. Shoshkov, *Opravdaniiu ne podlezhit: Ezhov i ezhovshchina 1936–1938* (St. Petersburg, 1998), pp. 35–36, 61.

14. A. Larina (Bukharina), *Nezabyvaemoe* (Moscow, 1989), pp. 269–70.

15. M. Shreider, *NKVD iznutri: Zapiski chekista* (Moscow, 1995), p. 35.

16. TsA FSB, Archival investigation case of Frinovskii, N-15301, t. 7, l. 193.

17. APRF, f. 3, op. 24, d. 241, l. 213; *Izvestiia TsK KPSS* 1989, no. 9: 39.

18. J. A. Getty and O. V. Naumov, *The Road to Terror: Stalin and the Self-Destruction of the Bolsheviks, 1932–1939* (New Haven, Conn., 1999), p. 273.

19. APRF, f. 3, op. 24, d. 242, ll. 173–74.

20. *Reabilitatsiia*, p. 248.

21. Ibid.

22. APRF, f. 57, op. 1, d. 176; RTsKhIDNI, f. 671, op. 1, d. 176, ll. 66–74.

23. Stenographic report of the December 1936 Central Committee Plenum, RTsKhIDNI, f. 17, op. 2, d. 575, ll. 6–68; "Fragmenty stenogrammy dekabr'skogo plenuma TsK VKP(b) 1936 goda," *Voprosy istorii* 1995, no. 1: 3–22, esp. pp. 3–7, 18–19.

24. RTsKhIDNI, f. 17, op. 2, d. 573, l. 2.

25. *Reabilitatsiia*, p. 225.

26. *Rodina* 1995, no. 10: 63–64; *Istochnik* 2001, no. 1: 63–77.

27. RTsKhIDNI, f. 17, op. 3, d. 983, l. 50.

28. I. V. Stalin, *Sochineniia*, vol. 1 (XIV) (Stanford, Calif., 1967), pp. 189–91.

29. "Materialy," *Voprosy istorii* 1992, no. 4–5: 3–16; 1993, no. 2: 24–33; no. 7: 23–24; *Reabilitatsiia*, pp. 252, 255–57; "Konets kar'ery," *Istoricheskii arkhiv* 1992, no. 1: 121–31, esp. p. 124; Larina, *Nezabyvaemoe*, p. 360; R. Conquest, *The Great Terror: A Reassessment* (London, 1990), p. 174.

30. "Materialy," *Voprosy istorii* 1994, no. 2: 19–29; no. 10: 13–27.

31. Getty and Naumov, pp. 421, 432.

32. *Voprosy istorii* 1995, no. 2: 25.

33. TsA FSB, f. 3, op. 4, d. 147, l. 34.

34. *Rossiiskaia gazeta*, 6 November 1993.

35. B. A. Starkov, in *Oni ne molchali* (Moscow, 1991), p. 217. See also, G. M. Ivanova, *GULAG v sisteme totalitarnogo gosudarstva* (Moscow, 1997), p. 152.

36. TsKhSD, f. 89, list 48, doc. 2.

37. Redens's statement to Beriia, 21 December 1938, TsA FSB, f. 3, op. 5, d. 84, l. 147; Frinovskii's statement to the same, 11 April 1939, ibid., Archival investigation case of Frinovskii, N-15301, t. 2, l. 44.

38. See interrogation of L. G. Mironov, 20 June 1937, ibid., op. 4, d. 71, l. 59.

39. See the report of Ezhov to the June 1937 Central Committee Plenum, ibid., d. 20, ll. 309–15.

40. *Genrikh Iagoda*, pp. 134–35, 163–65. For anyone with some knowledge of chemistry, Bulanov's confessions, confirmed at the 1938 trial, sound like complete nonsense. Mercury does not dissolve in sulfuric acid, as Bulanov testified—only in nitric acid—and even assuming that it was nitric acid, the resulting solution does not evaporate and would have been dangerous only when absorbed by the organism—that is, a victim would have had to lick the impregnated carpets and door curtains.

41. R. C. Tucker and S. F. Cohen, eds., *The Great Purge Trial* (New York, 1965), pp. 480, 482, 512, 578.

42. TsA FSB, Archival investigation case of Frinovskii, N-15301, t. 2, l. 40; ibid., f. 3-os, op. 6, d. 3, l. 374; G. Tsitriniak, "Rasstrel'noe delo Ezhova: Shtrikhi k portretu palacha," *Literaturnaia gazeta* 1992, no. 7.

43. "Poslednee slovo Nikolaia Ezhova," *Moskovskie novosti* 1994, no. 5; Briukhanov and Shoshkov, p. 151.

44. TsA FSB, f. 3-os, op. 6, d. 2, l. 163.

45. See V. Topolianskii, *Vozhdi v zakone* (Moscow, 1996), p. 314; I. B. Zbarskii, " 'Zhizn' 'mumii i sud'ba cheloveka: Iz vospominanii khranitelia tela Lenina," *Otechestvennaia istoriia* 1993, no. 5: 158–64, esp. p. 163.

46. *Reabilitatsiia*, pp. 238–39.

47. APRF, f. 3, op. 24, d. 409, l. 197; *Butovskii poligon, 1937– 1938 gg.: Kniga pamiati zhertv politicheskikh repressii*, vol. 2 (Moscow, 1998), pp. 39–40; A. Kokurin and N. Petrov, "GULAG: Struktura i kadry. Stat'ia piataia (Dmitlag)," *Svobodnaia mysl'* 2000, no. 1: 108– 23, esp. p. 114.

48. See Ezhov's order of 7 June 1937, TsA FSB, f. 66, op. 1, d. 395, l. 101.

49. Report of the NKVD personnel department, ibid., f. 3, op. 5, d. 996, ll. 188–89. Figures vary: this is the most accurate one available; it relates to state security officers properly, excluding the frontier and internal troops, militia, and Gulag people. Other figures available relate to different categories and/or periods. In 1963 a CPSU Central Committee Commission reported that from October 1936 to July 1938, "according to incomplete data," 7,298 NKVD employees had been re-

pressed (" 'Massovye repressii opravdany byt' ne mogut,' " *Istochnik* 1995, no. 1: 117–32, esp. p. 121). If the militia and NKVD troops are taken into account, this figure approximates the truth. From 1 October 1936 to 15 August 1938, 2,273 state security employees, 4,490 militia employees, and 813 frontier and internal troops employees were repressed (TsA FSB, f. 3, op. 5, d. 996, ll. 188–92); together that makes 7,576 people, approximating the 1963 CC Commission figure.

Yet another figure originates from Ezhov himself, who in his later trial claimed to have purged no less than 14,000 Chekists (D. Likhanov and V. Nikonov, " 'Ia pochistil OGPU,' " *Sovershenno sekretno* 1992, no. 4). This figure refers to the personnel of all NKVD subdivisions, including other categories of repressed NKVD employees: militia and registry office, frontier and internal troops, Gulag, fire service, weights and measures, and reserves inspection. Ezhov may also have included in his estimate people who had only been dismissed.

Still higher figures of 20,000 or more repressed NKVD people were launched by the KGB during perestroika in order to stress how much the Chekists themselves had suffered during the Stalinist terror. These figures relate to broader categories, however, and to a longer period, that is, 1933–39. According to this information, during these years 22,618 OGPU-NKVD employees were arrested, 9,462 of them during 1937–38 (TsA FSB, f. 3-os, op. 6, d. 33, l. 4). The figures include the militia, NKVD troops, Gulag, registry office, etc., the majority of whom were condemned for malfeasances in office (embezzlement, theft, forgery, and other nonpolitical crimes).

50. Starkov, "Narkom," pp. 30–32; B. A. Starkov, "The Trial That Was Not Held," *Europe-Asia Studies* 1994, no. 8: 1297–1315, esp. p. 1305; Conquest, *The Great Terror*, pp. 179–80; Likhanov and Nikonov; O. V. Khlevniuk, *1937-i: Stalin, NKVD i sovetskoe obshchestvo* (Moscow, 1992), p. 165 (for inducements).

51. Testimony of A. P. Radzivilovskii, *Pravda*, 29 April 1988; see also, Starkov, "Narkom," p. 33.

52. O. F. Suvenirov, *Tragediia RKKA 1937–1938* (Moscow, 1998), pp. 147–48.

53. TsA FSB, f. 3-os, op. 4, d. 6, ll. 53–54.

54. Ibid., f. 3, op. 4, d. 21, l. 8.

55. E. Gorbunov, "Voennaia razvedka v 1934–1939 godakh," *Svobodnaia mysl'* 1998, no. 3: 54–61, esp. pp. 55–57; *Oktiabr'* 1997, no. 2: 151.

56. *Istoricheskii arkhiv* 1995, no. 4: 53.

57. Gorbunov, p. 57. See also, TsA FSB, Archival investigation case of Frinovskii, N-15301, t. 15, l. 325.

58. RTsKhIDNI, f. 17, op. 162, d. 21.

59. *Svobodnaia mysl'* 1998, no. 8: 93; see also, Gorbunov, p. 55, and *Voenno-istoricheskii zhurnal* 1993, no. 2: 79.

60. Gorbunov, p. 58.

61. RTsKhIDNI, f. 17, op. 162, d. 21, l. 133.

62. *Svobodnaia mysl'* 1998, no. 8: 91; Gorbunov, p. 58.

63. Gorbunov, p. 59.

64. Ibid., p. 60; see also, TsA FSB, f. 3, op. 5, d. 77, *iskhodiashchii nomer* 107506.

65. Gorbunov, p. 60.

66. V. Kochik, "Sovetskaia voennaia razvedka: struktura i kadry," *Svobodnaia mysl'* 1998, no. 9–12: 98–117, esp. p. 98.

67. The Soviet intelligence officer Ignatii Reiss (Poretskii), who fled in 1937, was murdered on 4 September of the same year near Lausanne by NKVD agents, supervised by GUGB Foreign Department Deputy Chief Sergei Shpigel'glaz. Supposedly, Stalin wanted Reiss's deliberately demonstrative execution to serve as a warning to others. See N. Petrov, "Ubiistvo Ignatiia Reissa," *Moskovskie novosti* 1995, no. 63. That same month, on 22 September, the leading military émigré, General Evgenii Miller, was kidnapped in Paris by NKVD agents, also under Shpigel'-glaz's supervision. He was transferred to the Soviet Union and tried there. See N. Petrov and N. Gevorkian, "Konets agenta '13,'" ibid. 1995, no. 86.

68. TsA FSB, Archival investigation case of Frinovskii, N-15301, t. 3, ll. 117–22.

69. Ibid., ll. 122–23; see also, Petrov, "Ubiistvo."

70. A. Khinshtein and M. Gridneva, "Konets khoziaina Lubianki," *MK v voskresen'e*, 7 June 1998.

71. *Ocherki istorii Rossiiskoi vneshnei razvedki*, vol. 3 (Moscow, 1997), p. 17.

72. TsA FSB, f. 3-os, op. 4, d. 6, l. 29.

73. "M. N. Tukhachevskii i 'voenno-fashistskii zagovor.' " *Voenno-istoricheskii arkhiv*, no. 1 (Moscow, 1997): 149–255, esp. p. 179; *Pravda*, 29 April 1988.

74. S. Iu. Ushakov and A. A. Stukalov, *Front voennykh prokurorov* (Moscow, 2000), p. 71.

75. *Izvestiia TsK KPSS* 1989, no. 4: 50.

76. Report of the Party Commission headed by N. Shvernik, June 1964, *Voennye arkhivy Rossii*, no. 1 (Moscow, 1993): 29–113; "O masshtabakh repressii v Krasnoi Armii v predvoennye gody," *Voenno-istoricheskii zhurnal* 1993, no. 2: 71–80, esp. p. 72; *Reabilitatsiia*, pp. 282, 284, 289, 291, 295, 299, 308, 310; *Istochnik* 1994, no. 3: 80; N. Werth, "Un état contre son peuple," in S. Courtois et al., *Le livre noir du communisme* (Paris, 1997), pp. 43–295, esp. p. 220; "M. N. Tukhachevskii," p. 201; "M. N. Tukhachevskii," *Voenno-istoricheskii arkhiv*, no. 2 (Moscow, 1998): 3–81, esp. p. 43.

77. *Novaia i noveishaia istoriia* 1988, no. 6: 4.

78. "O masshtabakh," *Voenno-istoricheskii zhurnal* 1993, no. 1: 55–63, esp. pp. 56–57; no. 5: 59–65, esp. p. 63. See also: R. R. Reese, *Stalin's Reluctant Soldiers: A Social History of the Red Army* (Lawrence, Kan., 1996), pp. 132–34; "Massovye repressii," p. 126; *Voprosy istorii* 1997, no. 1: 164.

79. "Statistika antiarmeiskogo terrora," *Voenno-istoricheskii arkhiv*, no. 2: 105–17. Another figure in the same source (p. 114): 38,352 dismissed, 9,900 of them arrested. According to O. Suvenirov (*Tragediia, RKKA*, pp. 137, 301), during 1937–39 more than 11,000 Red Army officers and political commissars were arrested on charges of conspiracy, terrorism, counterrevolution, espionage, sabotage, etc. (excluding those arrested by the NKVD after dismissal).

80. A. G. Solov'ev, "Tetradi krasnogo professora (1912–1941 gg.)," *Neizvestnaia Rossiia, xx vek*, no. 4 (Moscow, 1993): 140–228, esp. p. 194.

81. Khlevniuk's opinion that the commission under Ezhov's leadership played a prominent role in preparing the repression is incorrect: O. V. Khlevniuk, *Politbiuro: Mekhanizmy politicheskoi vlasti v 1930-e gody* (Moscow, 1996), p. 191; see also, *Stalinskoe Politbiuro*, p. 58.

82. Khlevniuk, *Politbiuro*, pp. 237–39. According to Khlevniuk, the commission of five was designed primarily to examine questions relating to the NKVD's activity: O. Khlevnyuk, "The Objectives of the Great Terror, 1937–1938," in J. Cooper et al., eds., *Soviet History, 1917–53: Essays in Honour of R. W. Davies* (London, 1995), pp. 158–76, esp. p. 166.

83. Khlevniuk, *Politbiuro*, p. 251.

84. See Getty and Naumov, pp. 358–60, 463; S. Fitzpatrick, *Everyday Stalinism* (New York, 2000), p. 200.

85. O. Chlewnjuk, "Partei und NKWD: Die Machtsverhältnisse in den Jahren des 'grossen Terrors,'" paper for workshop "Stalinistischer Terror, Massenrepressalien, GULag," February 1998, Hamburger Institut für Sozialforschung, p. 9.

86. F. I. Firsov, "Stalin i Komintern," *Voprosy istorii* 1989, no. 9: 3–19, esp. p. 15.

87. A. Vatlin, "Kaderpolitik und Säuberungen in der Komintern," in H. Weber and U. Mählert, eds., *Terror: Stalinistische Parteisäuberungen 1936–1953* (Paderborn, 1998), pp. 33–119, esp. p. 82. Another source mentions Wilhelm Florin instead of Manuil'skii: S. Courtois and J.-L. Panné, "Le Komintern à l'action," in Courtois et al., pp. 299–364, esp. p. 327.

88. Vatlin, pp. 110–11.

89. F. I. Firsov, "Dimitroff, Komintern und Stalinsche Repressalien," paper for workshop "Stalinistischer Terror, Massenrepressalien, GULag," February 1998, Hamburger Institut für Sozialforschung, p. 12.

90. Ibid., p. 13; V. V. Mar'ina, "Dnevnik G. Dimitrova," *Voprosy istorii* 2000, no. 7: 32–55, esp. p. 36.

91. See note 90 above.

92. TsA FSB, f. 3-os, op. 4, d. 6, l. 21.

93. GUGB NKVD Directives, 14 February and 2 April 1937: N. Okhotin and A. Roginskii, "Iz istorii 'nemetskoi operatsii' NKVD 1937–1938 gg.," *Repressii protiv rossiiskikh nemtsev: Nakazannyi narod* (Moscow, 1999), pp. 35–75, esp. pp. 40–41.

94. Ibid., p. 45.

95. W. N. Chaustow, "Repressalien gegen Deutsche in den 30er Jahren," paper for workshop "Stalinistischer Terror, Massenrepressalien, GULag," February 1998, Hamburger Institut für Sozialforschung, p. 2.

96. S. V. Bezberezh'ev, "Mariia Aleksandrovna Spiridonova," *Voprosy istorii* 1990, no. 9: 65–81, esp. p. 81.

97. *Bol' liudskaia: Kniga pamiati tomichei, repressirovannykh v 30–40-e i nachale 50-kh godov* (Tomsk, 1991), p. 148.

98. D. B. Pavlov, *Bol'shevistskaia diktatura protiv sotsialistov i anarkhistov, 1917-seredina 1950-kh godov* (Moscow, 1999), pp. 96–98.

99. APRF, f. 45, op. 1, d. 729, ll. 93–95.

100. A. F. Stepanov, *Rasstrel po limitu: Iz istorii politicheskikh repressii v TASSR v gody "ezhovshchiny"* (Kazan', 1999), p. 154.

101. "O masshtabakh," *Voenno-istoricheskii zhurnal* 1993, no. 5: 59–65, esp. p. 61.

102. TsA FSB, f. 3, op. 4, d. 92, ll. 320–25.

103. Stepanov, p. 154.

104. TsA FSB, f. 3, op. 4, d. 20, ll. 117–22. I. P. Rumiantsev had been arrested on 17 June 1937 by Kaganovich, who had been especially delegated to Smolensk by the Politburo (in October he was tried and shot); the arrest initiated a great purge in the Smolensk provincial Party organization. See R. Manning, "Massovaia operatsiia protiv kulakov i prestupnykh elementov: apogei Velikoi Chistki na Smolenshchine," in *Stalinizm v rossiiskoi provintsii* (Smolensk, 1999), pp. 230–54, esp. pp. 232–33, 235–36, 247.

105. TsA FSB, f. 3, op. 4, d. 20, l. 297.

106. TsKhSD, f. 89, op. 48, d. 12. On 2 October 1937 Stalin and Molotov issued a similar order concerning sabotage in the livestock sector (ibid., d. 20). As a consequence, on 15 August 1937 the Western Siberian Party leadership ordered the regional Procuracy and NKVD within five days to prepare the organization of show trials in the districts against "enemies of the people—saboteurs of agriculture," to be attended by kolkhozniki and given broad press publicity. One such trial took place in the Northern district on 18–20 September. On 2 October the first secretary of the Western Siberian Provincial Party Committee, R. I. Eikhe, reported to Stalin on the results of these trials. All in all, during August–October 1937, as a result of Stalin's instruction of 3 August, more than thirty trials were organized in the rural districts; the sentences in these trials were predetermined by Stalin: I. V. Pavlova, "Sovremennye zapadnye istoriki o stalinskoi Rossii 30-kh godov (Kritika 'revizionistskogo' podkhoda)," *Otechestvennaia istoriia* 1998, no. 5: 107–21, esp. p. 117; S. A. Papkov, *Stalinskii terror v Sibiri 1928–1941* (Novosibirsk, 1997), pp. 214–15. For the execution of Stalin's orders in Kiev province: *Arkhivy Kremlia i Staroi Ploshchadi: Dokumenty po "delu KPSS"* (Novosibirsk, 1995), p. 20; for Smolensk: Manning, p. 242. See also, S. Fitzpatrick, "How the Mice Buried the Cat: Scenes from the Great Purges of 1937 in the Russian Provinces," *Russian Review* 1993, no. 3: 299–320; M. Ellman, "The Soviet 1937 Provincial Show Trials: Carnival or Terror?" *Europe-Asia Studies* 2001, no. 8: 122–33.

107. TsA FSB, f. 3, op. 4, d. 20, l. 344.

108. Ibid., ll. 341, 343, 347.

109. Minutes of the June 1937 Plenum, RTsKhIDNI, f. 17, op. 2, d. 614, ll. 1–4; d. 621, l. 14; V. Rogovin, *1937* (Moscow, 1996), pp. 440,

446–47; for biographies of expelled CC members, *Izvestiia TsK KPSS* 1989, no. 12.

110. According to Piatnitskii's relatives, at the Plenum a number of Central Committee members had intended to "publicly come out against the terror and, by consequence, against Stalin." Allegedly, during the Plenum Kaminskii and Piatnitskii had indeed protested against prolonging NKVD's full powers, as proposed by Ezhov and Stalin. This version is not supported by any documentary evidence, however. See V. Piatnitskii, *Zagovor protiv Stalina* (Moscow, 1998), pp. 45, 55, 61–67, 83, 100–101, 362–63, 365–66. Moreover, at the Plenum there could be no question of prolonging any extraordinary powers, since these had never been given to the NKVD.

111. Chlewnjuk, "Partei und NKWD," pp. 5–6.

112. TsA FSB, Archival investigation case of Frinovskii, N-15301, t. 9, ll. 190–91. According to one source, Nosov had already been pressured by the NKVD in April 1937 to sanction the arrest of some former Trotskiists working in Ivanovo; when he refused, he was accused of protectionism: Solov'ev, p. 192. See also, for attacks on Nosov, *Pravda*, 13 May and 4 July 1937.

Chapter 4

1. APRF, f. 3, op. 58, d. 212, l. 31.

2. TsA FSB, f. 3, op. 4, d. 97, ll. 222–23, 258–59.

3. O. Khlevnyuk, "The Objectives of the Great Terror, 1937–1938," in J. Cooper et al., eds., *Soviet History, 1917–53* (London, 1995), pp. 158–76, esp. p. 160.

4. *Spetspereselentsy v Zapadnoi Sibiri, 1933–1938 gg.* (Novosibirsk, 1994), pp. 70–72.

5. APRF, f. 3, op. 58, d. 166, ll. 151–54. See also, V. N. Zemskov, "Zakliuchennye v 1930-e gody: sotsial'no-demograficheskie problemy," *Otechestvennaia istoriia* 1997, no. 4: 54–79, esp. pp. 66–67; P. Hagenloh, " 'Socially Harmful Elements' and the Great Terror," in S. Fitzpatrick, ed., *Stalinism: New Directions* (London, 2000), pp. 286–308, esp. p. 300; G. Rittersporn, " 'Vrednye elementy,' 'opasnye men'shinstva' i bol'shevistskie trevogi: massovye operatsii 1937–38 gg. i etnicheskii vopros v SSSR," in T. Vikhavainen and I. Takala, eds., *V sem'e edinoi: Natsional'naia politika partii bol'shevikov i ee osushchestvlenie na*

Severo-Zapade Rossii v 1920–1950-e gody (Petrozavodsk, 1998), pp. 99–122, esp. p. 103.

6. N. Werth, "Un état contre son peuple: Violence, répressions, terreurs en Union soviétique," in S. Courtois et al., *Le livre noir du communisme: Crimes, terreur et répression* (Paris, 1997), pp. 43–295, esp. pp. 208–9.

7. RTsKhIDNI, f. 17, op. 162, d. 21, l. 89. See also, *Trud*, 4 June 1992, 2 August and 17 October 1997. For Ezhov's confirmation to the regional NKVD organs, 4 July, see M. M. Shytiuk, "Masovi represiï na terytoriï Mykolaïvshchyny (30-ti rr. XX st.)," *Ukraïnskyi istorychnyi zhurnal* 1998, no. 1: 94–98, esp. pp. 94–95.

8. RTsKhIDNI, f. 17, op. 162, d. 21, ll. 94–118.

9. *Trud*, 2 August 1997; the slight miscalculation seems to be Mironov's.

10. APRF, f. 3, op. 58, d. 212, l. 38.

11. TsA FSB, f. 3, op. 4, d. 147, ll. 348–49.

12. Ibid., Archival investigation case of Frinovskii, N-15301, t. 7, ll. 33–34.

13. M. Shreider, *NKVD iznutri: Zapiski chekista* (Moscow, 1995), pp. 41–42. During the briefing Radzivilovskii was not yet the Ivanovo NKVD chief: his predecessor, V. A. Styrne, had been invited there, and Radzivilovskii was only appointed on 20 July; he probably attended in his former capacity as Moscow NKVD deputy chief.

14. N. V. Petrov and K. V. Skorkin, *Kto rukovodil NKVD, 1934–1941: Spravochnik* (Moscow, 1999). For Agranov, see also, *Sovetskoe rukovodstvo. Perepiska. 1928–1941 gg.* (Moscow, 1999), pp. 364–65.

15. TsA FSB, f. 3-os, op. 6, d. 3, ll. 409–10.

16. See the testimony of the former Armenian NKVD deputy chief, N. V. Kondakov, May 1939: ibid., f. 3-os, op. 6, d. 4, l. 207; and ibid., Archival investigation case of S. F. Redens. According to R. Medvedev, probably citing oral sources, Ezhov explained that the Soviet Union was going through a dangerous period in which war with fascism was imminent and the NKVD must therefore destroy all nests of fascists in the country: "Of course there will be some innocent victims in this fight against fascist agents. We are launching a major attack on the enemy; let there be no resentment if we bump someone with an elbow. Better that ten innocent people should suffer than one spy get away. When you cut down the forest, woodchips fly." R. Medvedev, *Let History Judge:*

The Origins and Consequences of Stalinism, rev. ed. (Oxford, 1989), p. 603.

17. TsA FSB, Archival investigation case of Frinovskii, N-15301, t. 7, ll. 34–36.

18. Ibid., f. 3-os, op. 6, d. 3, ll. 409–10.

19. *Bol' liudskaia: Kniga pamiati repressirovannykh tomichei* (Tom piatyi; Tomsk, 1999), pp. 102–3, 110–11. See also: S. A. Papkov, *Stalinskii terror v Sibiri 1928–1941* (Novosibirsk, 1997), p. 211; A. G. Tepliakov, "Personal i povsednevnost' Novosibirskogo UNKVD v 1936–1946," *Minuvshee*, no. 21 (Moscow–St. Petersburg, 1997): 240–93, esp. p. 254.

20. TsA FSB, f. 3, op. 4, d. 147, ll. 377, 385.

21. Ibid., d. 2308, incoming telegram No. 22641/1303.

22. Order No. 00447, published in full in *Kniga pamiati zhertv politicheskikh repressii* (Ul'ianovsk, 1996), pp. 766–80, in shortened form in *Trud*, 4 June 1992. See also, *Moskovskie novosti* 1992, no. 25.

23. RTsKhIDNI, f. 17, op. 162, d. 21, ll. 116–17; J. A. Getty and O. V. Naumov, *The Road to Terror: Stalin and the Self-Destruction of the Bolsheviks, 1932–1939* (New Haven, Conn., 1999), pp. 478–80; A. F. Stepanov, *Rasstrel po limitu: Iz istorii politicheskikh repressii v TASSR v gody "ezhovshchiny"* (Kazan', 1999), pp. 49–50.

24. TsA FSB, f. 3, op. 4, d. 2241, l. 650.

25. *Bol' liudskaia*, pp. 102–3.

26. *Istochnik* 1999, no. 5: 85.

27. TsA FSB, f. 3, op. 4, d. 148.

28. Ibid., Archival investigation case of Frinovskii, N-15301, t. 5, ll. 110–11 (Ezhov and Frinovskii received Nasedkin together).

29. Tepliakov, "Personal i povsednevnost'," p. 254.

30. R. Gol'dberg, "Slovo i delo po-sovetski: Poslednii iz NKVD," *Rodina* 1998, no. 9: 85–87, esp. p. 87.

31. RTsKhIDNI, f. 17, op. 162, d. 22, ll. 113, 127; N. Geworkjan, *Der KGB lebt* (Berlin, 1992), pp. 224–36; *Moskovskie novosti* 1992, no. 25; *Trud*, 4 June 1992; *Svobodnaia mysl'* 1994, no. 7–8: 126–27; *Izvestiia*, 3 April 1996; O. V. Khlevniuk, *Politbiuro: Mekhanizmy politicheskoi vlasti v 1930-e gody* (Moscow, 1996), pp. 189–91.

32. These and the following figures have been calculated for a forthcoming publication by Arsenii Roginskii and Oleg Gorlanov (Memorial Society, Moscow).

33. See O. Hlevniuk, "Les mécanismes de la 'Grande Terreur' des années 1937–1938 au Turkménistan," *Cahiers du Monde russe* 1998, no. 1–2: 197–207, esp. pp. 201–2, 204; I. Chukhin, *Kareliia-37: Ideologiia i praktika terrora* (Petrozavodsk, 1999), pp. 13, 77.

34. See Hlevniuk, p. 200.

35. APRF, f. 45, op. 1, d. 57, ll. 107–8.

36. A. G. Tepliakov, "Portrety sibirskikh chekistov (1920–1953 gg.)," *Vozvrashchenie pamiati* no. 3 (Novosibirsk, 1997): 68–113, esp. p. 96; Papkov, *Stalinskii terror v Sibiri*, p. 213; *Moskovskie novosti* 1992, no. 25.

37. TsA FSB, f. 3-os, op. 4, d. 6, l. 61.

38. Ibid., Archival investigation case of Frinovskii, N-15301, t. 7, ll. 36–37.

39. *Sovetskoe rukovodstvo*, p. 388.

40. Tepliakov, "Personal," p. 254.

41. Testimony of a former Karelian NKVD deputy chief during interrogation, cited in Chukhin, *Kareliia-37*, p. 76.

42. NKVD instruction "On foreigners" of 22 August 1937, N. Okhotin and A. Roginskii, "Iz istorii 'nemetskoi operatsii' NKVD 1937–1938 gg.," *Repressii protiv rossiiskikh nemtsev: Nakazannyi narod* (Moscow, 1999), pp. 35–75, esp. p. 46.

43. Order of 28 October 1937, ibid., p. 47.

44. Okhotin and Roginskii, p. 35; F. I. Firsov, "Dimitroff, Komintern und Stalinsche Repressalien," paper for workshop "Stalinistischer Terror, Massenrepressalien, GULag," February 1998, Hamburger Institut für Sozialforschung, p. 9.

45. Operational order of the People's Commissar of Internal Affairs of the USSR, No. 00439, 25 July 1937: *Butovskii poligon, 1937–1938 gg.: Kniga pamiati zhertv politicheskikh repressii* (Moscow, 1997), p. 348.

46. Okhotin and Roginskii, pp. 54–57, 62–63, 67, 71. All in all, in the mass operations some 70,000 Germans were condemned (p. 71).

47. APRF, f. 3, op. 58, d. 254.

48. TsA FSB, Inventory of declassified orders, Order of the NKVD of the USSR, No. 00485; also published in *Butovskii poligon*, pp. 353–54.

49. Ibid.

50. TsKhSD, f. 6, op. 13, t. 6, ll. 8–51. The text of the letter has

been published (with a few minor distortions) in A. Sudoplatov, *Tainaia zhizn' generala Sudoplatova: Pravda i vymysly o moem ottse* (Moscow, 1998), 1: 363–93. On 5 September the Politburo permitted the Special Board to hand down prison sentences of ten years: APRF, f. 3, op. 58, d. 254, ll. 156–57.

51. V. Piatnitskii, *Zagovor protiv Stalina* (Moscow, 1998), pp. 72–73.

52. TsA FSB, f. 3, op. 4, d. 104, ll. 262–74.

53. TsKhSD, Materials of the "Shvernik Commission," d. 3, l. 79.

54. APRF, f. 3, op. 58, d. 254, l. 173.

55. N. V. Petrov and A. B. Roginskii, " 'Pol'skaia operatsiia' NKVD 1937–1938 gg.," *Repressii protiv poliakov i pol'skikh grazhdan* (Moscow, 1997), pp. 22–43, esp. p. 26.

56. Operational order of the People's Commissar of Internal Affairs of the USSR, No. 00593, 20 September 1937: *Memorial-Aspekt* 1993, no. 1; *Butovskii poligon*, pp. 355–56.

57. Petrov and Roginskii, p. 26.

58. For the Latvian operation, see N. Okhotin and A. Roginskii, " 'Latyshskaia operatsiia' 1937–1938 godov: arkhivnyi kommentarii," *30 oktiabria*, no. 4 (2000): 5; Shytiuk, "Masovi represii," p. 96. For the Finnish operation: Chukhin, *Kareliia-37*, pp. 60–61; an operation for the deportation of Iranians: N. F. Bugai and A. M. Gonov, *Kavkaz: narody v eshelonakh (20–60-e gody)* (Moscow, 1998), p. 105.

59. See Ezhov, January 1938, TsA FSB, f. 3, op. 4, d. 40, ll. 3–5.

60. Ibid., op. 6, d. 93, ll. 6–7.

61. Ibid., NKVD cipher communication No. 49721, 3 November 1937.

62. Ibid., NKVD postal telegram, No. 50194, 11 December 1937; NKVD cipher communication to regional organs, No. 233, 1 February 1938. See also, Firsov, "Dimitroff, Komintern und Stalinsche Repressalien," p. 8.

63. Firsov, p. 9.

64. TsA FSB, NKVD cipher communication, No. 1160, 28 May 1938.

65. Petrov and Roginskii, "Pol'skaia operatsiia," pp. 30–31; *Moskovskie novosti* 1992, no. 25.

66. Petrov and Roginskii, p. 33.

67. Ibid., pp. 33, 40.

68. Archive of Moscow Province FSB Directorate, Archival investigation case No. 52668; A. Paczkowski, "Pologne, la 'nation-ennemi,' " in Courtois et al., *Le livre noir du communisme*, pp. 397–428, esp. pp. 399–400.

69. M. M. Panteleev, "Repressii v Kominterne (1937–1938 gg.)," *Otechestvennaia istoriia* 1996, no. 6: 161–68, esp. p. 163.

70. Petrov and Roginskii, p. 33.

71. N. F. Bugai, *L. Beriia-I. Stalinu: "Soglasno Vashemu ukazaniiu"* (Moscow, 1995), pp. 9, 11; same author in *Istoriia SSSR* 1989, no. 6: 136; N. Bugaj, "Die Deportationen der Völker aus der Ukraine, Weissrussland und Moldavien," in D. Dahlmann and G. Hirschfeld, eds., *Lager, Zwangsarbeit, Vertreibung und Deportation* (Essen, 1999), pp. 567–81, esp. p. 569.

72. T. Martin, "The Origins of Soviet Ethnic Cleansing," *Journal of Modern History* 1998, no. 4: 813–61, esp. pp. 852–53.

73. "O vyselenii koreitsev iz Dal'nevostochnogo kraia," *Otechestvennaia istoriia* 1992, no. 6: 140–68; N. Bugai, in *Nezavisimaia gazeta*, 20 September 1997.

74. *Politicheskie represii na Dal'nem Vostoke SSSR v 1920–1950-e gody* (Vladivostok, 1997), p. 256.

75. Martin, "Origins," p. 851.

76. *Trud*, 17 October 1997.

77. *Memorial-Aspekt* 1993, no. 2–3; *Sbornik zakonodatel'nykh i normativnykh aktov o repressiiakh i reabilitatsii zhertv politicheskikh repressii* (Moscow, 1993), pp. 88–93.

78. Okhotin and Roginskii, "Iz istorii," pp. 56–57.

79. Werth, "Un état contre son peuple," p. 212; V. Rogovin, *Partiia rasstreliannykh* (Moscow, 1997), p. 164; Getty and Naumov, *The Road to Terror*, pp. 454–55.

80. *Sovetskaia Belorussiia*, 22 January 1988.

81. O. Chlewnjuk, "Partei und NKWD: Die Machtsverhältnisse in den Jahren des 'grossen Terrors,' " paper for workshop "Stalinistischer Terror, Massenrepressalien, GULag," February 1998, Hamburger Institut für Sozialforschung, p. 9.

82. S. Courtois and J.-L. Panné, "Le Komintern à l'action," in Courtois et al., *Le livre noir*, pp. 299–364, esp. p. 327; Panteleev, *Repressii v Kominterne*.

83. A. Vatlin, "Kaderpolitik und Säuberungen in der Komintern,"

in H. Weber and U. Mählert, eds., *Terror: Stalinistischer Parteisäuberungen 1936–1953* (Paderborn, 1998), pp. 33–119, esp. p. 84.

84. Piatnitskii, *Zagovor protiv Stalina*, p. 339.

85. *Arkhivy Kremlia i Staroi Ploshchadi: Dokumenty po "delu KPSS"* (Novosibirsk, 1995), p. 19.

86. RTsKhIDNI, f. 17, op. 162, d. 22, l. 7.

87. *Arkhivy Kremlia*, p. 20.

88. TsKhSD, f. 89, op. 29, d. 5, l. 1; Tepliakov, "Portrety," p. 93.

89. J. B. Dunlop, *Russia Confronts Chechnya* (Cambridge, Eng., 1998), p. 56; N. F. Bugai, "Pravda o deportatsii chechenskogo i ingushskogo narodov," *Voprosy istorii* 1990, no. 7: 32–44, esp. p. 35.

90. TsKhSD, f. 89, op. 73, d. 147, ll. 1–8.

91. Khlevniuk, *Politbiuro*, pp. 188, 192.

92. "O kul'te lichnosti i ego posledstviiakh," *Izvestiia TsK KPSS* 1989, no. 3: 128–70, esp. p. 137; Werth, "Un état contre son peuple," p. 214.

93. *Reabilitatsiia: Politicheskie protsessy 30–50-kh godov* (Moscow, 1991), p. 39; " 'Massovye repressii opravdany byt' ne mogut,' " *Istochnik* 1995, no. 1: 117–32, esp. p. 124. For the exact figures: APRF, f. 3, op. 24, d. 409, l. 3.

94. "Spravka," TsKhSD, f. 2, op. 1, d. 224, ll. 70–74; *Kommunist* 1990, no. 8: 103; *Istochnik* 1999, no. 5: 81, 83–84; Zhukov: *Molotov, Malenkov, Kaganovich, 1957: Stenogramma iiun'skogo plenuma TsK KPSS i drugie dokumenty* (Moscow, 1998), pp. 38–39. For Molotov on these lists: F. Chuev, *Sto sorok besed s Molotovym* (Moscow, 1991), pp. 439–40, 463.

95. TsA FSB, f. 3-os, op. 6, d. 11, l. 41.

96. Ibid., l. 42. From July 1934 on special collegia, forming part of the regular republican and provincial civil courts, examined NKVD cases. Unlike dvoikas, troikas, etc., they were fully official organs. In August 1938 they were abolished by the new Law on the Judicial System.

97. GARF, f. 9401, op. 1, d. 4157, l. 202.

98. Ibid., f. 9414, op. 1, d. 2877, l. 140.

99. M. Wehner, "Der Grosse Terror 1937–38: Bisherige Interpretationen und neue Erkenntnisse," paper for workshop "Stalinistischer Terror, Massenrepressalien, GULag," February 1998, Hamburger Institut für Sozialforschung, p. 3.

100. Khlevniuk, *Politbiuro*, p. 192.
101. *Istochnik* 1995, no. 1: 120.
102. Werth, "Un état contre son peuple," pp. 224–25.
103. Chuev, *Sto sorok*, pp. 390, 393–94, 416.
104. G. A. Kumanev, "Dve besedy s L.M. Kaganovichem," *Novaia i noveishaia istoriia* 1999, no. 2: 101–22, esp. pp. 113–14, 116.
105. "Demokratiia . . . pod nadzorom NKVD," *Neizvestnaia Rossiia*, no. 2 (Moscow, 1992): 272–81.
106. TsA FSB, f. 3-os, op. 4, d. 6, ll. 34–35, 38–39.
107. See Khlevniuk, *Politbiuro*, p. 195.
108. RTsKhIDNI, f. 17, op. 2, d. 617, l. 167.
109. Ibid., d. 626, ll. 40–41, 62.
110. I. V. Stalin, *Sochineniia*, vol. 1 XIV (Stanford, Calif., 1967), pp. 368–69.
111. "O proekte Konstitutsii Soiuza SSR," ibid., pp. 136–83.
112. TsA FSB, f. 3-os, op. 6, d. 1, ll. 1–2.
113. Ibid., ll. 2–3.
114. Gol'dberg, "Slovo i delo po-sovetski."
115. Hagenloh, "Socially Harmful Elements," p. 301.
116. TsA FSB, Archival investigation case of Frinovskii, N-15301, t. 2, ll. 32–35.
117. B. A. Starkov, "Narkom Ezhov," in J. A. Getty and R. T. Manning, eds., *Stalinist Terror: New Perspectives* (Cambridge, Eng., 1993), pp. 21–39, esp. p. 33; *Pravda*, 29 April 1988.
118. "M. N. Tukhachevskii i 'voenno-fashistskii zagovor,' " *Voenno-istoricheskii arkhiv*, no. 2 (Moscow, 1998): 3–81, esp. pp. 55–56.
119. Ibid., p. 50; see also, V. Shentalinskii, "Okhota v revzapovednike," *Novyi mir* 1998, no. 12: 170–96, esp. p. 180.
120. Papkov, *Stalinskii terror v Sibiri*, p. 269; "Tukhachevskii," *Voenno-istoricheskii arkhiv*, no. 1 (Moscow, 1997): 149–255, esp. p. 179.
121. D. Shepilov, "Vospominaniia," *Voprosy istorii* 1998, no. 4: 3–25, esp. p. 6.
122. O. F. Suvenirov, *Tragediia RKKA 1937–1938* (Moscow, 1998), p. 207.
123. *Reabilitatsiia*, p. 258.
124. APRF, f. 3, op. 24, d. 413, t. 5, l. 122.
125. *Rossiiskaia gazeta*, 19 April 1996; *Kubanskaia ChK: Organy gozbezopasnosti Kubani v dokumentakh i vospominaniiakh* (Krasno-

dar, 1997), p. 147; *Trud,* 17 October 1997; *Reabilitatsiia,* p. 40. At the Central Committee Plenum of June 1957 Kaganovich and Molotov confirmed that an instruction had been sent to the Central Committee members and all provincial committees, permitting the use of torture against prisoners; it had been written by Stalin himself during a Politburo meeting and had been signed by at least Kaganovich and Molotov. Khrushchev declared that during the time of the Twentieth Party Congress of 1956 the relevant document could not be found in the archives because the original had been destroyed; only a copy was found: *Istoricheskii arkhiv* 1993, no. 3: 88–89.

126. Firsov, "Dimitroff, Komintern und Stalinsche Repressalien," p. 6; *Pravda,* 7 April 1989; *Soiuz* 1990, no. 41; *Novoe vremia* 1997, no. 48: 42. See also, R. C. Tucker, *Stalin in Power: The Revolution from Above, 1928–1941* (New York, 1990), pp. 482–85.

Chapter 5

1. RTsKhIDNI, f. 17, op. 3, d. 989, l. 60; *Izvestiia,* 18 July 1937, with Ezhov's photograph.

2. *Izvestiia,* 28 July 1937; APRF, f. 57, op. 1, d. 270, ll. 121–24. *Izvestiia* printed photographs of Kalinin handing over the order to Ezhov (his head shaved) and of Ezhov making his speech.

3. *Izvestiia,* 30 July 1937. The saying was not exactly original: on 27 June the new GUGB Special Department chief in an official document reported that there was a new saying in the army: "This is no fruit [*iagodka*] for you, gentlemen, but hedgehog's gauntlets [*ezhovy rukavitsy*]." O. F. Suvenirov, *Tragediia RKKA 1937–1938* (Moscow, 1998), p. 146. Two weeks earlier, on 13 June, in a private conversation, People's Commissar of Justice Nikolai Krylenko had alluded to the same *ezhovy rukavitsy:* A. G. Solov'ev, "Tetradi krasnogo professora (1912–1941 gg.)," *Neizvestnaia Rossiia, xx vek,* no. 4 (Moscow, 1993): 140–228, esp. p. 194.

4. I. Deutscher and D. King, *The Great Purges* (Oxford, 1984), p. 111.

5. *Stalinskoe Politbiuro v 30-e gody* (Moscow, 1995), p. 159; O. V. Khlevniuk, *Politbiuro: Mekhanizmy politicheskoi vlasti v 1930-e gody* (Moscow, 1996), p. 216; J. A. Getty and O. V. Naumov, *The Road to Terror: Stalin and the Self-Destruction of the Bolsheviks, 1932–1939* (New Haven, Conn., 1999), pp. 462–63, 465.

6. B. Sultanbekov, *Stalin i "Tatarskii sled"* (Kazan', 1995), pp. 197–98. Another source says that Ezhov was preceded by Stalin and Voroshilov only: E. A. Rees, *Stalinism and Soviet Rail Transport, 1928–41* (London, 1995), p. 280.

7. At least in Leningrad: Suvenirov, *Tragediia RKKA,* p. 146.

8. APRF, f. 57, op. 1, d. 270, l. 141; *Izvestiia,* 10 December 1937.

9. *Izvestiia,* 11 December 1937, with Ezhov's photograph.

10. Suvenirov, p. 146.

11. Ibid., pp. 146–47.

12. *Izvestiia,* 21 December 1937.

13. M. Ebon, *Malenkov* (London, 1953), p. 39.

14. Suvenirov, p. 146; A. Khinshtein and M. Gridneva, "Konets khoziaina Lubianki," *MK v voskresen'e,* 7 June 1998. From May through October 1936 alone: Republican Courses of Party Activists, a Party district committee, a chemical industrial complex, a frontier detachment: RTsKhIDNI, f. 17, op. 3, dd. 977–78, 981, 989. See also: E. M. Pospelov, *Imena gorodov: vchera i segodnia (1917–1992)* (Moscow, 1993), p. 32; J. A. Getty, *Origins of the Great Purges: The Soviet Communist Party Reconsidered, 1933–1938* (Cambridge, Eng., 1985), p. 182.

15. "Kak Moska chut' ne stala Stalinodarom," *Izvestiia TsK KPSS* 1990, no. 12: 126–27; B. Starkov, "Narkom Ezhov," in J. A. Getty and R. T. Manning, eds., *Stalinist Terror: New Perspectives* (Cambridge, Eng., 1993), pp. 21–39, esp. p. 37; B. Starkov, "Wie Moskau fast zu Stalinodar geworden wäre," *International Newsletter of Historical Studies on Comintern, Communism, and Stalinism* 3 (1996), no. 7–8: 42–46; N. Zen'kovich, "Stalin protiv," *Parlamentskaia gazeta,* 22 October 1999.

16. Dzhambul, "Pesnia o batyre Ezhove," *Ogonek* 1937, no. 34: 2.

17. Dzhambul, "Poema o narkome Ezhove," *Novyi mir* 1938, no. 1: 92–96. The full text runs to 148 lines; the version here is somewhat abridged.

18. APRF, f. 57, op. 1, d. 270, ll. 67–68.

19. In January 1935 Ezhov lived on Malyi Palashevskii Lane (No. 4, Apt. 8), a side street of Tverskaia Street, not far from Pushkin Square: GARF, f. 1235, op. 15, d. 76, l. 53. Later, probably since 1935, he had an apartment in the Kremlin, in the First Building of the USSR Central Executive Committee (Apt. 87): ibid., op. 30, d. 99.

20. A. Polianskii, "Kak lomali 'zheleznogo narkoma,' " *Sekretnoe dos'e* 1998, no. 2: 68–77, esp. p. 69.

21. A. Polianskii, *Ezhov: Istoriia "zheleznogo" stalinskogo narkoma* (Moscow, 2001), p. 97; B. B. Briukhanov and E. N. Shoshkov, *Opravdaniiu ne podlezhit: Ezhov i ezhovshchina 1936–1938* (St. Petersburg, 1998), p. 122; V. Rogovin, *Partiia rasstreliannykh* (Moscow, 1997), p. 455.

22. Briukhanov and Shoshkov, p. 122.

23. Interview with A. I. Pirozhkova, *Nezavisimaia gazeta,* 16 January 1998.

24. TsA FSB, Archival investigation case of Frinovskii, N-15301, t. 7, l. 198.

25. G. Zhavoronkov, "I snitsia noch'iu den'," *Sintaksis,* no. 32 (1992): 46–65; Briukhanov and Shoshkov, p. 124; Starkov, "Narkom Ezhov," pp. 34–35; B. Kamov, "Smert' Nikolaia Ezhova," *Iunost'* 1993, no. 8: 41–43, esp. p. 41; V. Grossman, "Mama," *Znamia* 1989, no. 5: 8–15; M. Il'ves, "Doch' zheleznogo narkoma," *Moskovskie novosti* 1999, no. 1; M. Franchetti, "Daughter Fights to Clear Stalin's Hitman," *The Sunday Times* (London), 31 January 1999.

26. TsA FSB, f. 3-os, op. 6, d. 2, ll. 109–58.

27. APRF, f. 57, op. 1, d. 265, ll. 16–26-ob.

28. Ibid., f. 3, op. 24, d. 372, l. 119.

29. Ibid., l. 114.

30. *Politicheskii dnevnik,* vol. 2 (Amsterdam, 1975), p. 136.

31. Testimony of Z. V. Ivanova, APRF, f. 3, op. 24, d. 372, ll. 116–28. See also, Ezhov, ibid., f. 57, op. 1, d. 265, ll. 16–26-ob.

32. TsA FSB, f. 3-os, op. 6, d. 3, l. 57.

33. Briukhanov and Shoshkov, *Opravdaniiu ne podlezhit,* p. 34; E. Sinkó, *Roman eines Romans: Moskauer Tagebuch* (Berlin, 1990), esp. 408.

34. Testimony of L. Elisman, APRF, f. 3, op. 24, d. 376, ll. 82–83.

35. V. Shentalinskii, "Okhota v revzapovednike," *Novyi mir* 1998, no. 12: 170–96, esp. p. 179; Briukhanov and Shoshkov, p. 122.

36. TsA FSB, f. 3-os, op. 6, d. 4, l. 238.

37. Ibid., l. 241.

38. Execution lists, Memorial archives, No. 32D-1355.

39. TsA FSB, f. 3-os, op. 6, d. 1, l. 265; d. 3, l. 56.

40. Ibid., d. 1, ll. 266–69.

41. Ibid., ll. 269–70; ibid., Archival investigation case of Frinovskii, N-15301, t. 7, ll. 193–94.

42. Suvenirov, *Tragediia RKKA*, p. 23.

43. RTsKhIDNI, f. 17, op. 2, d. 628, ll. 115–16.

44. Getty and Naumov, *The Road to Terror*, pp. 465–67.

45. I. Takala notes a break from 5 to 20 January 1938; I. Chukhin notes inactivity of the Karelian troika between 31 December 1937 and 17 January 1938. But already on 14 January the NKVD center in Moscow ordered the regional organs to extend the troika activity. See I. Takala, "Natsional'nye operatsii OGPU/NKVD v Karelii," in V. Vikhavainen and I. Takala, eds. *V sem'e edinoi* (Petrozavodsk, 1998), pp. 161–206, esp. pp. 190–91; I. Chukhin, *Kareliia-37: Ideologiia i praktika terrora* (Petrozavodsk, 1999), pp. 18, 147. See also, O. Hlevniuk, "Les mécanismes de la 'Grande Terreur' des années 1937–1938 au Turkménistan," *Cahiers du Monde russe* 1998, no. 1–2: 197–207, esp. 201.

46. RTsKhIDNI, f. 17, op. 2, d. 639, ll. 3–7.

47. Briukhanov and Shoshkov, *Opravdaniiu ne podlezhit*, p. 125.

48. Khlevniuk, *Politbiuro*, p. 255; Getty and Naumov, p. 502.

49. RTsKhIDNI, f. 17, op. 2, d. 639, l. 13.

50. Ibid., d. 640, ll. 1–2.

51. *Pravda*, 19 January 1938; *KPSS v rezoliutsiiakh i resheniiakh s'ezdov, konferentsii i plenumov TsK*, vol. 5 (Moscow, 1971), pp. 303–11 (English transl.: *Resolutions and Decisions of the Communist Party of the Soviet Union*, vol. 3 [Toronto, 1974], pp. 188–95). See also: "Konets kar'ery Ezhova," *Istoricheskii arkhiv* 1992, no. 1: 124; R. W. Thurston, *Life and Terror in Stalin's Russia* (New Haven, Conn., 1996), p. 107; Zhdanov's report to the Eighteenth Party Congress: *XVIII s'ezd Vsesoiuznoi Kommunisticheskoi Partii (b): Stenograficheskii otchet* (Moscow, 1939), pp. 511–44.

52. Stenographic Plenum report: RTsKhIDNI, f. 17, op. 2, d. 630, containing agenda and decisions; see also, list of Plenum guests, 14 January, ibid., ll. 66–68.

53. *Moskovskie novosti*, 1992, no. 25.

54. O. Chlewnjuk, "Partei und NKWD: Die Machtsverhältnisse in den Jahren des 'grossen Terrors,' " paper for workshop "Stalinistischer Terror, Massenrepressalien, GULag," February 1998, Hamburger Institut für Sozialforschung, pp. 11, 19.

55. Politburo decisions of July 1931 (APRF, f. 3, op. 57, d. 36, l.

108) and 17 June 1935 (RTsKhIDNI, f. 17, op. 3, d. 965, l. 75); Central Committee instruction of 13 February 1937 (APRF, f. 3, op. 58, d. 6, l. 28). See also, Central Committee resolution of 23 June 1935 on errors by the Saratov Party Committee: *Izvestiia,* 24 June 1935.

56. TsA FSB, f. 3, op. 5, d. 14, ll. 19–20.

57. Ibid., ll. 20–21.

58. Ibid., Archival investigation case of A. A. Nasedkin, testimony of 16 July 1939.

59. Ibid., f. 3, op. 5, d. 14, l. 341.

60. Ibid., op. 4, d. 40, l. 54 and l. 3.

61. N. V. Petrov and A. B. Roginskii, "Pol'skaia operatsiia NKVD 1937–1938 gg.," *Repressii protiv poliakov i pol'skikh grazhdan* (Moscow, 1997), pp. 22–43, esp. p. 30; N. Okhotin and A. Roginskii, "Iz istorii 'nemetskoi operatsii' NKVD 1937–1938 gg.," *Repressi protiv rossiiskikh nemtsev: Nakazannyi narod* (Moscow, 1999), pp. 35–75, esp. p. 74.

62. TsA FSB, f. 3, op. 4, d. 40, ll. 42–43.

63. Ibid., l. 75.

64. *Izvestiia,* 28 January 1938.

65. TsA FSB, f. 3-os, op. 6, d. 1, ll. 285–86.

66. Ibid., d. 3, ll. 412–13.

67. Ibid., ll. 314–15.

68. Ibid., Case of A. I. Uspenskii.

69. Ibid., f. 3-os, op. 6, d. 1, ll. 266–68.

70. Ibid., f. 3, op. 5, d. 13, ll. 26, 31.

71. *Moskovskie novosti* 1992, no. 25.

72. D. Volkogonov, *Sem' vozhdei* (Moscow, 1995), 1: 341–42; S. Fedoseev, "Favorit Ezhova," *Sovershenno sekretno* 1996, no. 9; *Moskovskie novosti* 1995, no. 63; *Izvestiia,* 3 April 1996.

73. TsA FSB, Archival investigation case of Frinovskii, N-15301, t. 2, ll. 40–42; ibid., f. 3-os, op. 6, d. 3, ll. 375–76.

74. Ibid., Archival investigation case of Frinovskii, N-15301, t. 9, ll. 37–46.

75. TsA FSB, f. 3, op. 5, d. 86, ll. 32–34.

76. Ibid., Archival investigation case of Frinovskii, N-15301, t. 9, ll. 37–46.

77. Ibid., t. 7, l. 196.

78. APRF, f. 3, op. 58, d. 212.

79. Petrov and Roginskii, "Pol'skaia operatsiia," pp. 31, 37; Okhotin and Roginskii, "Iz istorii 'nemetskoi operatsii,' " p. 62.

Chapter 6

1. TsA FSB, Archival investigation case of Frinovskii, N-15301, t. 2, l. 39; ibid., f. 3-os, op. 6, d. 3, l. 374; *Reabilitatsiia: Politicheskie protsessy 30–50-kh godov* (Moscow, 1991), p. 239; *Rossiiskaia gazeta*, 26 January 1996; R. Conquest, *The Great Terror: A Reassessment* (London, 1990), p. 343.

2. APRF, f. 3, op. 24, d. 375, l. 42.

3. For the criticism, *Vodnyi transport*, 28 March 1938, and *Pravda*, 29 March 1938; *Izvestiia TsK KPSS*, 1989, no. 12, p. 108.

4. *Vodnyi transport*, 9 April 1938.

5. APRF, f. 57, op. 1, d. 265, ll. 16–26-ob.

6. See E. A. Rees, *Stalinism and Soviet Rail Transport, 1928–41* (London, 1995), p. 193.

7. *Izvestiia*, 30 May 1938.

8. B. Lewytzkyj, *Die rote Inquisition* (Frankfurt, 1967), p. 152.

9. *Vodnyi transport*, 16 April 1938.

10. Ibid., 18 and 26 April 1938; A. Sudoplatov, *Tainaia zhizn' generala Sudoplatova: Pravda i vymysly o moem ottse* (Moscow, 1998), 1: 406.

11. See Orders of the People's Commissariat of Water Transportation, RGAE, f. 7458, op. 3, dd. 158–62.

12. *Vodnyi transport*, 23 April 1938.

13. RGAE, f. 7458, op. 3, d. 158.

14. APRF, f. 57, op. 1, d. 265, ll. 16–26-ob.

15. See TsA FSB, Archival investigation case of I. I. Shapiro, R-24334, t. 1, l. 229.

16. See A. A. Andreev's report to Stalin of 25 April 1938: *Sovetskoe rukovodstvo: Perepiska 1928–1941 gg.* (Moscow, 1999), p. 393.

17. A. D. Coox, "*L'affaire* Lyushkov: Anatomy of a Defector," *Soviet Studies* 1967–68, no. 3: 405–20; D. Kunert, *General Ljuschkows Geheimbericht: Über die Stalinsche Fernostpolitik 1937/38* (Bern, 1977); *Revelations from the Russian Archives* (Washington, D.C., 1997), pp. 120–21; B. Sokolov, "Sud'ba perebezhchika," *Novosti*

razvedki i kontrrazvedki 2000, no. 13-14. Liushkov is supposed to have been liquidated by the Japanese in Manchuria in August 1945 in order to prevent his falling into Soviet hands.

18. *Istoricheskii arkhiv* 1995, no. 4: 60.

19. TsA FSB, Archival investigation case of Frinovskii, N-15301, t. 2, l. 173.

20. Ibid., ll. 173–75.

21. Ibid., ll. 177–78.

22. "Poslednee slovo Nikolaia Ezhova," *Moskovskie novosti* 1994, no. 5.

23. TsA FSB, Archival investigation case of Frinovskii, N-15301, t. 2, l. 179.

24. APRF, f. 57, op. 1, d. 265, ll. 16–26-ob.

25. TsA FSB, f. 3-os, op. 6, d. 1, ll. 357–83. For the suspicion against Bliukher, see Ezhov's reports to Stalin of 15 April 1938: ibid., f. 3, op. 5, d. 50, ll. 91–92, 211–14.

26. E. Shoshkov, "Ne v svoikh saniakh," *Rodina* 1997, no. 5: 91–94, esp. p. 92. On Mekhlis's contribution: *Voprosy istorii* 1998, no. 10: 78; Iu. Rubtsov, *Alter ego Stalina: Stranitsy politicheskoi biografii L. Z. Mekhlisa* (Moscow, 1999), p. 107. For Frinovskii's report of 28 August 1938 on Bliukher to Stalin et al.: TsA FSB, f. 3, op. 5, d. 72, l. 313.

27. A. G. Solov'ev, "Tetradi krasnogo professora (1912–1941 gg.)," *Neizvestnaia Rossiia, xx vek,* no. 4 (Moscow, 1993): 140–228, esp. p. 198.

28. "O masshtabakh repressii v Krasnoi Armii v predvoennye gody," *Voenno-istoricheskii zhurnal* 1993, no. 3: 25–32, esp. p. 27; "M. N. Tukhachevskii i 'voenno-fashistskii zagovor,' " *Voenno-istoricheskii arkhiv* no. 2 (Moscow, 1998): 3–104, esp. p. 61.

29. TsA FSB, f. 3-os, op. 6, d. 1, l. 350.

30. Ibid., d. 3, l. 316.

31. Ibid., l. 317.

32. The list, containing the names of 134 Chekists to be shot, had been approved by Stalin on 20 August: APRF, f. 3, op. 24, d. 417, ll. 248–53; most of them were shot immediately, on 26 and 29 August.

33. Politburo decision of 15 September 1938, *Moskovskie novosti* 1992, no. 25.

34. See A. I. Uspenskii, April 1939, during interrogation, TsA FSB, Archival investigation case of Frinovskii, N-15301, t. 9, ll. 160–61.

35. See APRF, f. 57, op. 1, d. 264: report by V. P. Cherepneva, 26 March 1938, on the situation in the Georgian Party organization, abuses by Beriia, V. G. Dekanozov, et al., persecution, etc.; and report by the director of the subtropical pavilion of the All-Union Agricultural Exhibition (VSKhV), M. F. Safonov, 21 July 1938, about style and methods of leadership of Beriia, Dekanozov, et al.

36. B. B. Briukhanov and E. N. Shoshkov, *Opravdaniiu ne podlezhit: Ezhov i ezhovshchina 1936–1938* (St. Petersburg, 1998), p. 105. The story's source is A. Antonov-Ovseenko.

37. *Istoricheskii arkhiv* 1995, no. 5-6: 10, 18.

38. Visitors' journal of Ezhov's office: TsA FSB, f. 3, op. 5, d. 92, l. 23.

39. Ibid., l. 25.

40. APRF, f. 57, op. 1, d. 265, ll. 16–26-ob.

41. S. Fedoseev, "Favorit Ezhova," *Sovershenno sekretno* 1996, no. 9.

42. Konstantinov: TsA FSB, f. 3-os, op. 6, d. 3, l. 258; Glikina: V. Shentalinskii, "Okhota v revzapovednike," *Novyi mir* 1998, no. 12: 170–96, esp. p. 180.

43. TsA FSB, Archival investigation case of Frinovskii, N-15301, t. 10, l. 148; t. 13, ll. 116–21.

44. O. V. Khlevniuk, *Politbiuro: Mekhanizmy politicheskoi vlasti v 1930-e gody* (Moscow, 1996), p. 211.

45. See P. Sudoplatov, *Novosti razvedki i kontrrazvedki*, no. 11-12 (1995): 3.

46. *Svobodnaia mysl'* 1997, no. 7: 109.

47. TsA FSB, f. 3-os, op. 6, d. 3, l. 367; ibid., Archival investigation case of Frinovskii, N-15301, t. 2, l. 32.

48. Ibid., Archival investigation case of Frinovskii, N-15301, t. 9, l. 44.

49. Y. Cohen, "Des lettres comme action: Stalin au début des années 1930 vu depuis le fonds Kaganovič," *Cahiers du Monde russe* 1997, no. 3: 307–45, esp. p. 327. Mamuliia preceded Beriia as Georgian First Party Secretary; later he was accused of "deviationism," and in 1937 he was arrested and shot.

50. *Beriia: konets kar'ery* (Moscow, 1991), pp. 374–75. Long before, in 1922, Beriia had been praised for his techniques as a Chekist in Baku, using torture methods in interrogations to force prisoners to con-

fess: B. S. Popov and V. G. Oppokov, "Berievshchina," *Voenno-isto-richeskii zhurnal* 1990, no. 3: 81–90, esp. p. 89; *Sotsialisticheskii vestnik* 1922, no. 16: 12.

51. See A. Chuianov, *Na stremnine veka* (Moscow, 1977), pp. 46–48.

52. M. A. Suslov, *Marksizm-leninizm i sovremennaia epokha* (Moscow, 1982), 1: 11–12.

53. TsA FSB, f. 3-os, op. 6, d. 3, l. 83.

54. *Pisatel' i vozhd': Perepiska M. A. Sholokhova s I. V. Stalinym 1931–1950 gody* (Moscow, 1997), pp. 76–106, 108–27.

55. "Poslednee slovo."

56. TsA FSB, Archival investigation case of I. I. Shapiro, R-24334, t. 1, ll. 93–94.

57. Ibid., Archival investigation case of Frinovskii, N-15301, t. 7, ll. 195–96.

58. Ibid., f. 3-os, op. 6, d. 3, l. 384; d. 4, ll. 158–59.

59. Ibid., Archival investigation case of Frinovskii, N-15301, t. 7, ll. 196–97.

60. J. Berger, *Shipwreck of a Generation* (London, 1971), pp. 123–24.

61. TsA FSB, f. 3–os, op. 6, d. 3, ll. 323–24.

62. Ibid., l. 259.

63. Ibid., Archival investigation case of Frinovskii, N-15301, t. 7, l. 194.

64. Ibid., f. 3-os, op. 6, d. 5, ll. 339, 374; d. 3, l. 86.

65. Ibid., Archival investigation case of E. G. Evdokimov, interrogation protocol of 17 June 1939.

66. Ibid., f. 3-os, op. 6, d. 4, l. 403.

67. Ibid., d. 3, l. 261.

68. Khlevniuk, *Politbiuro,* p. 212; J. A. Getty and O. V. Naumov, *The Road to Terror: Stalin and the Self-Destruction of the Bolsheviks, 1932–1939* (New Haven, Conn., 1999), pp. 529–30.

69. M. Ebon, *Malenkov* (London, 1953), pp. 38–39.

70. F. Chuev, "Chekist," *Molodaia gvardiia* 1996, no. 2: 82–126, esp. p. 86.

71. N. S. Khrushchev, *Vremia. Liudi. Vlast'* (Moscow, 1999), 1: 179.

72. APRF, f. 57, op. 1, d. 265, ll. 16–26-ob.

73. *Molotov, Malenkov, Kaganovich, 1957: Stenogramma iiun'-skogo plenuma TsK KPSS i drugie dokumenty* (Moscow, 1998), p. 44.

Chapter 7

1. *Istoricheskii arkhiv* 1998, no. 5-6: 22.

2. *Pisatel' i vozhd': Perepiska M. A. Sholokhova s I. V. Stalinym 1931–1950 gody* (Moscow, 1997), p. 150.

3. *Istoricheskii arkhiv* 1998, no. 5-6: 22.

4. P. Lugovoi, "S krov'iu i potom: Iz zapisok sekretaria raikoma partii," *Don* 1988, no. 8: 135–43, esp. p. 137; *Pisatel' i vozhd'*, p. 150.

5. *Pisatel' i vozhd'*, p. 148.

6. *Kubanskaia ChK: Organy gosbezopasnosti Kubani v dokumentakh i vospominaniiakh* (Krasnodar, 1997), pp. 144–46.

7. APRF, f. 3, op. 58, d. 212, l. 205.

8. Contrary to what Khlevniuk writes, the delay in preparing the decision was not connected with any rearrangements in the NKVD apparatus. Nor did Stalin have to fear surprises "before the decisive blow." The suspension of the terror was neither a blow to the regional leaders nor a surprise. See O. V. Khlevniuk, *Politbiuro: Mekhanizmy politicheskoi vlasti v 1930-e gody* (Moscow, 1996), p. 212.

9. "Konets kar'ery," *Istoricheskii arkhiv* 1992, no. 1: 121–31, esp. pp. 125–28; "Postanovlenie SNK SSSR i TsK VKP(b) ob arestakh, prokurorskom nadzore i vedenii sledstviia," 17 November 1938: *Organy gosudarstvennoi bezopasnosti SSSR v Velikoi Otechestvennoi voine. Sbornik dokumentov. Tom I. Nakanune. Kniga pervaia (noiabr' 1938-dekabr' 1940 g.* (Moscow, 1995), pp. 3–8; R. W. Thurston, *Life and Terror in Stalin's Russia* (New Haven, Conn., 1996), pp. 114–15.

10. See note 9 above.

11. Rossiiskii gosudarstvennyi arkhiv kinofotodokumentov (RGAKFD), Nos. 0292825 and 0292826.

12. TsA FSB, f. 3, op. 5, d. 83, *iskhodiashchii nomer* 109680.

13. F. Chuev, "Chekist," *Molodaia gvardiia* 1996, no. 2: 82–126, esp. p. 88; *A. I. Mikoian: "Kruglyi stol" k 100-letiiu so dnia rozhdeniia* (Moscow, 1996), p. 88.

14. APRF, f. 3, op. 58, d. 406, ll. 3–29.

15. Ibid., l. 2.

16. TsA FSB, f. 3-os, op. 6, d. 3, l. 385 (Uspenskii's testimony after arrest).

17. APRF, f. 3, op. 58, d. 406, l. 59.

18. *Voprosy istorii* 1992, no. 2-3: 87.

19. *Istoricheskii arkhiv* 1995, no. 5-6: 24.

20. Khlevniuk, *Politbiuro*, p. 214; "Konets kar'ery," p. 129; E. Radzinsky, *Stalin* (London, 1996), p. 412.

21. *Istoricheskii arkhiv* 1995, no. 5-6: 25; Khlevniuk, p. 214.

22. APRF, f. 57, op. 1, d. 265, ll. 16–26-ob.

23. *Stalinskoe Politbiuro v 30-e gody* (Moscow, 1995), pp. 168–71; A. Knight, *Beria: Stalin's First Lieutenant* (Princeton, N.J., 1993), pp. 89–90; "Konets kar'ery," pp. 129–31; B. Starkov, "Narkom Ezhov," in J. A. Getty and R. T. Manning, eds., *Stalinist Terror: New Perspectives* (Cambridge, Eng., 1993), pp. 21–39, esp. p. 38.

24. APRF, f. 45, op. 1, d. 58, ll. 61–62.

25. *Pravda,* 8 December 1938.

26. "Iz prikaza NKVD SSSR No. 00762 o poriadke osushchestvleniia postanovleniia SNK SSSR i TsK VKP(b) ot 17 noiabria 1938 g.," 26 November 1938: *Organy*, pp. 16–20.

27. TsA FSB, Archival investigation case of L. T. Iakushev-Babkin, N-13591, *Obzornaia spravka* of October 1955.

28. S. Fedoseev, "Favorit Ezhova," *Sovershenno sekretno* 1996, no. 9.

29. *Politicheskii dnevnik,* vol. 2 (Amsterdam, 1975), p. 136; B. Kamov, "Smert' Nikolaia Ezhova," *Iunost'* 1993, no. 8: 41–43, esp. p. 41; *Vsia nasha zhizn': Vospominaniia Galiny Ivanovny Levinson i rasskazy, zapisannye eiu* (Moscow, 1996), pp. 153–54.

30. V. Shentalinskii, "Okhota v revzapovednike," *Novyi mir* 1998, no. 12: 170–96, esp. pp. 180–81.

31. Ibid.

32. APRF, f. 45, op. 1, d. 729, ll. 96–97.

33. See TsA FSB, f. 3-os, op. 6, d. 9, l. 72.

34. B. B. Briukhanov and E. N. Shoshkov, *Opravdaniiu ne podlezhit: Ezhov i ezhovshchina 1936–1938* (St. Petersburg, 1998), p. 122.

35. Ibid., p. 123.

36. A. Khinshtein and M. Gridneva, "Konets khoziaina Lubianki," *MK v voskresen'e,* 7 June 1998.

37. TsA FSB, f. 3-os, op. 6, d. 3, ll. 56–58.

38. G. Zhavoronkov, "I snitsia noch'iu den'," *Sintaksis,* no. 32 (1992): 46–65, esp. p. 49.

39. Testimony of I. Dement'ev, APRF, f. 3, op. 24, d. 375, ll. 116–20.

40. Knight, *Beriia*, p. 250; G. Tsitriniak, "Rasstrel'noe delo Ezhova: Shtrikhi k portretu palacha," *Literaturnaia gazeta* 1992, no. 7; V. Topolianskii, *Vozhdi v zakone* (Moscow, 1996), pp. 326–27; Briukhanov and Shoshkov, pp. 123–24; B. Piliatskin, " 'Vrag naroda' Ezhov ostaetsia vragom naroda," *Izvestiia*, 4 and 5 June 1998.

41. APRF, f. 45, op. 1, d. 729, ll. 100–101.

42. TsA FSB, f. 3-os, op. 6, d. 3, ll. 257–58.

43. APRF, f. 3, op. 24, d. 375, ll. 120–21.

44. Shentalinskii, "Okhota v revzapovednike," p. 179.

45. TsA FSB, f. 3-os, op. 6, d. 3, ll. 332–33. According to Dement'ev's testimony, Ezhov had said, "I'll send her a medicine that will make her fall asleep so profoundly that she won't ever wake up again." Ibid., ll. 276–77.

46. TsA FSB, f. 3-os, op. 6, d. 3, ll. 59–60; Briukhanov and Shoshkov, p. 124.

47. TsA FSB, f. 3-os, op. 6, d. 3, ll. 420–23.

48. Ibid., d. 1, ll. 269–70; d. 3, ll. 59–60, 67.

49. Ibid., d. 3, l. 256.

50. Ibid., l. 266; APRF, f. 3, op. 24, d. 375, l. 116.

51. TsA FSB, f. 3-os, op. 6, d. 3, ll. 247–50.

52. Ibid., l. 252.

53. Ibid., d. 1, ll. 266–68.

54. APRF, f. 3, op. 24, d. 375, ll. 69–70.

55. J. A. Getty and O. V. Naumov, *The Road to Terror: Stalin and the Self-Destruction of the Bolsheviks, 1932–1939* (New Haven, Conn., 1999), p. 542.

56. TsA FSB, f. 3-os, op. 6, d. 3, l. 61.

57. Ibid., l. 84.

58. Ibid., Archival investigation case of Frinovskii, N-15301, t. 7, l. 197.

59. APRF, f. 57, op. 1, d. 265, ll. 29–41, 67, 71.

60. *Voprosy istorii* 1992, no. 2-3: 87.

61. Piliatskin, " 'Vrag naroda.' "

62. APRF, f. 57, op. 1, d. 287, ll. 7–18.

63. A. Fadeev, "Nikolai Ivanovich Ezhov: Syn nuzhdy i bor'by," RTsKhIDNI, f. 671, op. 1, d. 270, l. 78; *Izvestiia* and *Pravda,* 15 May 1936; Ezhov to Stalin, 5 October 1935: APRF, f. 45, op. 1, d. 729, ll. 71–72.

64. Draft: TsA FSB, f. 3-os, op. 6, d. 1, ll. 1–6; final version: APRF, f. 3, op. 58, d. 409, ll. 3–9.
65. Briukhanov and Shoshkov, *Opravdaniiu,* p. 130.
66. TsA FSB, f. 3-os, op. 6, d. 3, l. 61.
67. Briukhanov and Shoshkov, p. 161.
68. Photograph with text: *Pravda* and *Izvestiia,* 22 January 1939.
69. Briukhanov and Shoshkov, p. 161.
70. TsA FSB, f. 3-os, op. 6, d. 3, l. 71. On the district Party conference, see *Izvestiia,* 20–21 February 1939.
71. TsA FSB, f. 3-os, op. 6, d. 3, l. 71.
72. APRF, f. 45, op. 1, d. 20, l. 53.
73. N. G. Kuznetsov, "Krutye povoroty: Iz zapisok admirala," *Voenno-istoricheskii zhurnal* 1993, no. 7: 50.
74. R. Medvedev, *Let History Judge: The Origins and Consequences of Stalinism,* rev. ed. (Oxford, 1989), pp. 458–60.
75. TsA FSB, f. 3-os, op. 6, d. 4, l. 159.
76. N. G. Kuznetsov, *Nakanune* (Moscow, 1969), p. 230.
77. Ibid., p. 231; *18 s'ezd VKP(b), stenograficheskii otchet* (Moscow, 1939), p. 477.
78. Kuznetsov, *Nakanune,* pp. 233–34.
79. TsA FSB, Archival investigation case of Frinovskii, N-15301, t. 1, l. 54; APRF, f. 3, op. 24, d. 373, ll. 75–87.
80. Briukhanov and Shoshkov, p. 132; "Overcome the Arrears in Water Transportation" (lead article), *Pravda,* 2 April 1939.

Chapter 8

1. R. Medvedev, *Let History Judge: The Origins and Consequences of Stalinism,* rev. ed. (Oxford, 1989), pp. 458–60; V. Topolianskii, "Ezhov: portret palacha," *Nezavisimaia gazeta,* 4 December 1991.
2. Three on 29 March, eight on 1 April, one on 2 April, two on 3 April, one on 4 April, six on 7 April, one on 8 April, three on 9 April: RGAE, f. 7458, dd. 5222-23.
3. Ibid.
4. *Vodnyi transport,* 10 April 1939.
5. B. B. Briukhanov and E. N. Shoshkov, *Opravdaniiu ne podlezhit: Ezhov i ezhovshchina 1936–1938* (St. Petersburg, 1998), p. 132; A. Polianskii, "Kak lomali 'zheleznogo narkoma,'" *Sekretnoe dos'e*

1998, no. 2: 68–77, esp. pp. 68, 73; A. Malenkov, *O moem ottse Georgii Malenkove* (Moscow, 1992), p. 34.

6. TsA FSB, f. 3-os, op. 6, d. 3, l. 57.

7. D. Likhanov and V. Nikonov, " 'Ia pochistil OGPU,' " *Sovershenno sekretno* 1992, no. 4; G. Tsitriniak, "Rasstrel'noe delo Ezhova: Shtrikhi k portretu palacha," *Literaturnaia gazeta* 1992, no. 7; B. Piliatskin, " 'Vrag naroda' Ezhov ostaetsia vragom naroda," *Izvestiia*, 4 and 5 June 1998.

8. J. A. Getty and O. V. Naumov, *The Road to Terror: Stalin and the Self-Destruction of the Bolsheviks, 1932–1939* (New Haven, Conn., 1999), p. 538.

9. According to information in *Izvestiia TsK KPSS* 1990, no. 7: 94, Ezhov was arrested on 10 June 1939.

10. O. V. Khlevniuk, *Politbiuro: Mekhanizmy politicheskoi vlasti v 1930-e gody* (Moscow, 1996), p. 215.

11. V. V. Mar'ina, "Dnevnik G. Dimitrova," *Voprosy istorii* 2000, no. 7: 32–55, esp. p. 55.

12. S. Iu. Ushakov and A. A. Stukalov, *Front voennykh prokurorov* (Moscow, 2000), p. 69.

13. Khlevniuk, p. 215; P. Sudoplatov et al., *Special Tasks: The Memoirs of an Unwanted Witness—A Soviet Spymaster* (Boston, 1994), p. 63.

14. Polianskii, p. 75; "Pokazaniia Ezhova," *Volia*, no. 2-3 (1994): 87–100.

15. TsA FSB, f. 3-os, op. 6, d. 3, ll. 420–23.

16. Ibid., l. 265.

17. Testimony of M. I. Shabulin and Z. V. Ivanova, APRF, f. 3, op. 24, d. 372, ll. 114, 123.

18. TsA FSB, f. 3-os, op. 6, d. 2, ll. 109–58. Two months earlier, on 30 January 1939, Beriia had asked Stalin's permission to arrest Ivan Ezhov, but Stalin seems to have been in no hurry; probably he did not want to alarm Nikolai Ezhov: APRF, f. 3, op. 24, d. 372, l. 115.

19. According to his son Oleg, Frinovskii was arrested on 5 April: TsA FSB, f. 3-os, op. 6, d. 3, l. 6 (the arrest may have taken place on the night of 5–6 April); Briukhanov and Shoshkov, pp. 131–32.

20. TsA FSB, Archival investigation case of Frinovskii, N-15301, t. 2, l. 2.

21. APRF, f. 3, op. 24, d. 374, ll. 3–47; Shvernik Report (1964): "O

masshtabakh repressii v Krasnoi Armii v predvoennye gody," *Voenno-istoricheskii zhurnal* 1993, no. 5: 59–65, esp. pp. 61–62.

22. Piliatskin, " 'Vrag naroda' "; APRF, f. 3, op. 24, d. 368, ll. 18–25.

23. TsA FSB, f. 3-os, op. 6, d. 3, l. 75; d. 5.

24. Memorial archives, execution lists, Nos. 25D-928 and 25D-959; *Vlast' i khudozhestvennaia intelligentsiia: Dokumenty TsK RKP(b)-VKP(b), VChK-OGPU-NKVD o kul'turnoi politike. 1917–1953 gg.* (Moscow, 1999), p. 774.

25. Briukhanov and Shoshkov, p. 123.

26. Piliatskin.

27. APRF, f. 3, op. 24, d. 375, l. 74.

28. Memorial archives, execution lists; APRF, f. 3, op. 24, d. 369, ll. 41, 130–44.

29. S. Povartsov, *Prichina smerti—rasstrel: Khronika poslednikh dnei Isaaka Babelia* (Moscow, 1996), p. 148.

30. V. Chentalinski, *La parole ressuscitée: Dans les archives littéraires du K.G.B.* (Paris, 1993), pp. 69, 82, 95–96.

31. B. Sopel'niak, "On veril Stalinu do kontsa," *Novye Izvestiia*, 10 January 1998; *Rasstrel'nye spiski*, vol. 1 (Moscow, 1993), p. 32.

32. APRF, f. 57, op. 1, d. 265, ll. 16–26-ob.

33. Ibid., f. 3, op. 24, d. 377, l. 109.

34. Ibid., l. 115.

35. APRF, f. 3, op. 24, d. 377, ll. 116–35.

36. Ibid., l. 136.

37. Ushakov and Stukalov, *Front voennykh prokurorov*, pp. 65, 69–70, 72.

38. Likhanov and Nikonov, " 'Ia pochistil OGPU' "; Tsitriniak, "Rasstrel'noe delo Ezhova."

39. Briukhanov and Shoshkov, p. 145. According to A. Polianskii, *Ezhov: Istoria "zheleznogo" stalinskogo narkoma* (Moscow, 2001), p. 291, Ezhov *was* charged with pederasty. Since 1933 "pederasty" (*muzhelozhstvo*) had indeed been punishable by law: *Trud*, 24 February 2000; B. de Jong, " 'An Intolerable Kind of Moral Degeneration': Homosexuality in the Soviet Union," *Review of Socialist Law* 1982, no. 4: 341–57, esp. p. 342.

40. Briukhanov and Shoshkov, p. 145; "Poslednee slovo Nikolaia Ezhova," *Moskovskie novosti* 1994, no. 5.

41. Likhanov and Nikonov; Tsitriniak.

42. Ushakov and Stukalov, p. 74.

43. "Poslednee slovo."

44. Ushakov and Stukalov, p. 74.

45. Ibid., p. 75. One highly embellished account of dubious authenticity describes how after the verdict Ezhov was half-unconscious and paralyzed with fear. In the prison corridor, on the way from his cell to the execution spot in the basement [not a separate building], he was ordered to undress and was conducted naked through a line of former subordinates. Somebody hit him first. Then the blows showered down. They hit him with their fists and feet, escorts smashed him with their butts. He screamed, fell on the stone floor, was picked up and dragged on, while they continued to beat him. He was dragged to the execution place hardly alive, possibly even already dead. All those present were disorderly and without a command started to shoot with their pistols and revolvers at the bloodstained body of the once all-powerful and frightening former People's Commissar. See Briukhanov and Shoskov, pp. 154–55; also B. Kamov, "Smert' Nikolaia Ezhova," *Iunost'* 1993, no. 8: 41–43, esp. p. 43. Another completely different account has it that Ezhov sang the "International" while being taken to his execution: Sudoplatov, *Special Tasks*, p. 63.

46. Ushakov and Stukalov, p. 75.

47. Chentalinski, *La parole ressuscitée*, pp. 96–97; information from O. Kapchinskii, Moscow, October 1997.

48. *Komsomol'skaia pravda*, 29 September 1989; G. Zhavoronkov, "I snitsia noch'iu den'," *Sintaksis*, no. 32 (1992): 46–65; B. A. Starkov, "Narkom Ezhov," in J. A. Getty and R. T. Manning, eds., *Stalinist Terror: New Perspectives* (Cambridge, Eng., 1993), pp. 21–39, esp. p. 39; S. Beriia, *Moi otets—Lavrentii Beriia* (Moscow, 1994), p. 81; V. Nekrasov, *Trinadtsat' "zheleznykh" narkomov* (Moscow, 1995), p. 211; Briukhanov and Shoskov, pp. 124–25; Polianskii, "Kak lomali," p. 69; M. Il'ves, "Doch' zheleznogo narkoma," *Moskovskie novosti* 1999, no. 1; M. Franchetti, "Daughter Fights to Clear Stalin's Hitman," *The Sunday Times* (London), 31 January 1999.

49. E. Shur, "Reabilitiruiut li Ezhova?" *Sovershenno sekretno* 1998, no. 4: 4–6; Piliatskin, " 'Vrag naroda.' "

50. Shur, pp. 4–6; Piliatskin; A. Khinshtein and M. Gridneva, "Konets khoziaina Lubianki," *MK v voskresen'e*, 7 June 1998.

51. *Segodnia*, 5 June 1998; *Algemeen Dagblad* (Rotterdam), 5 June 1998.

52. Il'ves, "Doch' zheleznogo narkoma."

53. E. Shoshkov, "Ne v svoikh saniakh," *Rodina* 1997, no. 5: 91–94, esp. p. 94; *Knizhnoe obozrenie* 1989, no. 49. Frinovskii's wife and son were also condemned to death: *Otechestvennaia istoriia* 1996, no. 4: 176–77.

54. Khinshtein and Gridneva.

55. Information from the Main Information Center of the Russian Ministry of Internal Affairs.

56. Memorial archives, execution lists, No. 23D-768.

57. Ibid., Nos. 23D-765 (Anatolii Babulin), 23D-848 (Ivan Ezhov).

58. Memorial archives, execution lists, No. 23D-827.

59. Ibid., Nos. 23D-785 (Koriman), 39D-2480 (Glikina).

60. Ibid., No. 25D-987; V. Shentalinsky, *Arrested Voices: Resurrecting the Disappeared Writers of the Soviet Regime* (New York, 1993), pp. 67–71.

61. *Rasstrel'nye spiski,* 1: 32.

62. Memorial archives, execution lists, No. 25D-928.

63. Ibid., No. 25D-959.

64. *Vecherniaia Moskva,* 22 February 1999.

65. Briukhanov and Shoshkov, p. 35.

66. Ibid., p. 154.

67. At one point, not long after World War II, when Natasha was fourteen years old, her former nanny came to see her and even had plans to adopt her; but she gave up the idea after realizing that she could not cope with the girl: Zhavoronkov, "I snitsia noch'iu den'," pp. 55–57.

68. *Organy gosudarstvennoi bezopasnosti SSSR v Velikoi Otechestvennoi voine. Sbornik dokumentov. Tom I. Nakanune. Kniga pervaia (noiabr' 1938 g.–dekabr' 1940 g.* (Moscow, 1995), p. 9. There are a number of errors in this source, however. For example, Leplevskii was arrested in April and not in late 1938, not all regional chiefs were arrested, e.g., not T. M. Borshchev (Turkmenistan), S. A. Goglidze (Georgia, then Leningrad), or A. K. Uralets (Murmansk), and V. A. Tkachev (Buriat-Mongoliia) was dismissed only in September 1939 and A. E. Rasskazov (Arkhangel'sk) in late May 1939.

69. Act for the transmission of NKVD cases, TsA FSB, f. 3-os, op. 6, d. 1.

70. Information of the NKVD personnel department, GARF, f. 9401, op. 8, d. 51, l. 2.

71. See Ul'rikh to Stalin and Molotov, 14 June 1939: Getty and Naumov, *The Road to Terror,* pp. 548–49.

72. *Argumenty i fakty* 1989, no. 45; V. Rogovin, *Partiia rasstreliannykh* (Moscow, 1997), p. 457.

73. *Revelations from the Russian Archives* (Washington, D.C., 1997), pp. 26–27; *Nezavisimaia gazeta,* 29 April 1998 (suppl. *Khranit' vechno,* no. 2).

74. A. G. Tepliakov, "Personal i povsednevnost' Novosibirskogo UNKVD v 1936–1946," *Minuvshee,* no. 21 (Moscow–St. Petersburg, 1997): 240–93, esp. pp. 261–62.

75. APRF, f. 3, op. 58, d. 177, ll. 68–69.

Chapter 9

1. B. B. Briukhanov and E. N. Shoshkov, *Opravdaniiu ne podlezhit: Ezhov i ezhovshchina 1936–1938* (St. Petersburg, 1998), p. 10.

2. V. Iantemir, "Preliudiia k 'ezhovshchine,' " *Ioshkar-Ola,* 28 November 1996; A. Polianskii, "Kak lomali 'zheleznogo narkoma,' " *Sekretnoe dos'e* 1998, no. 2: 68–77, esp. p. 71.

3. Briukhanov and Shoshkov, p. 6.

4. D. Shepilov, "Vospominaniia," *Voprosy istorii* 1998, no. 4: 3–25, esp. p. 8.

5. A. Uralov, *The Reign of Stalin* (Westport, Conn., 1975), p. 44.

6. Shepilov, p. 8.

7. G. Zhavoronkov, "I snitsia noch'iu den'," *Sintaksis,* no. 32 (1992): 46–65, esp. p. 52.

8. A. Khinshtein and M. Gridneva, "Konets khoziaina Lubianki," *MK v voskresen'e,* 7 June 1998.

9. B. Piliatskin, " 'Vrag naroda' Ezhov ostaetsia vragom naroda," *Izvestiia,* 4 and 5 June 1998; L. Razgon, *Plen v svoem otechestve* (Moscow, 1994), p. 50.

10. Shepilov, p. 8.

11. TsA FSB, f. 3-os, op. 6, d. 1, l. 265.

12. Ibid., l. 269.

13. Ibid., l. 5.

14. "Poslednee slovo Nikolaia Ezhova," *Moskovskie novosti* 1994, no. 5.

15. APRF, f. 57, op. 1, d. 266, l. 80.
16. Briukhanov and Shoshkov, p. 8.
17. Shepilov, p. 6.
18. Zhavoronkov, p. 52.
19. "Bolshevik Marat"—thus he was praisingly called by both Aleksandr Bezymenskii and Aleksandr Fadeev. See Briukhanov and Shoshkov, p. 108; A. Fadeev, "Nikolai Ivanovich Ezhov: Syn nuzhdy i bor'by," RTsKhIDNI, f. 671, op. 1, d. 270, ll. 69–86.
20. Briukhanov and Shoshkov, pp. 17–18.
21. Ibid., pp. 23–24; Iantemir, "Preliudiia k 'ezhovshchine.' "
22. Briukhanov and Shoshkov, p. 35; Razgon, pp. 104–6.
23. V. I. Vernadskii, "Dnevnik 1938 g.," *Sovetskoe obshchestvo: Vozniknovenie, razvitie, istoricheskii final* (Moscow, 1997), 1: 446–92, esp. p. 453.
24. Testimony of I. Ia. Dagin of April 1939: APRF, f. 3, op. 24, d. 375, l. 43.
25. *Rasstrel'nye spiski: Moskva, 1937–1941* (Moscow, 2000), p. 465.
26. Ezhov to Stalin, 6 September 1936: APRF, f. 45, op. 1, d. 94, l. 43.
27. Memorial archives, execution lists, No. 22N-2565.
28. TsA FSB, Archival investigation case of Frinovskii, N-15301, t. 7, l. 195.
29. Ibid., t. 2, l. 35. At his trial, Ezhov admitted to having ordered that Mar'iasin be beaten: "Poslednee slovo."
30. Ezhov's bodyguard, V. N. Efimov: TsA FSB, f. 3-os, op. 6, d. 1, ll. 266–68.
31. APRF, f. 57, op. 1, d. 265, ll. 16–26-ob.
32. D. S. Azbel' answering questionnaire of S. F. Cohen, Princeton, N.J., August 1983, photocopy, kindly made available by N. Adler.
33. V. Topolianskii, *Vozhdi v zakone: Ocherki fiziologii vlasti* (Moscow, 1996), p. 301.
34. Ibid., p. 295.
35. O. V. Khlevniuk, *Politbiuro: Mekhanizmy politicheskoi vlasti v 1930-e gody* (Moscow, 1996), pp. 207–8, 290–91; "Posetiteli kremlevskogo kabineta I. V. Stalina," *Istoricheskii arkhiv* 1994, no. 6; 1995, nos. 2–6.
36. Khlevniuk, p. 210.

37. I. B. Zbarskii, " 'Zhizn' 'mumii i sud'ba cheloveka: Iz vospominanii khranitelia tela Lenina," *Otechestvennaia istoriia* 1993, no. 5: 158–64, esp. p. 160.

38. See, e.g., Babulin's and Konstantinov's testimony: TsA FSB, f. 3-os, op. 6, d. 3, ll. 72, 258, 261.

39. I. Takala, "Natsional'nye operatsii OGPU/NKVD v Karelii," in V. Vikhavainen and I. Takala, eds., *V sem'e edinoi* (Petrozavodsk, 1998), pp. 161–206, esp. pp. 196–97.

40. S. A. Papkov, *Stalinskii terror v Sibiri 1928–1941* (Novosibirsk, 1997), pp. 230–31.

41. See S. Konstantinov, "Malen'kii chelovek," *Nezavisimaia gazeta*, 13 April 2000.

42. A. Iakovlev, *Tsel' zhizni*, 2d ed. (Moscow, 1970), p. 509.

43. Reference to 1938 in A. Iakovlev, *Tsel' zhizni: Zapiski aviakonstruktora* (Moscow, 1966), p. 179.

44. RTsKhIDNI, f. 558, op. 4, d. 672, l. 10.

45. F. Chuev, *Sto sorok besed s Molotovym* (Moscow, 1991), pp. 398–400, 402, 438.

46. F. Chuev, *Tak govoril Kaganovich* (Moscow, 1992), p. 89.

47. A. Avtorkhanov, "Memuary," *Oktiabr'* 1992, no. 8: 142–68, esp. p. 158.

INDEX